WHY
THINGS ARE &
WHY THINGS
AREN'T

ALSO BY JOEL ACHENBACH
PUBLISHED BY BALLANTINE BOOKS

WHY THINGS ARE
WHY THINGS ARE, VOLUME II: The Big Picture

WHY THINGS ARE & WHY THINGS AREN'T

Joel Achenbach

Illustrated by Richard Thompson

BALLANTINE BOOKS • NEW YORK

Sale of this book without a front cover may be unauthorized. If this book is coverless, it may have been reported to the publisher as "unsold or destroyed" and neither the author nor the publisher may have received payment for it.

Copyright © 1996 by Joel Achenbach
Illustrations copyright © 1996 by Richard Thompson

The essays in this book were previously published in somewhat different form in *The Washington Post*. Copyright © 1992, 1993, 1994, 1995 by The Washington Post Company.

All rights reserved under International and Pan-American Copyright Conventions. Published in the United States by Ballantine Books, a division of Random House, Inc., New York, and simultaneously in Canada by Random House of Canada Limited, Toronto.

Library of Congress Cataloging-in-Publication Data
  Achenbach, Joel.
    Why things are & why things aren't / Joel Achenbach; illustrated by Richard Thompson.
      p. cm.
    "Originally appeared, in slightly different form, in The Washington Post"—T.p. verso.
    Includes index.
    ISBN: 0-345-39288-4
    1. Questions and answers. I. Title.
  AG195.A34 1996
  031.02—dc20   95–50293
                                                          CIP

Cover illustration by Richard Thompson
Cover design by David Stevenson

Manufactured in the United States of America
First Edition: February 1996
10 9 8 7 6 5 4 3 2 1

For Emily Notestein,
with her mellifluous voice and sunny personality and polysyllabic
way of saying the word "Hello" when she answers the phone.
Thanks, Mom.

CONTENTS

ACKNOWLEDGMENTS

Contrary to the vicious rumors, the Why staff is not just some fictional construct used as a narrative gimmick. The Why staff is real. It is a nonhierarchical collectivist intellectual enterprise in which no single person's opinion or thought is any less worthless than anyone else's.

Gene Weingarten has been the Why editor from the start, making him one of the few people who can knowledgeably say, "Didn't we already do the one about why you don't get grossed out when you pick your own nose?"

Alan Shearer, Anna Karavangelos, Heather Green, Suzanne Whelton, Mary Fleming, Grace Hill, and Geoffrey Johnson at The Washington Post Writers Group have heroically endured the idiosyncratic production schedule of the Why staff (we ignore the calendar and file when biorhythms dictate).

Pat Myers, the chief of the Style section copy desk, has policed this material with the kind of rigor that brings to mind East German border guards in the days of the Berlin Wall.

Elizabeth Zack of Ballantine Books has patiently edited all three of the Why books, the first of which was a titanic bestseller and second of which we probably are legally prohibited from mentioning since it sold only dozens of copies and is now out of print. (Nonetheless we expect this third book to outsell *Valley of the Dolls*.)

In recent years bountiful research assistance has come from Katherine Wanning, David Jackson, Elizabeth Schandelmeier, Cristina Dragomirescu, Dana Hull, and Bebe Gribble, all of whom have worked hard for little credit until this very moment of worldwide fame.

The news research department of *The Washington Post* has been of immeasurable help with its expertise in finding primary sources and trolling through computer databases and getting many an item jump-started.

Thanks also to: Peggy Hackman, Bill Smart, Jeanne Smith, Bob Park, LeRoy Doggett, Tom Shroder, Brian Dickerson, Mary Hadar, Dave Barry, Mike Baker, and Michael Congdon.

And thanks, for the love and inspiration, to Mary, Paris, and Isabella.

WHY THINGS ARE, SO FAR

"Why Things Are" is more than a weekly newspaper column. It has become, over the years, an institution, a beloved American tradition, like leaving work early on Fridays, falling asleep during baseball games, and lying to children.

To get you started on this volume we will give you a concise review of what we have learned since the elevator shafts to the Why bunker went into operation in December 1988.

The skin on your fingers doesn't shrivel in a bathtub; it expands.

Sound moves seven to eight times as fast underwater as in the atmosphere. Of all the human beings who were ever born, about 7.7 percent are alive today. Avoiding eye contact with someone passing on the street is called "polite inattention."

Individual jet packs like those used on *Jonny Quest* are impractical due to the weight of the fuel.

The Halsey-Taylor two-hole water fountain is designed to make the two streams of water converge at the apex of the arc of water, thus creating a fuller, wider, broader, rounder, more watery drink.

Although Herb Woodley and the mailman in "Blondie" look disturbingly alike, they are not, repeat, not the same person, and Herb, on closer examination, has a stronger jawline and a cleft chin. The reason Nixon taped his own nefarious conversations was he figured he could edit the tapes later. As turkeys have been bred for fatness, they have lost some of their innate cunning.

The birth of Jesus is celebrated on December 25, as opposed to some other day, because the Romans needed to replace the pagan holiday called the Feast of the Unconquered Sun.

The lowest score one can get on either the math or verbal SAT is 200 because the College Board didn't want anyone to feel that he or she had zero intelligence.

You get a runny nose when you cry because the tears drain into the nose through the tiny hole at the corner of your eye, called the *puncta lacrimalia*. Porous objects get darker when they get wet because they become more transparent to light, thus reflecting less of it.

The YKK on a zipper stands for Yoshida Kogyo Kabushiki-gaisha.

A football team on offense can't launch a midget carrying the football up and over the defensive line for a touchdown because it would violate Rule 17 of Section 6 of the Official Football Rules: "No player of the side in possession of the ball shall use his hands, arms or body to push, pull or hold upon his feet the player carrying the ball."

The myth of mass suicide by lemmings was promulgated in part by a filmmaker who herded a bunch of lemmings off a cliff for the 1958 Disney documentary *White Wilderness*. Because movie producers used to get top billing instead of directors, nobody remembers who directed *Gone With the Wind* and *The Wizard of Oz*; it was Victor Fleming. The giant fetus at the end of *2001: A Space Odyssey* is the ultimate evolved human, a Nietzschean superman, capable of surviving in the vacuum of space.

Within an 80-light-year radius of the Earth are about one thousand sunlike stars that conceivably could have planets with intelligent civilizations. If you go out to 160 light-years the number increases by a factor of ten. Scientists are listening for signals from these star systems, but they do not send any intentional signals themselves for fear that aliens will come to Earth and either kill or enslave us.

Birds do not love their mates, and in some cases will try to kill one another in a caged environment because they don't even recognize each other.

A fetus is about 90 percent water, a newborn about 70 percent water, and a mature adult about 60 percent water. Possums lie motionless because they know that many predators, wary of spoiled meat, eat only creatures that are writhing in agony.

A monkey pounding randomly on a typewriter would very likely write *Hamlet* given an infinite amount of time—but that outcome is not an absolute certainty.

If you went back in time, you could conceivably alter the course of history—but you wouldn't. Because you didn't.

Some quarters have residual red or black paint on them, marked by bar owners to use in jukeboxes to get the joint jumping; they belong to the bar rather than the vending machine company.

Humor is funny because of overlapping but incompatible frames of reference.

We exist to spread love in a large, cold universe.

READER INSTRUCTIONS

It would behoove the readers to take several things into consideration while reading this book:

1. This book is a collection of columns and stories that have appeared, in different form, in *The Washington Post*. If you read something that seems outrageous, immature, vulgar, irresponsible, or simply vile, please appreciate that we managed to get this stuff printed in the paper that broke the Watergate story. It wasn't easy.

2. As in the previous paragraph, there are numerous instances in which the narrator uses the first-person plural pronoun, with very occasional, and potentially confusing, uses of the first-person singular pronoun. The explanation for this is simple: The official "author" of the book is a single individual, but he is merely a *news medium*. The "we" refers to the collective consciousness of civilized man. In effect the reader is not merely a passive consumer of the material herein, but rather a collaborator. You are the we.

3. We will say anything for money.

4. One humor technique that appears in the book, perhaps clumsily at times, is the blatant lie. The purported humor behind this rhetorical device is that, as you are reading along, you expect to read things that are true because this is fundamentally a book of factual information, and so when we jump out with something that is preposterously false, you are supposed to laugh heartily, both hands clapped loosely on your jiggling gut. The problem is that on certain occasions we have

noticed that readers haven't gotten the joke, as, for example, when we wrote a while back that "as everyone knows, a raisin is a very young prune." We were barraged with letters. People were shocked. We had to write back to each one to reassure them that we fully understood that a prune was actually a withered tomato.

5. In compiling this volume we've tried to bring things up to date and weed out obsolescent material. Nonetheless, the subjects included tend to be of a dynamic nature. Theories change. Answers fluctuate. Someone discovers that neutrinos have mass after all. We stand firmly behind the intellectual content of this volume but at the same time are prepared, should new and contradictory data be presented, to renounce it, to the point of denying that we wrote it at all. We would be thrilled to know that readers see this material not as a final delivery of known fact, but rather as a guide and an inspiration for further inquiry. We can tell you where we think the answers lie—but ultimately you are the one who must find them.

From Dinosaurs to Bugs:
The Wacky World of Creatures with Legs That Are Too Fat or Too Numerous

Why did no one discover the dinosaurs until the 1800s, even though dinosaur bones had been lying around for millions of years?

Ask any historian and you'll find out the unsettling truth about history: Until fairly recently, people were dumb as rocks. When they'd by chance stumble across the thighbone of a stegosaurus, they'd say something like, "Now that there was one heck of a dawg."

The truth is that there are few intact dinosaur skeletons to be found in the ground. You mostly find individual bones or teeth.

"Most of what anybody finds, including the professionals, are bits and pieces," says Nick Hotton, a research paleontologist at the National Museum of Natural History. "To find a complete, articulated skeleton is a very rare event."

But obviously there were chance encounters between people and dinosaur bones long ago. We have no way of knowing what prehistoric man thought, although we do have a record of subsequent misapprehensions.

We have to remember that science is a fairly recent invention. There was no systematic look at these bones until the 1800s. Geology didn't exist, by and large, until the nineteenth century. No one knew about the origin and extinction of species. People didn't even know the world was old! The scientists who had discovered the laws of physics and the existence of distant planets still didn't realize that the Earth had been around for millions of years and that many species had arisen and then become extinct. Discoveries take place within intellectual frameworks, and the discovery of the dinosaurs had to wait until the Earth became, in the minds of scientists, an old planet.

For much of human history, people assumed that big bones belonged to the giants of mythology. Indeed, dinosaur bones may have been the inspiration for religious and mythical tales of giants.

When the Reverend Robert Plot of Oxford examined a gigantic leg bone in 1677 he declared that it was the bone of an elephant and that this elephant had been taken to the British Isles by the Romans many hundreds of years earlier. He was off by about, oh, 100 million years or so.

In 1806, during the Lewis and Clark expedition, William Clark found what was probably a dinosaur rib jutting from the bank of the Missouri River. He wrote in his journal that it was the rib of a fish.

In the Connecticut Valley, behemoths had left unmistakable reptilian footprints in the ancient sandstones. Amherst College president Edward Hitchcock collected these fossils and published a book about them. He said they must have been big birds.

Finally, in 1841, anatomist Richard Owen of the British Museum announced that all these mysterious fossils were part of a separate tribe of extinct and gigantic reptiles, which he named "Dinosauria." That's from the Greek, "deinos," terrible, and "sauros," lizard. A few decades later the people building railroads in the American West stumbled across all sorts of bones, launching the dinosaurmania that persists to this day.

The real question, of course, is what, prior to 1841, did little boys get obsessed about?

Why can't some really clever scientist figure out how to grow dinosaurs from little scraps of dinosaur DNA preserved in amber?

Before we figure out how to make the plot of *Jurassic Park* come true (dinosaurs are regenerated from DNA and within hours they're flossing their teeth with human legs), we have to figure out the scientific trick that's crucial to the plot of *The Boys from Brazil*. (That's the one with the Hitler clones.)

You see, there are two major obstacles to reconstituting dinosaurs:

1. We aren't good at cloning. No animal has ever been cloned from mere DNA. So before we started generating dinosaurs from old DNA scraps, we'd have to figure out how to do the same trick with the DNA of a living animal (simultaneously coming up with a way to prevent Ross Perot from cloning himself 100 million times and ordering the offspring to elect him president).

Every cell in your body contains DNA, the blueprints necessary to make another person who looks just like you. But you can't just take a little fleck of skin, stick it in a test tube, and wait for your clone to come crawling out in a few months, wondering where's the keg. This is because that fleck of skin is a differentiated cell—it has a specific design and function. If cells didn't differentiate we'd all grow up to be giant piles of goop.

What we'd need to do, somehow, is de-differentiate cells and make them act like fertilized eggs. This way they'd replicate into an entirely new organism.

2. DNA is fragile. It degrades over time. Although scientists can obtain DNA from some fossils, it's never in great shape. Dinosaur bones are worthless—no DNA surviving there. To generate a new organism, you'd need to find a way to find pieces of DNA, repair the stuff, and get all those little genes lined up in the right sequence (otherwise you might get a dinosaur with no teeth, and people would get gummed to death).

Are these problems insurmountable? For the foreseeable future, certainly.

"It's great science fiction, but that's about all it is," says Rob DeSalle, an entomologist at the American Museum of Natural History who has obtained DNA from a 30-million-year-old termite preserved in amber.

But molecular biology is an explosive field. A few years ago no one thought it would be possible to alter, for therapeutic purposes, the genes of a living person—a feat recently accomplished.

"I think eventually we'll be able to come up with something," says George Poinar, a paleobiologist at the University of California at Berkeley. Poinar has reason to be intrigued: He has found amber-preserved insects from the dinosaur era (a discovery that parallels the plot of *Jurassic Park*). These insects presumably feasted on dinosaur blood. "They very likely have dinosaur cells in their guts," he says.

The Why staff has just one request of the scientific community: Please, no pterodactyls.

Why do apes stagger when they walk on two legs? Why can't they stride along smoothly, with style, the way humans can?

Apes stagger because they have to shift their weight from leg to leg. Humans don't do this because our thighbones are slanted inward, toward the knee, so that our knees are close together. This makes it easy to stand on one leg and shift to the other—each leg is already nearly underneath our center of gravity.

Moreover, humans have pelvic muscles that apes don't have. You can feel them contracting when you walk. These muscles keep our pelvis level and stable.

Why humans are bipedal to begin with is a major scientific mystery. Most people don't wonder about this because they assume that going from four legs to two legs is simply what happens when you evolve. They figure that's what evolution is: learning to stand up straight. But the truth is that bipedalism is a quirky trait. To be smart and technological we don't have to walk on two legs. We could just as well be knuckle-walkers, like gorillas or chimpanzees. (Is "The Knuckle-Walk" a dance craze yet? Why not?)

Theories about bipedalism often are inspired by the latest political fashion or cultural obsession, notes Alison Brooks, a professor of anthropology at George Washington University. During the Vietnam War, she says, everyone talked about bipedalism as a mechanism for allowing men to throw spears and act belligerent.

This is related to the old theory that we learned to walk so that we could free our hands to use tools. But the fossil record shows clearly that we started walking long before we started using tools.

Bipedalism probably has something to do with the need to carry stuff. Geologic changes in Central East Africa caused a shift in climate and a drying of the ecosystem. Jungle became savanna. If you were an ape, you couldn't just hang out in the trees anymore and swing from branch to branch, but rather had to travel over the ground and carry food long distances. Human bipedalism isn't particularly fast, but it is smooth, and much more efficient, in terms of energy expended, than simian quadrupedalism. (We believe this to be the cheapest book on the market with the phrase "simian quadrupedalism.")

So we probably walked on two feet because it was easier to lug our dinner around.

A new theory is that by standing up we stay cooler. That's right. We're up in the breeze. At midday we have a smaller shadow, less skin exposed to direct sun. This matters in hot climates. The theory is that "bipedalism is basically a heat loss mechanism," summarizes Brooks.

Incidentally, John Eccles in *Evolution of the Brain* gives a good summary of how a human walks: "Each leg alternately is thrust forward ('the swing leg') while the weight is supported by the 'stance' leg. The swing leg is flexed to clear the ground and the step is over as its heel strikes the ground, the body weight moves forward, and the initial stance leg soon becomes the swing leg, beginning with a thrust exerted from the big toe by the *flexor hallucis longus* contraction."

Yeah, but try to contract your *flexor hallucis longus* and chew gum at the same time. Impossible.

Why are there no wild cows?

We do a lot of cow items. Maybe we should just do a weekly column about meat. We could call it the Meat Beat.

We began thinking about cows again after noticing, during a recent trip to the zoo, that there is no cow exhibit. You'd think there'd be at least some kind of obscure, little-known Wild Cow of Borneo. Instead, cows are completely snubbed, just like cats and dogs.

Primitive man just didn't know squat about cows.

The obvious reason for this is that zoos are for wild and exotic animals and cows are neither. There are no wild cows anymore. But this is actually a fairly recent development.

All the domestic cows on Earth are descended from a single species of wild cow, called *Bos primigenius*. This wild cow is now referred to as the aurochs, or sometimes the urus. (Aurochs is a singular word; depending on whom you are talking to and on what continent, the plural is either aurochs, or aurochsen.)

The Asian and African aurochs disappeared thousands of years ago, but the European aurochs continued to linger in the forests of Europe. The last wild cow on Earth is believed to have died in Poland in 1627. (We don't know the details of the death. But we are guessing that the meat was tough.)

Since then, a few zoos have tried to "re-create" the aurochs. The silly things people think of! "Back-breeding" techniques can produce a cow with scary horns and a shy temperament, but that doesn't make it a real aurochs, much less a genuinely wild animal. (It's hard to be a wild cow when you're stuck in a zoo.)

When was the first aurochs domesticated and turned into a "cow"? Beats the Meat Beat. But the archaeological record shows traces of domesticated cattle as long ago as 6400 B.C.

"It is impossible to say that at such and such a place, at such and such a time, the first domesticated aurochs calf was born. It is more than likely to have been domesticated quite independently by different peoples in different places at different times," says the book *Cattle: A Handbook to the Breeds of the World* (soon to be a television movie starring Roseanne).

The descendants of the aurochs come in two subspecies: humped and humpless. All told, there are about 250 breeds within those subspecies. An argument can be made that there are other wild cows still in existence, in the form of yaks, bison, buffalo, and oxen. All these creatures are even-toed ungulates, members of the *Artiodactyla* order of mammals and of the family within that order called *Bovidae*. (Yes, there will be a test.)

But we would argue that it's a terrible mistake to lump all even-toed ungulates together and call them cows. A yak is just not a cow. For one thing, there are domesticated yaks, and they aren't called cows, they're called "domesticated yaks."

You would say, "This here is our family yak, Bessie."

Why do cows have four stomachs? Why do they "chew the cud"?

W e've been ruminating on the latter question for years. The whole concept of cud-chewing seems so gross, so backward, it's hard to believe cows still do that.

The first thing we learned is that cows don't actually have four stomachs. They have just one, but it has four compartments. We will mention that these compartments are called the rumen, the reticulum, the omasum, and the abomasum because this will make our book seem classier.

What happens is, the cow swallows a bunch of grass without even chewing it, and it goes into the rumen, which is like a fifty-gallon fermentation tank, full of microbes that can break down and soften the grass. Later the cow will hawk up a bolus of "cud" and chew it, breaking it down further.

Here's why such an unsavory process evolved: Grazing is a high-profile activity. Dangerous. You have to stand out in the open, in full view of predators. So cows and other ruminants developed the low-profile method of digestion. You can scarf down a full tank of grass in half an hour and then lie down in the shade, or among the underbrush, for a leisurely mastication of the aforesaid cud. Vile, but safe.

Why do ostriches bury their heads in the sand?

They don't. Not ever. Don't tell Gary "The Far Side" Larson, but ostriches do not bury their heads in the sand, even if they have a spare. So why is ostrich head burying a bedrock belief of Western civilization?

Fred Beall (whenever we see his name we think "and End-all"), who is curator of birds at the Baltimore Zoo, has an explanation: Ostrich chicks are prone to predation. They can't outrun their enemies the way an adult ostrich can. So when attacked, they sometimes flop to the ground and lie there motionless, hoping to blend in with the grassy surroundings of their habitat. Their long necks are usually beige, with black stripes, which blends perfectly with stalks of grass and their shadows.

"It looks as though there's just this dome of a body with no neck attached to it," Beall says.

Maybe that won't fool a ravenous leopard, but it sure fooled us.

Why do birds sing so gay?

Outside the dormitory wing of the Why bunker, the birds start performing around five in the morning. We stumble from bed, open a window, and scream SHADDUP ALREADY, but they won't listen. What possesses them? Are they discussing something interesting, or is this twittering and twerping, as we suspect, *total and complete gibberish*?

The first thing to understand is that birds do not have a language. Language involves symbolic representation. Birds are just making sounds that convey the most rudimentary information imaginable, basically "I am here" and "I am ready to get funky." The singing achieves two functions: It stakes out a territory, and it attracts a mate.

But you sorta knew that, probably. What you didn't know was that, in temperate zones like the United States, the male birds do all the singing, and for the most part they are being irresponsible. They should be foraging. Feeding themselves. A bird does all that flying around, all that hopping from branch to branch, and yet it's so tiny (no meat on them bones!), it obviously has little storage capacity and needs to constantly refuel itself. You can't eat and sing at the same time (try it!), so by singing instead of foraging, the male birds are bragging. They're strutting their stuff.

"To be able to sing like crazy first thing in the morning and not look for food means you're a pretty good bird. I'd even say they handicap themselves," says Gene Morton, a research biologist and leading bird expert at the National Zoo.

Birds form pair-bonds, just like humans. But the birds don't really get to know each other. (You can add "just like humans" if you want.)

In the tropics, birds mate for life (and females also sing), but even so, says Morton, they have shockingly little attachment to one another. A female may suddenly abandon her mate and join another male who has a better territory. The spurned male will immediately start advertising for a new mate. There's no grace period, no sense of decency. They never pause to ask, "What about the children?"

Seriously, not only do birds not love each other, they don't really recognize each other. Males have killed their mates when confined in cages, not because of the terror of the confinement but simply because the male didn't recognize the female, says Morton. Birds would have a hard time picking their mate out of a lineup.

But let's remember, they have a good excuse. They're bird-brained.

Why do birds often stand on one leg?

Because they get cold feet. They're tucking one foot up in those feathers for insulation. Another wonderfully logical answer! (You had probably assumed the poor thing had lost a limb in a tragic encounter with, who knows, a helicopter.)

But birds don't really mind cold feet the way we do. Their main concern is that they not radiate away too much of their body heat from those featherless appendages. Indeed, they want their legs to be cold, recognizing the simple principles of heat conduction.

"They shunt the blood away from the legs and the legs cool down. Their legs get colder than the body," says Morton of the National Zoo, "although they won't let the leg freeze; that would kill it." One trick is to go for a swim; a foot in liquid water cannot freeze.

On the flip side, if a bird gets too hot, it will increase blood flow to the feet to cool itself down. In fact, turkey vultures and black vultures urinate on their legs and exploit the cooling effects of evaporation. The uric acid leaves a whitish substance on their legs. It's nasty, but when you are a vulture you don't worry a lot about appearances.

Why are there no giant insects?

Whenever you're feeling kind of mopey, or bored, or discontented with your lot in life, just remind yourself: At least you're not being borne aloft by a wasp the size of a helicopter.

We are not the type to say negative things about insects . . . in fact we consider the word "bug" to be pejorative . . . but we will confess that we are glad that the hideous little monsters are small enough to squish.

Why is there not a single gargantuan species of insect, other than in horror movies?

Ventilation.

Bugs, you see, don't transport oxygen to their body parts the way we do. We have a circulatory system in which blood cells take oxygen from the lungs to the cells. Bugs don't have lungs. They don't have blood quite like we do. The way they get oxygen is through vents.

Tiny holes in the surface of the insect allow oxygen to enter the body. These hollow passages branch into ever-finer tubes, carrying oxygen to all the bug parts. This is an excellent system for a small creature, says Chris McGowan, curator of vertebrate paleontology at the Royal Ontario Museum and author of *Diatoms to Dinosaurs: The Size and Scale of Living Things*.

The problem is that a "tracheal system," as it's called, wouldn't be effective for larger creatures. "As you get bigger, the area-to-volume ratio gets smaller," says McGowan. In other words, you have relatively more body mass compared with your surface area. You have much more to ventilate but only a little bit more surface for ventilation holes.

"It puts a limit on their body size, so you don't get whacking great big insects," he says.

Why can't some insect just develop lungs and a circulatory system? Because that would require a wholesale change in anatomical strategy. Once we go down a certain evolutionary path we don't back up completely and take a new route. (See, in our chapter "The Glorious Temple That Is the Human Body," the discussion about why our eating and breathing systems share some of the same plumbing.)

There's another reason insects stay small: It works. Have you noticed how many bugs there are? By being small, they're capable of reproducing in enormous numbers without using up too many nutrient resources in the environment. There's a cost to getting big.

Then again there's a cost to staying small. You can get eaten! This is one major reason small creatures like flies don't live very long, while large or well-protected creatures like elephants or tortoises do. Creatures that run the risk of being eaten tend to live speeded-up lives, with early maturity and passels of offspring.

Another cost of being small . . . and here we are basically flipping the whole item around so that we can explain why there are no one-inch-tall humans . . . is your brain won't be large enough and complex enough to get you into a good college. In fact, an insect is largely controlled by decentralized nerve ganglia, minibrains spread around the body. McGowan writes that if you surgically remove the pinhead-sized brain from an insect, the creature will continue to function, only confusedly. It might try to eat, fly, and walk all at the same time.

Whereas a human will just run for public office.

Why don't ants drown when it rains heavily?

It's awfully hard to drown an ant. You can immerse one in water, keep it there for hours, even days, and it won't die. Instead, when you pull it out, it'll appear dead—but will revive in a couple of hours. Fun science trick!

The reason they don't drown is that water doesn't penetrate their tiny breathing tubes. Water has a lot of surface tension and merely surrounds the ants. If our own breathing tubes were blocked, we'd die from the lack of oxygen, but ants don't. They just suffer carbon dioxide narcosis, which knocks them out. Eventually they'll die, of course, but it's amazing how long they'll last.

(You wonder, do they have brain damage when they wake

up? Apparently not. But these are ants, remember, so they don't write existential novels even on a good day.)

Obviously, this is not the standard way ants deal with rain. Usually they just go deep underground (the nests of tropical leaf-cutting ants go down as far as six feet beneath the surface) and then dig their way back out.

Another trick: Fire ants in the Deep South will link their bodies together and float on flood waters. They will just drift downstream until they wash up somewhere. The queen, naturally, is right in the middle, high and dry.

Why do bugs always die on their backs?

Bugs have a standard choreography of death. Tremble. Lurch. Collapse. Flip. Wriggle. Expire.

The lurching part is unsettling to watch, the flip is puzzling, and the wriggling is absolutely disgusting. We realize some of our readers are squeamish about insects, so we will only mention one last time that as they die their legs are constantly wriggling, wriggling, wriggling.

We spoke to Dick Froeschner, an entomologist at the Smithsonian Institution who has watched many bugs die in various situations in the laboratory—another example of a job that's fun *and* you get paid to do it—and he said the back flip is merely a function of gravity and inertia.

Think of a barstool. The seat is perched high atop long legs. If one or two of those legs were to suddenly collapse, the barstool wouldn't drop straight down but would topple over to one side. The same thing happens to bugs, and that gets things rolling, so to speak, for them to turn upside down.

We should remember that insects have six legs, spiders eight (Rush Limbaugh ten). In a diagram you'll see the legs evenly spaced and roughly in the same position. In reality, they are continually moving in different directions, some splayed wide, some pulled in close. When the insect starts to die, its legs will fold up, but not simultaneously. One or two or three legs will collapse first. The insect doesn't collapse straight down but topples over with some angular momentum.

It doesn't always roll onto its back, of course. Sometimes it will be on its side, a-wrigglin' like there's no tomorrow. The flailing will usually knock it the rest of the way over. Once on its back, there's no return. The legs are up in the air and they have nothing to push against.

"It's just the physical condition of things; there's nothing psychic or fancy. It's just what happens and how gravity works on it," says Froeschner.

There are exceptions. If a bug has something on which to clamp the claws on the end of its legs—there are itty-bitty claws down there—it can die standing up straight, with legs locked in place.

Makes you want to rush right out and get some Roach Motels, huh?

Why are killer bees in such a bad mood? And why can't we just wipe them out with some napalm or whatever?

The strange thing about killer bees is that they do, in fact, kill people. You would expect that the "killer" label would be just some kind of media hype. It ain't. These are some bad bees. They've been known to sting a victim a thousand times or more. If Winnie the Pooh were to go looking for honey around these bees, he'd wind up scattered on the ground like confetti.

"When they really go berserk, unless you're protected, your life is in danger. But they don't go berserk that often," says Orley "Chip" Taylor, an entomologist at the University of Kansas who has studied killer bees for twenty years. Once, he said, he was covered with protective clothing except for one square inch of skin. That square inch got seventeen stings, he said.

The killer bees also are called African bees or, perhaps more exactly, neotropical African bees. A Brazilian geneticist in 1957, hoping to get the domestic Brazilian bees to be a little more active, had the brilliant idea of crossing them with some extremely aggressive bees from southern Africa. The problem is, a local beekeeper stumbled across the experiment, didn't realize what was going on, and allowed the imported queens to escape into the wild during the swarming season.

They've been on their way here ever since. The killer bees will mate with domestic bees, but the ferocity remains. And the domestic bees are simply dying out.

"They're being outcompeted," says Taylor.

The killer bees are not only more aggressive, they're more

numerous. Their colonies are huge. As of 1994, about two hundred people had been killed by the bees in Latin America and two in the United States after the bees crossed the border into Texas in October 1990.

What should we, the general public, do about this, other than garb ourselves twenty-four hours a day in protective netting?

The best hope is that geneticists will find a way to "improve" the killer bees to make them less fierce, says Taylor. The bees are already being used commercially by beekeepers, but by and large the beekeeping industry has collapsed in many Latin American countries because the killer bees are just too nasty. If they can be selectively bred for docility, then they'll pose less of a threat. But at the moment, no one's stepped forward with the money or the courage to take on that task.

Yet another reason to be thankful for the invention of the Great Indoors.

Why do owls seem to turn their heads 180 degrees without turning their bodies?

Owls are constantly doing that *Exorcist* thing. The head seems to rotate on ball bearings. As you approach an owl from behind, you think you're dealing with a cuddly, soft bird, but then suddenly the head pivots obscenely and it stares at you directly over its back with those big appalled eyeballs that seem to be communicating the idea that you will roast agonizingly in the Lake of Fire.

(But maybe we are weirded out by owls because we always ask "Why?" and they always ask "Who?")

(Ba-dum bum.)

The swivel-headedness of owls is a necessity. "Unlike many birds, they have significantly forward-positioned eyes," says Pam Osten, curator of birds at the Baltimore Zoo. Owls, with their flat facial disk, have a visual field of only 110 degrees, compared with about 180 degrees for humans and 340 degrees for a homing pigeon.

The limited visual field is more than compensated for by the improved binocular vision. Owls can see distant objects clearly. An owl is basically a pair of eyeballs with wings attached. It is a sit-and-wait predator, scanning the terrain for any sign of movement. It sees clearly at night. If it hears something in the

woods behind it, the head can silently pivot and search for the noise-making creature, the body remaining still.

"The neck is fairly short and composed of 14 cervical vertebrae, which allows for enough rotation of the neck that an owl can turn its head and peer directly over its back," writes Paul A. Johnsgard in *North American Owls*.

An owl's softness is related to is quietness. The tiny fibers that make up the owl's feathers are not bonded together on their outermost edges as in most birds. This makes it a bit harder to fly but easier to fly quietly.

Owls, we have learned, not only can turn their heads 180 degrees, but in fact can keep turning them even further, a full 270 degrees. In other words an owl can turn its head to the right and look over its left shoulder. Try *that*, Linda Blair.

Why have numerous cultures come up with the silly idea of mermaids?

Sea cows. No lie. The dugong, or sea cow, which is related to the manatee, nurses its young in an upright posture. The mother's teats resemble human breasts. The babies are held against the mother with a single fin, like a human holding a baby with one arm.

The problem is that it is hard to imagine that sailors would look overboard, see some large, blubbery, hairless mammal, and find themselves irresistibly attracted. You'd have to be at sea a *long* time to get to that point.

Richard Grinker, an anthropologist at George Washington University, says that mermaids are part of a broader phenomenon, the concept of the half-human, half-beast. Half-human creatures are pre-Darwinian transitional forms. They're like missing links.

"One of the most important things human beings do is try to separate themselves from the animal world," Grinker says. "And one way they do that is invent such mythical creatures."

You can't ignore the fact that there's a slap at women in the myth of the mermaid. The mermaid is always alluring, sitting on the rocks combing her hair and looking in a little mirror, but she's also exceedingly dangerous, deceptive, ultimately elusive. This is the basic male take on women.

"That age-old idea of the gorgeous and deadly woman has powered much myth and art. Mermaids crystallize the fear," writes Diane Ackerman in her book *A Natural History of Love*.

"For men of the sea, mermaids combine the self-destructiveness of the ocean, to which they are nonetheless wedded, with their loneliness for the women they've left behind," she writes.

Go too close to them and your ship crashes on the shoals. Odysseus had to lash himself to the mast to keep himself from being lured to his doom by the song of the sirens. (We understand that particular strait, the Dardanelles, now just plays the Muzak version.)

Why do squirrels get hit by cars even though they're incredibly spry animals?

This is not to suggest that the squirrels are to blame when they are smushed. This is not some blame-the-victim thing. But you have to admit that it's amazing how squirrels can leap around in a tree, elude cats, scramble across rooftops and power lines, bury nuts in the ground and sometimes actually find them later, and yet still have a hard time just crossing the street safely.

The obvious answer is that squirrels evolved long before the automobile age and don't know how to deal with cars. But it's not simply that cars befuddle them. The amazing thing is that squirrels really cannot see the car at all. The motion of the car

SQUISHY SQUIRREL SAYS

KIDS! If you've got to cross a street, next time try scampering along a power line!

American Council for Unwise Safety Advice

is so bizarre, compared with other things in nature, that the squirrel's brain can't even register it.

"They don't appreciate the movement toward them of these objects," says Richard Restak, author of *The Modular Brain*. He says he pondered the squirrel paradox for twenty-five years before figuring it out. "They can't appraise speed and movement coming at them like that. There's nothing in their life to correspond to that."

Tree branches don't move much. Cats don't bear down on them from a block away. As for power lines, squirrels probably just think they are a new variety of vine.

The point is, the brain of a squirrel, or any creature, including a human being, is a carefully calibrated sensorium. It doesn't just suck in the whole world and discern it. Each creature's brain is evolved, in tandem with sensory organs, for a particular environment. We might think we humans discern the world around us perfectly, but in fact we lack the kinesthesia of squirrels, the sonar skills of dolphins, the keen vision of owls, and the brilliant olfaction of dogs. Squirrels might even think it's weird that we can't remember where we put our eyeglasses.

Why are animals so healthy even though they don't seem to eat a balanced diet? Why don't anteaters need to eat vegetables?

We just read today that the spotted owl in California eats wood rats and not much else. How can you survive on one source of food? Isn't that unhealthy *and* tedious? You can imagine conversations in the spotted owl nest:

"Mom, what's for dinner?"

"Wood rat."

"AGAIN????"

The secret to staying healthy on a monotonous diet is that you have to eat the entire animal. Owls don't sit there picking off the good parts of the rat. They just wolf the thing down, if you don't mind that metaphor applied to an owl. Then at some point they hawk up (ha!) a bolus of bones and hair. Miss Manners probably advises against this move when you are a dinner guest, but it's a great way of gleaning all the nutrients from your prey.

Anteaters don't eat much of anything other than ants, but ants are highly nutritious. Kent Redford, a biologist with the Nature Conservancy, says he and his kids routinely fry up the fat-rich winged ants they find in their yard. The neighbor kids eat them too. "I made sure the neighborhood kids went back and asked permission from their mother," he notes.

Our own policy is never to eat anything that has a larval stage.

HABITUALLY BAD HABITS

Why is it that you find nothing wrong with picking your nose but are totally grossed out if you see someone else do it?

Okay, we will try to be adult about this. We will try not to be disgusting. We will try not to mention terms like "bodily excretions" more often than is strictly necessary since they (terms like "bodily excretions") are almost as revolting in print as the things they represent in real life (bodily excretions).

What's odd, though, is that we all have such a double standard. Such hypocrisy. For example, you might be the kind of person who, when you remove a little flake of earwax, will scrutinize it as though it contains the answer to some cosmic riddle, like the significance of the gravitational constant. And yet the same behavior in another person repels you. You think: Where did this guy come from, the Ozarks? (Our address, for those of you who live in the Ozarks, is c/o *The Washington Post*, 1150 15th St. NW, Washington DC 20071.)

An even more obvious example of this phenomenon: Smells. You like yours. Hate others'.

Here's why: You have invested time and energy into yourself, and your "self" is a much vaster enterprise than you realize.

That may sound like a typically glib, superficial answer, but we'd argue that it's a profound statement about the nature of existence. A "self" is not the same thing as a body. A "self" is a

multitentacled enterprise. Anything that is yours, even ear wax, is not merely tolerated, it's cherished.

"A sense of self is always much larger than just the body. We're reflected in our work, we're reflected in our furnishings, we're reflected in our attire," says Herbert J. Freudenberger, a New York City psychoanalyst.

"We have an investment in ourselves," says Stephen Franzoi, a psychologist at Marquette University. The self is anything and everything that reflects an investment of our psychological energies, he says. He adds, "The self is not necessarily rational."

For example, says Franzoi, before he had children he thought the idea of changing a diaper was disgusting. He simply didn't understand how parents could do it. But then he had kids, and he found that diaper changing didn't faze him in the slightest. The child is an extension of the parents.

We may possess an evolutionary trait of being attracted to and valuing the things we identify as our own. There's an obvious competitive advantage in this—if people didn't care that much about their looks, the state of their home, or which kids belonged to them, they wouldn't have much evolutionary success.

One other thing: You can't see yourself when you're picking your nose. If you could, you wouldn't.

Why does almost everyone drive faster than the speed limit?

We are a nation of criminals. We routinely and blithely break the law. Even those of us who are not "speeders" in the classic sense are still fudgers.

If the speed limit is thirty mph we will routinely drive about thirty-seven or thirty-eight mph. Unless, of course, we see a police cruiser. Then we slam on the brakes so hard that the back of the car lifts in the air, and we drive past the cop at fifteen mph with both hands firmly gripping the wheel, eyes concentrating on the road and checking left and right rearview mirrors at 0.5-second intervals, doing everything we can to project the image of the Safe Driver.

Here is the tough intellectual question: Do we drive faster than the speed limit because the speed limit is set artificially low, or do we speed because we have an innate desire to get away with whatever we can get away with? If the speed limit on a typical city street were raised from thirty to forty, would we stop driving thirty-eight and start driving forty-eight?

The answer is: The speed limits are too low.

Most speed limits are set by a city council or county commission or state department of transportation. They cover entire jurisdictions—for example, a city might say that every city street has a maximum speed limit of thirty mph. But many of those streets can easily handle faster traffic without any additional danger of accidents.

Indeed, Julie Cirillo, acting director of the Office of Highway Safety of the Federal Highway Administration, says that most motorists drive at safe, rational, reasonable speeds and that these speeds are not determined by the speed limit signs so much as by the nature of the street or road.

"Many, many speed limits are set legislatively, and therefore they have no relevance to anything, and they beg to be violated, and of course they are," Cirillo says.

What happens if you raise or lower a speed limit? Hardly anything. An October 1992 study by the Federal Highway Administration said that even if you changed the speed limit by fifteen mph the average car speed would only change about one or two mph.

Sometimes traffic engineers will study a given street to see what the best speed limit would be. They look at the cars flowing by. The general industry rule, Cirillo says, is to set the speed limit at the 85th percentile. What this means is that eighty-five out of one hundred cars will be going at or below that speed. The other 15 percent will be going too fast.

Traffic engineers tend to be conservative, though. If they find that the 85th percentile is going at forty-nine miles an hour they will likely put the speed limit at forty-five. They round down. In fact, even when traffic engineers get involved, the average speed limit is set around the 43rd percentile, Cirillo says.

We have obtained a graph from the Federal Highway Administration that clearly shows that on rural highways and freeways it is more dangerous to go a little bit too slow than to go a little bit too fast. For cars going ten to fifteen miles under the speed limit, the accident involvement rate is 449 accidents per 100 million miles. For cars going ten to fifteen mph over the speed limit, there are only fifty-one accidents per 100 million miles. In fact, the safest speed appears to be five to ten mph over the speed limit, with only twenty-four accidents per 100 million miles.

The reason is easy to understand: It's safest to go with the flow. Since speed limits are usually set artificially low, the safest and most efficient speed on a highway is right in that fudge zone of seven or eight mph over the posted speed limit. The October 1992 FHA study showed that when posted speed limits were raised, accidents actually decreased.

So why are the speed limits so low? It's not a plot to allow cops to write traffic tickets. Much of it is pressure from residents who don't want cars zooming by their house. For a person who has to cross the street, a car going sixty is more dangerous than one going thirty.

But it's not merely a concession to pedestrians that speed limits are set low. No one has the time and money to survey every street to find out what the most efficient speed would be. So the officials pass laws affecting entire categories of streets. In the District of Columbia the speed limit is thirty miles an hour, tops, everywhere, regardless of the type of road. For highways, the fifty-five mph national speed limit (repealed in 1995) reflected the desire to conserve gasoline.

The fifty-five mph law was passed in 1973 at the height of the oil crisis.

We do not write this as an encouragement for people to speed. In fact the numbers show that going *way* too fast is extremely dangerous, more so than going way too slow. Cars going twenty-five to thirty miles an hour over the speed limit have 7,072 accidents per 1,000,000 miles.

And these accident figures are for highways and freeways only. One should probably fudge a lot less on a city street—particularly in the neighborhood where the Why staff lives because there are millions of sweet little children running around trying to dodge cars. In fact, when you drive into our neighborhood, we suggest you get out and push.

Why does cigarette smoking cause lung cancer?

The Why staff refuses to join the media crusade to demonize the tobacco industry simply because it has sought, in the name of profit, to serve the whims of Satan. You'll have to look elsewhere if you want to read another diatribe against the cancer-stick peddlers.

That said, we think it's a good time to figure out what's going on in the lungs of a smoker. Why does cigarette smoke incite tumors, and why only sometimes?

The proof of the smoking/cancer link comes from several different categories of evidence. The first is epidemiological. People who smoke have seventeen times as great a chance of getting lung cancer as people who don't. If the ratio were just two to one, then you might argue that it was merely a reflection of the fact that smokers aren't health fanatics, that they are more likely to eat nothing but chili dogs, and so forth. But a seventeen-to-one ratio can't be explained away. "Lung cancer is almost exclusively a smoker's disease," says Donald Shopland, a spokesman for the National Cancer Institute.

A hundred years ago there was no such thing as lung cancer in medical literature. It wasn't officially registered as a disease until 1930. That's probably because before about 1910, people, being primitive, thought that what you were supposed to do with tobacco was chew it, or smoke it in cigar form, in which the smoke isn't inhaled. Camel, the first major national cigarette brand, was introduced in 1913.

Cigarettes grew in popularity because of tuberculosis. The public feared that the spitting of tobacco was spreading TB. So they started smoking *as a health measure*.

The next indication of a link is what Michael Siegel, an epidemiologist at the Centers for Disease Control in Atlanta, calls "biologic plausibility." This is the fact that tobacco smoke has been shown to cause cancers in laboratory animals. Tobacco smoke contains more than forty known carcinogens.

A third type of evidence comes from the study of lung tissue. Autopsies of some smokers who didn't have lung cancer have shown that they did have precancerous, abnormal, "neoplastic" cells in their lungs—in other words, sort of lung cancer in progress.

Now we come to the hard part. What actually happens inside the cells of a smoke-enshrouded lung? The most truthful answer, and one that probably would warm the heart of a tobacco executive, were he or she to have one, is that we don't really know. Somehow the carcinogens are damaging the internal regulatory systems of cells and causing them to divide uncontrollably.

The dastardly thing about cancer is that it is not a freakish, unnatural development. Cancer is nothing more than your own cells dividing and forming masses where they don't belong. A cell normally regulates and suppresses its own ability to divide. If that suppression mechanism is damaged, you can get cancer.

Maybe cigarette smoking will turn out to be a strictly twentieth-century fashion, like jousting in the eleventh century or dying of plague in the fourteenth. Our guess is that within a quarter of a century smoking will be considered a bizarre and antiquated behavior.

Naturally that's when we plan to start.

Why does drinking too much cause a hangover?

The serious drinker will point out that, technically, it is stopping drinking that causes a hangover.

A hangover, for those of you who haven't experienced it, involves headaches, lethargy, nausea, shakiness, body pains, a bad taste in the mouth, sensitivity to light, regret, guilt, shame, and a desperate struggle to remember what you might have

Quick cure for hangover.

Remove your head and
have it cryogenically
frozen till you feel better.

said or done the night before. There are two explanations for
why this happens, and perhaps both are right.

The first is that a hangover is a mild case of alcohol withdrawal symptoms. Basically, while tanked up, your body gets
used to operating with alcohol in the blood, and the brain factors in the depressant effects of alcohol when it synthesizes
neurotransmitters. Then suddenly the alcohol starts disappear-
ing from the blood because the person has gone to sleep or
passed out and the kidneys are working overtime to get rid of
the toxin. The brain chemistry can't adjust fast enough, and
you get all jittery and headachy.

"The body doesn't like change. It likes to keep things as they
are," says Walter Hunt, a neuropharmacologist at the National
Institute on Alcohol Abuse and Alcoholism. "The body gets
used to the alcohol as though [its presence] is normal."

The second explanation is: congeners. This is the culprit
Hunt favors. Congeners are chemical substances that are created by the same fermenting process that creates alcohol, and
they add to the taste. For example, when juniper berries fer-
ment, they create substances that add flavor to gin and make it
taste different from vodka. But these exotic congeners are

toxic. They ride the alcohol to all parts of your body where they don't belong.

The nasty thing about alcohol is that it's a terrific solvent. All those grubby little congeners become nicely dissolved in your alcoholic beverage, which in turn, because it's full of alcohol, becomes dispersed throughout your body, mixing with your bodily fluids right down to the cellular level. The alcohol smoothes the way for congeners to go anywhere in your body where there's water—which is just about everywhere.

That's why a hangover is an all-body experience. The alcohol's euphoric effects are gone and you're left with this toxic gunk in your body.

Vodka and white wine have fewer of these congeners than, say, gin or rum or red wine, and so they are less likely to cause a bad hangover. But the safest thing to do is just stick with the soda pop.

Why do people look at the ground when they're walking toward you? Why are people always refusing to look at each other?

In the old days, encounters were simpler. This is because society was stratified in clearly delineated social classes. If you walked by someone in your own social class, you said hello. If the person was in a lower class, you pretended the person did not exist.

Of course, there was a downside to the system. If you were a gentleman and another guy in your own social class didn't say hello to you—if he "cut" you—then you were absolutely obliged to challenge him to a duel with swords, or burn down his village, or defile his womenfolk, or whatever. So it was kind of a drag: One minute you're happily strolling down the sidewalk, the next you're elbow-deep in the entrails of your neighbor.

In today's classless society, we're still trying to sort out the rules of encounters. In the countryside and small towns, people still say hello. When high-powered city people go to small towns they practically jump out of their skin when total strangers in the grocery store or the filling station say hello. (How does one answer? Invite these strangers to do lunch? Ask them to come by the house for cocktails? *Do they want money?*)

In the city, you just can't say hello to everyone. Too many people. And there *are* dangerous loons out there. So the standard operating procedure for sidewalk cruising is to keep one's eyes down. You walk around as though shrouded in shame.

This isn't wrong, necessarily. Even a brief verbal exchange on a sidewalk is an immensely complicated bit of theater. You don't want to impose on the other person by insisting on an elaborate conversation, but neither do you want to be too superficial. So you have to make a reasoned, carefully calibrated decision about what to do.

Why can't you simply say hello to everyone? Because that wouldn't be polite. That's too demanding of others. Staring at the ground is called "polite inattention," says Margaret Visser, author of books on the rituals of everyday behavior.

"A lot of politeness is not taking any notice of people," she says. At the same time, "The rules are not clear. This causes a lot of pain. People don't know what to do, how to react."

The most painful of these superficial sidewalk encounters are with acquaintances. You have to make a snap judgment: How friendly am I with this person? Should I just say "Hi" or is something more prolonged appropriate? What if this person doesn't even acknowledge me? Does this person secretly hate me? Did this person somehow find out that my soul is diseased?

Even worse by far is when you are walking down a long hallway and see someone you know at the end of it, coming toward you, but still far away. When, and how, do you enter into the encounter ritual? To acknowledge the person immediately would require either a shout or a foolish-looking physical gesture. You could always stare, but to stare at someone without saying anything is kind of creepy and Ted Bundyish.

So what you do is: Pretend you don't see the person. Stare at the ground. Then, when the person is closer, you act surprised. "Oh, hi!" you say. You, a supposedly sane person, have just performed a little bit of encounter theater.

Why are so many of us so darn fat, and why is it so hard to lose weight?

Whenever you make your New Year's resolutions you probably start with a vow to lose weight this year. What you don't realize at that moment is that you are about to enter what will be, for you, the Year of the Pizza.

Fat's an epidemic. You might be under the delusion that society is slimming down thanks to trends like aerobic exercise and low-fat food. The tragic truth is that, despite $33 billion a year spent on dieting, ours is an ever-widening society. According to the National Academy of Sciences, in 1980 about 25 percent of Americans were overweight. A decade later, 33 percent of Americans were overweight.

How fat do you have to be to be "overweight"? Scientists say you're overweight if you're 20 percent heavier than your ideal weight. In other words, you're overweight if you're fat. Many of us aren't technically overweight; we just have ten pounds of pudge that we plan to lose very soon, but which, of course, will outlast the pyramids.

"We're getting fatter," says Susan Yanovski, an obesity researcher at the National Institutes of Health. "Kids are also becoming more obese."

So why is this?

For a long time there was an idea that people are just weak. They just have no willpower. They are fat because they don't behave, they eat too much, they can't resist slamming those pizzas and cheeseburgers and whatnot. This theory is wrong.

The fundamental problem is that we are not biologically designed for this world. That is to say, human evolution prepared us for times of feast and famine, for a world in which food was often hard to come by. We have a natural craving for fatty foods, so that we can pork up a little in anticipation of going hungry down the road. We are not designed with Taco Bell in mind. We have paleolithic bodies trapped in a world of fast food.

What no one knew until recently was why some people are fatter than others. Now, finally, there's an explanation, thanks to Jeffrey Friedman and his colleagues at the Howard Hughes Medical Institute at Rockefeller University.

As you probably heard, Friedman found the fat gene, or at least *a* fat gene. After seven years of searching he discovered a gene causing a certain breed of mouse to become extremely obese. From there he quickly found the same gene in humans. The gene instructs fat cells to make a certain protein, which Friedman calls leptin. From the fat cells, the leptin travels to the brain and tells the brain to stop eating so much and start burning more calories. But if there aren't many fat cells, there won't be much leptin produced, and thus the brain will tell you that you need to keep eating. In mice with a defective copy of the gene, no leptin is produced, and thus the brain thinks that it is trapped in a starving body even though the body is morbidly obese.

Friedman's research is stunning because this simple feedback mechanism applies to everyone, whether you're thin or a little bit pudgy or extremely fat. The discovery of leptin confirms an old theory, which is that everyone has a set point for how fat he or she will be. This is the lipostatic model of fat. In the same way that a thermostat regulates heat, a lipostat regulates lipids, or fats. Of course there is no organ in the body called a lipostat: There is just this tiny protein, found in extremely low concentrations in the blood, which travels from fat cells to the brain.

If leptin injections can be proven safe in animals and humans, and proven to be effective in humans, then in a matter of years it may become a widely used treatment for obesity.

What's kind of unnerving, though, is that the same drug would work in those of us who just want to lose five or ten pounds. One batch of normal, healthy mice in Friedman's laboratory were given leptin injections, and in only four days they went from 12 percent body fat to less than one percent body fat. You have to wonder: In the next century will some people stick themselves with a needle every morning just so they can lose their love handles? Will they have their daily leptin injection just so they can have a washboard stomach?

Why do we behave stupidly and do things we know are not in our best interests?

People are irrational. They smoke cigarettes. They have romances with creeps. They convince themselves they can reach the green by hitting the ball over the trees with a three-wood. What happens? The ball gets lost in the woods, and during the search a former spouse appears and starts yelling, and in the chaos someone drops a cigarette on the ground and ignites a forest fire. This is the price of bad judgment.

Not every disastrous decision is truly stupid. "We may be unduly harsh on ourselves," says Baruch Fischhoff, a psychology professor at Carnegie Mellon University. Even if we attempt an impossible golf shot or say "I do" to a known psychotic, we may be showing an admirable characteristic of perseverance. "Part of our job in life is not to accept limits, and to give it one more try," says Fischhoff.

Another possibility is that failure is a kind of success— because it vindicates your carefully constructed image as a total loser. You gotta believe in something, and so maybe you believe you are the kind of person who, for example, deserves to stub his toe a lot. You wander around your house at night, barefoot, with the lights off, and WHANG!, you're hopping up and down and saying, "I'm such an idiot." Though blinded by pain, at least *you know who you are*.

But the explanation we like most comes from Seymour Epstein, a psychologist at the University of Massachusetts. He says we literally have two separate minds, one of them logical and analytical and one of them emotional, instinctive, nonrational.

"They're working so smoothly together, people are not normally aware that there are two minds," he says.

The nonrational mind is dominant, he says. It's basically your animal mind; you make decisions the same way an animal does, through an emotional reaction to a given stimulus. When a rabbit hears a strange noise nearby, it doesn't think, "Uh-oh, a predatory species may want to turn me into *hasenpfeffer*." Instead, it just gets scared and runs. Just because human beings have other ways of making decisions (like logic) doesn't mean we no longer use the more ancient, nonrational methods.

Which is why TV commercials and political ads appeal to emotion, not reason. "Politicians and advertisers know what I'm talking about very well," Epstein told us.

So maybe that's why we make illogical decisions. We're not as logical a species as we think. How obvious!

On the other hand, Epstein's theory seems kind of hard to prove. So we can't decide what we think. You might say we're of two minds about this.

THE OUTER LIMITS

Why are we so sure there aren't tiny universes, complete with intelligent civilizations, contained within the atoms on the end of our fingernails?

One of the explicit policies of the Why staff is: Never Be Sizist.

Just because most adult human beings are between two and eight feet tall doesn't mean this is by any means the normal size of intelligent creatures. Maybe there are entire civilizations on the surfaces of atomic nuclei, right? Maybe when we clip our fingernails we are butchering billions of tiny beings who had been minding their own business until the gigantic clippers appeared up in the sky and everyone started screaming in extremely squeaky voices.

Okay, so maybe not. But even though we all know this is a pretty stupid question, how many of us can honestly say we know why it's stupid?

We called someone who ought to know: Steve Weinberg, the University of Texas physicist and author of *Dreams of a Final Theory*, which is about the search for an ultimate theory of physics that will explain everything that exists. Weinberg is definitely a 'spert.

He said the main evidence that there aren't miniature worlds or universes is that when we look at tiny objects like electrons they're all the same. Sameness increases as you move

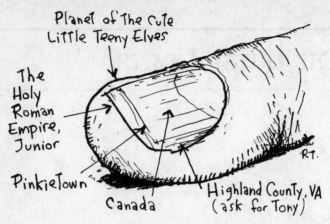

Planet of The Cute
Little Teeny Elves

The
Holy
Roman
Empire,
Junior

PinkieTown

Canada

Highland County, VA
(ask for Tony)

RT.

Some Civilizations now living on your fingernail.

down the size scale. This tips us off that we're reaching the
fundamental units of matter.

"There are reasons for strongly suspecting that there isn't
anything very complicated inside the electron, and one of the
reasons is that every electron is exactly like every other electron. If they had whole universes inside them, presumably they
would all be a little different," Weinberg said.

Look around you and you'll see that everything looks different. Your spouse or lover, for example, looks nothing at all like
your couch. We hope. Because things look different we know
they are expressions of tinier building blocks arranged in different ways. Electrons aren't like that. They come in only one
make and model. They're pretty insipid.

"They're interesting because they're boring," says Weinberg.

There are, to be sure, things other than electrons in the sub-
atomic realm. Atoms were once thought of, by definition, as
the smallest units of matter, but we know now that atoms are
made up of protons and neutrons, and they in turn are made
up of tiny particles called quarks, which supposedly come in
different "flavors" and "spins" and whatnot, and it may be that
quarks are made up of tiny looplike "strings," but any way you
slice it, you find that it's basically mush down there.

Now if we go to the opposite end of the size scale we find a
lot more scientific uncertainty. One of the big cosmological
revelations of this century was the discovery that there are bil-

lions of galaxies besides our own. And now some cosmologists think that our universe is just a fraction of the greater cosmos, that, as Weinberg puts it, "this universe which we call the Big Bang is just a small piece of a much larger universe, in which most parts are expanding very, very rapidly and are basically empty, and it's only a few places like here where the expansion is slower and you have matter and the possibility of life."

In other words: *We* are on the fingernail.

Why do we have a moon?

Imagine the Earth without a moon. The night sky would seem desolate. There'd never be an eclipse of the sun. Our ancestors might not have been inspired to become scientists. Poetry would be missing something. The word "lunacy" wouldn't exist. The *Apollo 11* astronauts, when they took one giant leap for mankind, would have tumbled screaming into empty space.

The incredible thing is, after all these years we don't know where the moon came from. "It's a major puzzle that we still haven't solved," says Bruce Hapke, a planetary scientist at the University of Pittsburgh.

What we do know is that the moon is a highly unusual object. Of the four rocky, inner planets—Mercury, Venus, Earth, and Mars—only Earth has a moon worth writing home about (Mars has two silly rocks, which appear to be a couple of captured asteroids). The four big gasbags beyond Mars (Jupiter, Saturn, Uranus, Neptune) have gobs of moons because those planets are like miniature solar systems. The gas giants and their moons formed simultaneously.

But Earth and the moon probably didn't form at the same time—they're too different. For example, Earth has a big iron core, the moon hardly any iron at all. And there's stuff here on Earth that doesn't exist on the moon.

For a long time scientists thought the moon split from the Earth in a kind of fission. The theory even suggested that the Pacific Ocean was the scar left by the moon's exit. Hardly anyone believes that anymore. Planets don't just spit out moons.

Another popular theory is that the moon is a captured planetoid. The problem there is that gravity doesn't work that way, usually. An object can't easily drift near a planet and then go into a holding pattern like an airplane around an airport. Without brakes, you'll just get whipped around the back side and slungshot (we say it's a word!) back into space. In special circumstances, if everything's just so, a moon can be captured—but "a capture would be a highly improbable event," says Hapke.

That leaves the reigning hypothesis: About 4.5 billion years ago an object the size of Mars smashed into the Earth, possibly a glancing blow. Stuff spewed into space. Some of it recondensed into the moon. This would explain why the moon is so dry. Water is volatile enough to have evaporated into space in such a situation. So would potassium and sodium, of which there are no trace on the moon.

This theory of a cataclysm-born moon has been around only a decade or so and comes from the study of moon rocks. It's also trendy: The eighties were the Impact Theory Decade.

Here's something to chew on: If that chance collision long ago hadn't occurred, and we didn't have a moon, it's possible that life itself might never have formed. What does the moon have to do with life on Earth? Tides. Life may have first appeared in evaporating tidal pools. On some rocky shoreline, a depression in a rock got splashed with water from a high tide. The water then sat there in a puddle, slowly evaporating. All those molecular compounds in the primordial soup of the young Earth would have gotten only more concentrated as the water evaporated.

Not only that, the moon's gravity stabilizes the motions of the Earth. Earth has only the slightest wobble on its axis, from about 22 to 24.6 degrees of tilt. The tilt is what gives us seasons; the stability of the tilt is what makes the seasons fairly predictable. Without the moon, the Earth might wobble a lot more, with dramatic changes in just a few million years. The result would be weather so wacky that higher forms of life might never have evolved.

Why do the sun and moon appear neither near nor far? Why do they just kind of hang there in the sky, as though someone pasted them there?

The other day the sun set fat and bloody. We knew it was 93 million miles away, roughly, but it didn't *look* 93 million miles away. Something that is 93 million miles away ought to be a speck, even if it is a star.

On the other hand, we couldn't honestly say how far away it appeared. It was just . . . there. Kind of godlike. Apollonian.

Why is it so hard, indeed impossible, to perceive the distance to the sun and the moon?

You probably think that's a dumb question. You are thinking we are doodoo-brains for not realizing that it's all because of the vacuum of space. You think the explanation is that there's nothing but *clear stuff* between us and the sun and the moon. If there were a haze between the Earth and, say, the sun, maybe you could tell how far away it was, right?

Nah, it's just geometry.

The way we perceive depth in everyday life is through stereoscopic vision. Hold up a finger in front of you, look at it first with one eye, then with the other. The eyes have slightly different angles on the finger, so the finger seems to shift against the background. This is a simple example of what is called parallax. Our brain combines the two images into a single perception with depth of field.

This trick works only for things within a few yards of us. As we write this column, we easily perceive the three spatial dimensions around our desk, but as we look across the Why bunker, toward the tennis courts and the putting green and the personal yacht basins, objects and shapes tend to become flattened out.

Fortunately a second clue kicks in, which is that we know how tall people are, how high the ceiling is, etc., and we know that if we see a very small but normally proportioned human being it is probably someone far across the room and not a midget right in front of us.

But you see the problem with the sun and moon: They are not close, nor is their size obvious. So basically there's no way to tell where they are or even what they are (spheres? disks?).

Did ancient people think they could build a tower tall enough to reach the moon or sun? Did they shoot arrows at them and wonder why they never got there?

Actually it was always obvious that the sun and moon were far away. They didn't get larger when you climbed a tree or a mountain.

A couple of thousand years ago, the Greek astronomer Eratosthenes came up with an essential piece of cosmological information: the size of the Earth. He dug a well in what is now the Egyptian city of Aswan. One day a year, at the summer solstice, the sun would be directly overhead and shine on the water at the bottom of the well. That same day, Eratosthenes would measure the angle of the sun's rays on a stick far to the north in the city of Alexandria. Because he knew how far it was between Alexandria and Aswan, and because he knew geometry, he was able to calculate that the Earth was about 29,000 miles in circumference, which was a bit high but not a bad estimate.

If you know the size of the Earth, then it's possible to estimate the distance to the moon. The secret is to let the Earth's rotation assist your observation of the moon.

"You look at the moon when it's on the horizon and then you look at the moon when it's straight overhead, and you see that it's displaced by a degree with respect to the fixed stars," says Al Van Helden, author of *Measuring the Universe*.

The moon, in other words, has parallax just like the finger held up in front of your face. You just have to wait a few hours (in six hours you will move a distance equal to one Earth radius) and do some fancy equations. Thus the ancients were able to calculate that the moon was roughly sixty Earth radii away.

The sun's distance was much harder to figure. Ptolemy, the Alexandrian astronomer of the second century A.D. who created a cosmology that lasted until the Copernican revolution thirteen centuries later, figured the sun was 1,200 Earth radii away. But that's only about 5 million miles. (What a dunce!)

In 1672, when astronomers were finally figuring out once and for all which objects orbited around which, an important experiment helped clear up matters. An astronomer in Paris recorded the position of Mars, as did an astronomer on the coast of South America. They compared notes and spent years crunching the numbers. There was enough parallax to give them a sense of the distance to Mars.

Since the relative positions of the sun and planets were well understood by then (they correctly supposed that Mars was about 1.5 times as far from the sun as Earth), the astronomers were eventually able to extrapolate their data and come up with a pretty good estimate of the distance between the Earth and the sun.

Nowadays if you want to know precisely how far it is to the moon you can bounce a laser beam off a reflector left on the surface of the moon by the *Apollo 11* astronauts. The speed of light is constant, so we can use light to calculate distance.

Better yet, you could just look up the number in an encyclopedia.

Why didn't the Russians ever make it to the moon?

It would have been a complete bummer if the lunar rover had gotten a flat tire from running over a vodka bottle. That was a real possibility for a while there. Physicist Edward Teller, asked in the early sixties what we would find if we landed on the moon, answered simply, "Russians."

Remember, the Soviets had a great space program. In 1957 they launched the first artificial satellite, *Sputnik*, to which Americans had a calm, measured response (diving into bomb shelters, screaming in the streets, etc.). In 1961 the Soviets put the first man in space. Throughout the 1960s they sent probes to the moon. If for some reason you look at a map of the far side of the moon you'll see that all the big craters have Russian names.

So why'd the Soviets lose the biggest race of all?

A lousy surgeon was partly responsible. The Soviet space program's mastermind, Sergei Korolev, who was even more important to the Soviets than Wernher von Braun was to the Americans, went to the hospital for routine polyp surgery in January 1966. The inexperienced surgeon discovered a cancerous tumor and labored eight hours to remove it, until finally the bleeding Korolev checked out permanently.

That was a devastating loss, but the Soviets probably wouldn't have beaten us to the moon anyway. For one thing, the U.S. was moon-crazy, pouring about 3 percent of the entire federal budget into the space program. Our best minds were involved. The Soviets, by contrast, waffled for a couple of years in the early sixties before deciding to shoot for the moon. Even then they were more interested in bombs than spaceships.

"They were never as excited about space flight as they were about ballistic missiles," says Jim Harford, former head of the American Institute of Aeronautics and Astronautics, who's writing a book on Korolev.

You could probably trace the Soviet missile obsession back to American superiority in making airplanes. We had B-52s that could fly intercontinental distances and potentially drop nukes on Moscow and the like, but the Soviets lacked long-range bombers—there was no Soviet version of Boeing. To make up for that, they built intercontinental missiles (stashing medium-range missiles in Cuba was another idea but it kind of backfired, as you may know). The best Soviet rocket designer, Valentin Glushko, wouldn't work for the space program, in part because he wanted to use exotic, toxic fuels that worried Korolev.

The result was that, even as the Americans were polishing the *Saturn V* rocket that would eventually take us to the moon, the Soviets were dithering with a huge go-nowhere contraption called the *N1*. They already had a lunar lander built and wanted to go to the moon in 1968, ahead of *Apollo*. But four times they tried to launch the *N1* and every time it fizzled or blew up. The problem wasn't the rocket so much as the diagnostic equipment used to test it. Rockets are impressive, but what's more important are the unseen gadgets that measure temperature, pressure, and so forth with extreme precision.

"When it came to the difference between our two capabilities, far and away the biggest difference was not so much in the rockets but in the instrumentation we had, our ability to test things," says Robert Seamans, who was deputy administrator of NASA during the 1960s. "Before the *Saturn V* was launched, we'd check around seventy thousand different points in the last few minutes before liftoff, and if something was out of tolerance, one of the launch crew at their console inside the launch facility would get a signal that something was wrong and electronically could move in and find out which item was out of tolerance."

The Soviets had rockets more reliable than the *N1*, but they just weren't big enough for a moon voyage. Putting men in orbit around Earth doesn't require a particularly large booster, but a moon shot is another story: Not only do you need enough oomph to get your spaceship to the moon, you also have to lug along all kinds of extra boosters and rockets for getting it back.

When the spacecraft reaches the moon it has to brake itself so it won't just whip around the back side and zip right back to Earth. A key strategy for both the Americans and the Russians was to keep the command module in lunar orbit, with one astronaut, and only send a largely disposable landing craft to the moon itself. Neil Armstrong and Buzz Aldrin left the moon by crawling into the equivalent of a tin can and launching themselves back into orbit for a rendezvous with the command module, which then fired off more rockets for the return to Earth. Had NASA not used this tricky lunar orbit rendezvous strategy the *Saturn V* would have had to be twice as large. (Maybe they would have called it the *Saturn X*.)

The Soviets considered going to the moon until the late 1970s, when they gave up. Then they tried to cover up their moon program so no one would know that they had failed.

But of course the Soviet Union failed in bigger ways, which is why, although someday there may be Russians on the moon, there will never be Soviets.

Why were the *Apollo* astronauts quarantined after they got back?

Let's say you're the person in charge of the moon program. (This is a "hypothetical" situation.) You have to make an important decision. What do you do with the astronauts when they get back?

You know that, of all the dangers of the mission, the most far-fetched is that the astronauts might be exposed to, and bring back to Earth, a killer bacterium or virus. You know the moon has no atmosphere, no water, no sign of anything biological, and the surface temperature of any given spot varies by hundreds of degrees from day to night. You are convinced the moon is sterile.

On the other hand, you know that it would be bad for your career if the astronauts came back infected by a Lunar Death Microbe that eventually wiped out life on Earth.

Your decision? Right. Quarantine. (Though you are tempted to let the astronauts shake hands first with President Nixon.)

"In retrospect we really didn't have to do this," says Richard S. Johnston, the former director of NASA's Lunar Receiving

Symptoms of the Lunar Flu

MOO

Your head exhibits swelling & you tend to bob off the floor. Dogs howl at you and cows jump over you. Charles Schulz may try to draw you.

Lab, where the *Apollo 11* astronauts were sealed for twenty-one days. He still groans about the money it cost. "Let's not go into the dollars. Tens of millions."

The astronauts were inside protective suits when they were plucked out of the ocean by the crew of an aircraft carrier. They were immediately placed in a pod called the Mobile Quarantine Facility. The pod was flown to Houston and transferred on a flatbed truck to the Lunar Receiving Lab. The MQF had a portal that could be tightly sealed against the LRL (that's just FYI). The astronauts then went inside, where a staff of doctors, scientists, cooks, and other NASA employees joined them in quarantine.

Another part of the lab was reserved for moon rocks. The rocks were kept in a vacuum and handled with special pressurized gloves. When one of the gloves came off, an alarm went off, the lab was evacuated, and the "contaminated" worker and anyone else standing nearby were quarantined.

Lunar dust, meanwhile, was scrutinized and even injected into lab mice.

Hardly anyone at NASA actually thought there might be moon microbes, says Johnston, but people in the agriculture industry as well as some university professors and disease specialists said, "Something might be there and we might endanger the whole world."

The idea for this elaborate procedure came from a government panel, formed in 1963, called the Interagency Committee for Back Contamination.

"There are some really intelligent people who go off on some very deep ends," Johnston says.

It goes without saying that there wasn't any "back contamination" from the moon.

Though maybe the symptoms don't show up for twenty-five years.

Why is Jupiter so big? And why doesn't it have a surface?

Jupiter could eat Earth for lunch, with room for a Pluto dessert. You could fit a thousand Earths inside Jupiter. Jupiter is one big hunk-o-planet.

How did this thing get there? Partly it's just a random event. During the formation of the solar system a lot of matter accreted in that area. Big things get bigger: All that matter has lots of gravity, pulling in yet more matter.

Here's a critical fact, should you decide to recall any of this answer: Jupiter has enough gravity to keep its hydrogen gas from floating away. You, by contrast, cannot hold on to your gas. Neither can Earth. Any hydrogen gas on this planet just leaks off into space.

Why does hydrogen float away on Earth? Because hydrogen is so puny. It heats up easily. If a hydrogen molecule bumps into a big ugly nitrogen molecule, the hydrogen goes flying and sometimes careens into space.

"When the light guy hits the fat guy, the light guy bounces off at a higher speed," explains NASA spokesman Steve Maran.

A gas giant like Jupiter probably couldn't form close to the sun because it would get too hot. That solar radiation would heat up the Jovian hydrogen. Hot means fast, and fast means you reach escape velocity.

Because it has all this gas, Jupiter doesn't have a surface, exactly. If you could descend into the atmosphere you would find yourself in an increasingly dense, muggy, soupy, pressurized environment. You would be crushed.

If you could somehow keep going, you might reach a surface of sorts: a core of liquid metallic hydrogen. This stuff would behave a little like mercury (the metal, not the planet). We can't make liquid metallic hydrogen on Earth because it requires so much pressure.

Finally, deeper still, you'd hit a rock core. Or so scientists think; they're not really sure.

We've assumed there was some water vapor down there. When the comet Shoemaker–Levy 9 slammed into Jupiter, everyone expected to see signs of water vapor rising toward the top of the atmosphere. It didn't happen. No one is sure why. For now, astronomers are assuming that the comet just didn't penetrate far enough to reach the water vapor.

In other words, scientists presume they had the right theory—it was the comet that messed up.

Why is the universe expanding?

Actually there's a rather wonderful answer: The universe is expanding because the universe has to do *something*. The laws of physics say that the universe can't stand still. It can expand, it can contract, it can do the hokeypokey and turn itself around, but it can't just lie there in a cosmic torpor.

Gravity's to blame. Gravity ensures that everything we see, whether it is a spinning moon or an expanding universe, is going somewhere.

Let's say you pick up a rock. The first thing you notice is, they don't make rocks like they used to when you were a kid. Back then, a rock wasn't just a rock, it was a stone, something far more upscale and interesting. But never mind. You got this rock and you want to do something with it. What can you do? You can throw it toward the ground. You can toss it up into the air. You can continue to apply enough muscular pressure to the rock to keep it from falling to the ground. But what you can't do is place it into the air in front of you and make it stay there.

The rock must move. So too must the universe.

As for why the universe began expanding a long time ago, no one knows. It wasn't *because* of the Big Bang. The expansion *is* the Big Bang. There's no causality there. (In fact there wasn't even a bang!) There's no way for us to see all the way back to the dawn of time, when the expansion began. We can, however, detect light and radiation from about 300,000 years after the birth of the universe, and what we see is a very hot and very dense cosmos that is becoming less so over time, in the same way that steam shoots out of a teakettle in an expanding cloud and cools into visible liquid water.

Science can't tell us who lit the fire.

THE MAILBAG

Chuck Hansen of Richmond, Virginia, read our remarks on the Big Bang and the expansion of the universe, and he asked, "Where did the matter in the hot, dense ball come from to begin with, if the matter cannot be created or destroyed?"

Dear Chuck: We make it a policy to pause, at least once a day, to appreciate the matter around us. It is so nice to live in a solid world. It is hard to see how a world of pure energy could possibly be enjoyable, especially in regard to the things we feel most passionately about, like lunch.

As for your question, first you should forget that daffy notion that matter can't be created or destroyed. Matter can be converted to energy, and energy can be converted to matter. It is this principle that was behind the decision to spend a billion dollars or so constructing the vast tunnel in Texas for the Superconducting Super Collider. (Congress later voted to save money by filling in the hole.)

This is also the principle behind the decision to make nuclear bombs and nuclear reactors. You remember $E=mc^2$? That's the energy/matter conversion formula. A hunk of matter represents a tremendous concentration of energy, which is why you can convert a relatively small chunk of plutonium into an explosion capable of wiping out an entire city.

So, as for why there is matter at all, it's basically just an alternate state of energy. The universe started in a state of pure energy and, after expanding and cooling a little bit, matter formed, specifically quarks and electrons and other tiny particles. Later, bigger stuff like protons appeared, and then atoms, and finally after about a billion years your galaxies got it together.

Now, here's the bad news: There's no solution yet for the real mystery, which is why there was a little bit more matter than antimatter in the early universe. Matter and antimatter annihilate one another, but fortunately there was just enough excess matter to leave some solid stuff in the universe to form the stars and planets and, eventually, human beings. But no one knows why there was that "symmetry break," as physicists put it.

"That is precisely the question the Super Collider was to address," says Bob Park, a physicist with the American Physical Society.

In other words, Chuck, your curiosity cannot be sated unless you are willing to pony up about $10 billion yourself. Some "Why Things Are" answers are more expensive than others.

Why are we suddenly menaced by asteroids from space?

There is a fear industry out there that refuses to shut down. No longer a big market in nuclear terror? Let's try selling the fear of rocks from space.

The timing is awfully suspicious—the Soviet Union becomes defunct and almost within minutes there is talk about Earth-crossing asteroids. Among those discussing this new threat are scientists associated with the Strategic Defense Initiative—instead of shooting down incoming Soviet nukes, they say, we can destroy or divert incoming 'roids.

For years no one worried about asteroids or comets striking Earth because such events are so rare. But then last year NASA issued a report saying there was a one in ten thousand chance that during "our lifetime" an asteroid at least one third of a mile wide would strike Earth and "possibly end civilization as we know it."

Which would be a very unpopular outcome, as it were. Now you have to ask yourself: Why play the lottery, which offers you only about a one in a million chance of a big payday, when there's an even better chance that the sky will fall?

You can answer this one yourself by figuring out where this scary one in ten thousand figure comes from. The thinking is that once every million years or so, a big rock or comet hits Earth. Thus any given period of one hundred years—every "lifetime" in the NASA calculus—has a one in ten thousand chance of having an asteroid problem.

But the reason you play the lottery is that you know there will be a payoff. There's always a winner. The reason you shouldn't worry about asteroids is that, in most centuries, there won't be a payload (can we say "as it were" again?). No asteroid of appreciable size will hit. No one will die.

"Numerically the odds of yourself dying from this [impact] are similar to the odds of dying in a tornado or an airplane crash," says Clark Chapman, a planetary scientist for Science Applications International Corporation in Tucson. "I can't imagine losing sleep over this."

Asteroids are a psychological issue as much as an astronomical one. How do we perceive risk? What level of menace can we tolerate before we have to take defensive action? What's absurd about this is that even as we worry about hypothetical asteroid collisions we are already doing our best to wreck the planet.

"There are lots of risks that we will face in the next century. There are things that are right in our face, but people have a tendency to think of things that are way up in the sky," says Steven Ostro, who studies asteroids for NASA's Jet Propulsion Laboratory in Pasadena. He says we should perhaps survey the near-Earth asteroids better than we have so far because "it would be nice to know if there's something coming toward us, say, in the next century."

Doomsayers we ain't, but we'd bet that if civilization comes to an end in the next century it will be either because of the environmental and economic costs of human overpopulation or because some highly educated, well-meaning world leaders manage, somehow, against all odds, to start a nuclear war. Which would, of course, simulate rather strikingly the effects of a rogue asteroid.

Why can't we see other planets outside our own solar system?

Look at Jupiter some night. Most brilliant! And Venus is so bright it is sometimes mistaken for a UFO. At least that's what we've read. The Why staff would never make that mistake, of course, because we're so sophisticated we'd be more likely to make the opposite mistake—if we ever saw a huge rotating saucer emit a blinding beam of light and suck a pickup truck off a remote country road, we'd probably say, "Hey, lookit that! Venus!"

It is worth noting that extrasolar planets might not even exist. But the planetary community presumes they do and figures they're fairly common.

The official reason why you can't see any planets around other stars is that the stars are too bright, relative to planets. But the truth is that our telescopes are simply not good enough.

Stars are far brighter than planets (stars generate light and planets only reflect it). To get a measure of the difference you need only compare Venus or Jupiter to the sun. You can't even look at the sun, it's so bright. If there were a big, fat, Jupiter-sized planet orbiting a nearby star, it would reflect enough light to be seen in a sensitive telescope if it were not washed out by the light coming from the star.

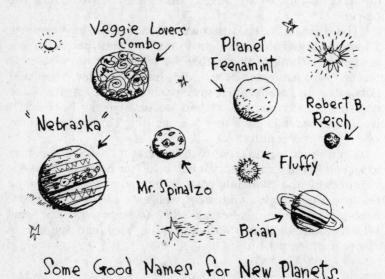

Some Good Names for New Planets.

"There are enough photons coming from the [hypothetical] planet for it to be detectable," says Eugene Levy, a planetary scientist at the University of Arizona. But the planetlight is buried by starlight. Starlight is splashy, it scatters within the telescope itself, and appears as a smudge rather than a nice, neat point.

Levy and several colleagues say they can fix this. For several hundred million dollars it would be possible to build a space-based telescope that, using something called a "coronagraph," would extract the light from a star and leave only the surrounding light sources, such as dust and planets. This technique already has been used to detect a vast dust cloud, the type of thing that spawns planets, around the star Beta Pictoris.

"We believe it will be possible to observe planets around other stars," Levy says. "It's a funding question, not a technological question."

In the meantime, scientists are using "astrometry"—the study of the motion of stars—to look for signs of planets. A large planet would give a star a slight wobble in its motion.

"The discovery of planetary systems will be an historic occasion," Levy says.

Yeah, and better yet: You'd never have to write a grant proposal again.

Why did people in ancient times decide that constellations of stars look like bears and crabs and horses and so forth even though you can stare at them for hours and not see anything that remotely resembles a bear or a crab or a horse?

There are only a few constellations that make any sense. The Big Dipper is clearly a big dipper (though the ancients bizarrely called it Ursa Major, Latin for "a really major bear"). Scorpius is another tolerable constellation because it's basically scorpionlike, and Orion does have a nifty belt-and-sword ensemble. We're told by smarter people that Cygnus is vaguely swanlike. But the rest are simply ridiculous. (The Milky Way doesn't look anything like a candy bar!) So what were the ancients thinking?

Here's one preliminary thought that is certainly not an answer by itself: A couple of thousand years ago, there were no streetlights. There was no smog. The sky was clear. So the an-

cients saw more stars. The Big Dipper actually has 227 visible stars, not just the big 7 we see at night in the city and the suburbs. Some constellations, seen in full on a clear night, may have looked slightly more like a mythological figure or creature.

But there's a better, more realistic answer, and it's this: The ancients *didn't* think the constellations looked like bears and crabs and soldiers or whatnot. They simply needed a way to discuss the night sky. They had to name the parts of the celestial map. If you look at a map of the United States, you wouldn't say that Florida looks like a "Florida." In fact, let's not even think about what it looks like.

Modern astronomers still refer to Orion and Cassiopeia and Hercules and so forth: When talking about stars and galaxies and quasars, they have to have some way of identifying where these things are in the sky.

The big picture is, we are a naming species. We give ourselves names, our cities names, even our dogs names. No other creature does this as far as we know, and it's certainly not necessary. Admit it: There's no reason you couldn't just refer to your dog as "The Dog." If you have two dogs they can be Dog One and Dog Two. But you won't do this because you prefer to give things names; it makes them more familiar. Thus we name the heavens. Though let's be honest: Most of us can only name about two or three constellations. The rest of the night sky is just a big ol' splotch.

Why is it that we're scanning the heavens for signals from alien civilizations, but we're not sending any messages ourselves?

B ecause space is dark and scary. We don't want anyone to know we're here. We're just trying to be a fly on the wall.

Seriously, this has been a topic of scientific discussion. Earthlings are not exactly silent, of course, because radar, radio, and TV signals have been leaving the planet for more than sixty years. Within an eighty-light-year radius of the Earth are about one thousand sunlike stars that conceivably could have planets with intelligent civilizations. If you go out to 160 light-years the number increases by a factor of ten. Any day now, six-legged Beetle People could pick up the antics of Milton Berle. ("Hilarious!" they'll say. "Let's take them as pets.")

The early broadcasting signals were weak, however, and would be difficult to detect. Even the stronger signals of recent years would likely be fuzz by the time they reached a distant radio telescope (electromagnetism isn't destroyed as it passes through the near vacuum of space, but it spreads out and gets weaker). It's likely that only an intentional, look-here signal can be easily detected across vast stellar distances.

Once, in 1974, astronomers Frank Drake and Carl Sagan sent a message describing who we are and where we live, from the Arecibo antenna in Puerto Rico toward a cluster of stars in the constellation Hercules. But it'll take that signal about twenty-six thousand years to reach those stars.

The general thinking is that communicating with other beings ought to be done after much deliberation. "When you don't know what you're going to encounter, you don't start yelling out there," says Louis Friedman, executive director of the Planetary Society.

But he says he doesn't think aliens would actually try to come and get us. We were also assured by John Billingham, chief of the SETI (Search for Extraterrestrial Intelligence) program at NASA's Ames Research Center in Northern California, that any aliens we might detect out there are probably peaceful.

"If we detect anyone with our search, they're bound to be very much older than we are," he says. "Say they're ten million years older than us. They must have achieved some sort of structure in their society which has permitted longevity and stability over an enormous period of time."

Of course, we're able to send signals and no one would accuse us of being a "stable" civilization. Why wouldn't we pick up signals from a young, crazy, testosterone-poisoned alien race? Well, for one thing, older civilizations presumably have superior signal-sending technology and are easier to detect.

Now we should deal with the real issue: What do we do if the new, expanded SETI program conducted by NASA actually comes up with something? Recently new computer programs allowed NASA to increase dramatically the search of the sky. Make no mistake: SETI is still a long shot. The enterprise is full of presumptions. Why, for example, would anyone send a signal? *We're* not! Besides, intelligent life doesn't just grow on trees. Most of the universe is probably like most of the solar system—lots of cold, vacant real estate.

But just in case, scientists from around the world recently came up with something called the "Declaration of Principles Concerning Activities Following the Detection of Extraterrestrial Intelligence."

It's a silly document, frankly. It asks that anyone who detects the fabulous beep of E.T. immediately inform responsible scientists (who can verify the signal), and then "national authorities," and then various scientific organizations ("Commission J of the International Radio Science Union," for example, and "the Central Bureau of Astronomical Telegrams of the International Astronomical Union"), and, of course, the secretary general of the United Nations.

Ridiculous. Let's get this straight: If we discover life on Neptune, we're calling our local TV station, pronto. We're shrieking into the camera: ALIENS FROM SPAAAAAAAAAACE.

INSIDE THE NOGGIN

Why did Freud think women suffer from "penis envy" when that is obviously absurd?

Sure it's easy to criticize Freud these days. But when you look at what ol' Sigmund wrote, at the actual *text*, is it really so offensive? He wrote that women "fall a victim to envy for the penis which will leave ineradicable traces on their development and which will not be surmounted in even the most favorable cases without a severe expenditure of psychical energy."

He went on to say that because of this trauma, women suffer from "narcissism" and "physical vanity" and have a weak sense of justice, that they are rigid and inflexible, that "to be loved is a stronger need for them than to love," that "they are bound to value their charms more highly as a late compensation for their original sexual inferiority."

So what's the problem????

Seriously, Freud spewed out a lot of ideas in his day, and not all of them were as dumb as the penis envy theory. Freud, we must note, deserves some respect: He's the Aristotle of modern psychology, an irrepressible genius who was almost too prodigious for his own good. We consider him an auxiliary Why staffer for sheer chutzpah in trying to explain why people are the way they are, even at the risk of sometimes giving a preposterous answer.

You have to remember that at the end of the nineteenth century, no one knew much about human psychology. Freud was

If Freud had gone into obstetrics.

practically operating in a vacuum, and he had to fashion his own scientific field from the scraps of neurology and philosophy. Among other things he is credited with discovering the unconscious—not a bad thing to put on one's résumé! He also invented a number of concepts that we take for granted today, like infantile sexuality, repression, and the Oedipus complex. He even invented the whole lying-on-the-couch routine.

The notion of penis envy isn't entirely concocted. It's grounded in the observation that little girls sometimes explicitly express a desire to have one of those things. For example, Freudian apologist Lucy Freeman, in her book *Freud Rediscovered*, quotes a four-year-old girl on a playground saying, "I'm growing a penis under my arm so I can get everybody's attention."

But even though penis envy is real, it's not very important. Freud's great error was in thinking that penis envy was the path by which a girl identified herself as feminine—and thus as sexually inferior. In fact, subsequent research has shown that little girls are aware early in life that they are girls, and they don't have to envy a penis to understand that. And boys are envious too—for example, they are envious of their mother's and father's power. Penis envy is thus nothing more than a "subclass of envy," says psychoanalyst David Scharff, director of the Washington School of Psychiatry.

"The trouble was, Freud had about a million ideas, and you couldn't expect them all to hold up," Scharff says.

(Actually, it looks as though Freud's brand of therapy, psychoanalysis, is rapidly becoming a historical curiosity. Increasingly, people forgo the couch and instead try to find a cure in something like Prozac, a "serotonin reuptake inhibitor." Freud would be appalled.)

Surely Freud was a victim of his own culture, in which it was orthodox to see women as not only inferior but basically as inexplicable. Freud asked: "What do women want?" (There may be one or two men today who ask the same thing, we guess.) Scharff says, "Freud was much more generous to women than most of his peers. He wasn't actually trying to put them down."

Also, he was blunt. It did not occur to him to worry about how women (and late-twentieth-century feminists) would react to his theories. Thus perhaps he did not choose his words carefully enough when he described the female child as "the little creature without a penis" and when he said that a woman was happiest giving birth to a son because the son brings "the longed-for penis with him."

Bonus Freud Item:
Why was Freud so enamored of his cigar?

Freud smoked twenty cigars a day, from when he awoke at 7 A.M. to when he went to bed after midnight. We can almost smell him from here.

Freud declined to assign any symbolic significance to his cigar. He's purported to have said, "Sometimes a cigar is just a cigar" (though the American Psychiatric Association says the quote is apocryphal, or at least without any known citation). But Freud may have been guilty of repressing the symbolic significance of the cigar. It was his security blanket.

Evan J. Elkin, a New York psychiatrist, told us that a Freudian analysis of Freud's cigar smoking might probe whether the cigars revealed an oral dependency. "We know that he was extremely attached to his mother. So is this someone who is orally dependent, orally motivated? Probably yes," Elkin said. But he said that's just one part of the picture.

Elkin recently wrote of Freud's cigar habit in the magazine *Cigar Aficionado* (which reminds us: Why isn't there a magazine called *Dorito Aficionado*?). Elkin wrote that Freud grew up watching his industrious father smoking cigars in his long hours at the fabric factory in Vienna. "From early on, young Sigmund associated his father's smoking with his great capacity for hard work and self-control," wrote Elkin.

Freud himself said the malodorous cancer tube "served me for precisely 50 years as protection and a weapon in the combat of life . . . I owe to the cigar a great intensification of my capacity to work and a facilitation of my self-control."

The cigar was also a guy thing. Guys stood around smoking cigars, bonding, discussing psychoanalysis, trying to come up with demeaning theories about why women are so weird.

Eventually the cigars imperiled Freud's health. He developed cancer of the soft palate and the jaw. His doctors told him to stop smoking. He refused. When he did go cold turkey he became depressed. So he smoked almost until he died at eighty-three of cancer.

"His very own inability to modify his smoking habit illustrates a basic mechanism in human psychology that Freud termed 'knowing and not knowing,' where an individual, faced with rational understanding, may still be unable to act appropriately," writes Elkin.

Also there's the little matter of addiction. Freud was a heavy user of not just nicotine but also cocaine. Freud toyed with his own addiction theory, something about finding a replacement for compulsive masturbation as a child. (Can we say that word? "Compulsive"?)

A cigar is now a quaint old thing, suggesting a bygone world where men in top hats drank port after dinner and proudly patted their tenured bellies. And believed in Freud.

Why does altruism exist in a dog-eat-dog world?

The existence of altruism is one of those things that consternate people in lab coats but offer no mystery whatsoever to regular people. Regular people know, with utter certainty, that they do things out of love, and caring, and goodwill toward fellow man and woman. But to a scientist, charity seems, at first glance, maladaptive. You say you give money to the United Way? How un-Darwinian of you!

The fact is, however, there are other species that do the same thing. It's not a dog-eat-dog world after all (isn't that a Disney song?). Rats in a cage will eat less if doing so stops the electric shocks given to another rat. Dolphins will physically support another injured dolphin and keep it from drowning. The worker honeybee sacrifices herself for the good of the hive. Monkeys take turns picking lice from one another's back.

So why aren't all these creatures merely self-interested?

The answer is that altruism, though not necessarily benefiting an individual, benefits the genes that the individual is carrying. (Yet another Hallmark card sentiment from the Why staff.)

The classic example is the lioness sacrificing herself for the safety of her cubs. She dies, but her genes survive within those cubs. And among those genes is the gene that says it is better to sacrifice oneself than to let one's cubs die.

We might say the behavior of the lioness is a particular kind of altruism called nepotism. That's simply the investment of energy in the support of offspring and kin, and it's common in humans, apes, birds, mammals, insects—you name it. What's far more rare is "social reciprocity." You find it in the lice-picking chimps. But you find it most of all among humans. Humans are constantly being reciprocal. We constantly cut deals with, or work with, people who aren't kin. When you buy a burger at McDonald's you're engaging in social reciprocity of sorts. Our entire human civilization is a monument to reciprocity. Do you think birds would ever do a deal like NAFTA?

The good thing about social reciprocity is that, on the whole, we prosper because we can accomplish more working together than working individually. Economies of scale and all that. Scratch someone's back, and later he'll scratch yours when you're really itching. It works! There are 5 billion of us!

But the bad thing about all this is that, as an individual, you might get the shaft. Social reciprocity is risky. People may cheat you. Maybe that guy won't scratch your back after all. Richard Alexander, an evolutionary biologist and author of *The Biology of Moral Systems*, says human intelligence may be an evolutionary response to the risks of our social structures. We might have needed savvy brains in order to detect cheaters and frauds. They say journalists are too cynical, but maybe cynicism is the essential function of human gray matter.

"We're all lie detectors in a sense," Alexander says. "When you start that business of potential cheating, you have to have a defense against that."

So look where we are: a tit-for-tat social structure. Big ol' brains. What's next? Ethics. Morals. Religious beliefs. Cultural rules. Government laws. All of these things are designed on top of our primitive impulses to govern social relations among people who are, for the most part, genetically unrelated.

We teach these values to our young. We try to create a decent world, not simply as a biological instinct but as an intellectual and moral choice. We may be animals, but we're not *just* animals.

We are gifted, most of us, with the ability to empathize, to understand how another feels, and to feel that feeling ourselves. But the power to empathize has one drawback, notes Frans de Waal, a primatologist at the Yerkes Regional Primate Research Center of Emory University:

"Empathy makes it also possible to be cruel," he says.

Animals are not cruel, intentionally. They may be tricky, deceptive, bloodthirsty, but they are not sadistic.

Perhaps that is another reason it is better to give than to receive: There's so much evil in the world, you have to try your best to tip the scales back in the direction of love.

Why is it that humans recognize faces easily, while computers have never figured out the trick?

Someone might hand you an old photograph and you'll instantly realize it's a picture of, say, Richard Nixon as a boy. You just see it. The incipient ski-slope nose. The juvenile jowls. The tape recorder slung over the shoulder. How does your brain pick up these subtle details so easily?

We know that vision works in multiple stages. Light enters your eyes. Your brain first detects the spots of light and dark. Then, at another neuronal level, it discerns color. Then it registers the horizontal and vertical lines of objects. Then it checks out the corners of objects. All this happens quickly but not instantaneously. What's amazing is that there's an even higher level of detection: A tiny but distinct portion of the brain, in the inferotemporal cortex, appears to be devoted to facial recognition. (We're not sure yet which part of the brain comes up with words like "inferotemporal.")

That's basically all this little section of the brain does. It tells you that you're looking at California governor Pete Wilson and not Texas governor George W. Bush. (Though we privately think they are the same person.)

"It's an awesome capability that the brain has," says Robert Desimone, a neuroscientist at the National Institute of Mental Health.

Desimone says this multistep process is poorly understood: It's not quite as simple as Step A leads to Step B leads to Step C. No one doubts that it's fundamentally a mechanical, deterministic process (i.e., it's not a miracle), but for the moment it remains inscrutable. Computer scientists would love to know how the brain does the trick because then maybe they could copy the scheme.

Which leaves us with nothing but the Darwinian answer:

"Faces are incredibly important for primate social life," says Charles Gross, professor of psychology at Princeton University, "so the brain has developed an exquisite set of mechanisms so that we can recognize faces well."

Now if the brain would only hurry up and develop a way of remembering the name of the acquaintance who is rapidly approaching with hand extended in greeting.

Why are men better than women, on average, at reading maps?

The better question is: If men are so great at navigation, why can't they ever find anything? Not once in recorded human history has a man been able to find, without assistance, the napkin rings.

"Male and female brains differ. That's a given," says Christina Williams, chairman of the psychology department at Barnard College. She argues that both types of brains are basically perfect—they just have different strengths. "It's like the difference between a Macintosh and an IBM computer," she says.

Navigational skill is a good example. Men and women are equally fast at learning their way through a maze. But they use different techniques. Men tend to use geometry, and women use landmarks. In the basement of the psychology building at the University of Rochester, psychologist Tom Bever and his colleagues built an elaborate maze and asked men and women to run through it. The sexes performed equally well.

Then came a follow-up test: The participants were asked to look at a series of maps and identify which one corresponded to the maze they had run. Bever says about half the men made the right selection, while only about 25 percent of the women chose correctly. Men also were better at creating maps based on the maze. But women were better at looking at a photograph taken within the maze and identifying where it was taken.

"Men are better at reading and creating conventional maps," says Bever—with an emphasis on the "conventional."

So maybe the problem isn't that women can't read maps but rather that your average map is designed by men and sold by men for use by men. Maybe if women controlled the map industry, instead of little grids and dots and lines there would be drawings of landmarks, a pictographic rather than geometric representation of reality.

Indeed, one problem with debating the difference between male and female brains is that the argument is always stated in terms of the male way of doing things. Notice that no one poses the question "Why aren't men as good as women at recognizing landmarks?"

The next issue is: Why aren't the male brain and the female brain identical? What purpose does this serve?

One theory that's going around is that during much of human evolution, the men were the primary hunters and had to wander a larger territory than the women. They needed the skill of "dead reckoning," a form of geometrical navigation that requires a keen sense of distance traveled and changes in direction. The problem with this theory is that it's not clear that prehistoric sex roles were so dramatically defined—women didn't just sit around the campfire in a sewing circle all day.

Another possible answer: Two systems are better than one. Rather than conflicting, the male and female brains can work together for the best possible result.

And finally: Maybe it doesn't matter. The two systems may have evolved not for any purpose, but just by accident, another evolutionary quirk. If the net result is that men and women are equally skilled at navigating, then the forces of evolution won't select against either way of doing things.

"When things don't matter, you get evolutionary differentiation," Bever says.

This male/female stuff doesn't always hold true—we know guys who can't find their way home from the front yard. And just because you have no idea which way north is doesn't mean you can't be the next Mozart. For a long time, everyone presumed that the brain was just a big computer and some were better than others. The new theory is that the brain is broken up into a lot of little special-purpose computers.

You've got your language computer, your facial-recognition computer, your music computer, etc. As Lynn Nadel, psychologist at the University of Arizona, puts it: "Spatial cognition, or cognitive mapping, appears to have its own brain module."

In any case, map-reading skill isn't always such a great thing. It can backfire. "According to the map, this dirt road is a great shortcut back to the interstate," the guy will say. Hours later, your car is out of gas in a primeval forest and you're going "Shoo, shoo" to Bigfoot.

Why do we sometimes get "the willies"?

The reference books reveal no known origin of the term. *The Oxford English Dictionary* defines the willies as "a fit of nervous apprehension." We'd argue that a true case of the willies is a general sensation of fear that is unaccompanied by a single, or obvious, trigger. It strikes you in the same manner as déjà vu, in which you have a sensation (familiarity) without the obvious cause (a specific memory).

You don't get the willies when you encounter a scary-looking dog. You do get the willies late at night, in a quiet house, when all you can hear is a dripping faucet, or when you enter the attic of your grandparents' house and see a rocking chair covered with cobwebs next to a sepia-toned photograph of one of those grim-faced relatives who probably ate nails for breakfast, or when a bat flies through your bedroom window and transmogrifies into a man with slicked-back hair.

Elliot Weiner, a psychologist in Portland, Oregon, says the willies are "the yellow light for a red light that could be dangerous." They warn you that your security might be threatened. A silent house reminds you that you are alone and defenseless. Of course, chances are, you're just imagining the danger. But sometimes your fear will save you. We're supposed to be on guard, like any other animal. "Basically humans are very efficient machines," Weiner says. But he notes, "I've not heard the willies come up in professional meetings as a concept."

Alan Entin, a psychologist in Richmond, Virginia, told us, "When people go into new, unknown, novel situations, they react with anxiety. Some anxiety is good anxiety, and it's motivational, and it gets you to do something. And some of it is not so good anxiety that becomes paralyzing. And the more paralyzing, we might think of as the willies."

He adds, "It would be a subclinical form of anxiety."

We forgot to ask him about the heebie-jeebies, but we'll guess that's subclinical too.

Why do some people think they've been abducted by aliens from space?

Why staffers tend to be extremely calm and rational, so when we hear stories about alien abductions we respond with hoots, sneers, and guffaws. If we're really amused we remove our rubber human masks and emit beeping noises from our antennae.

Lately the alien thing has gotten out of hand. We live in a society where you are basically nobody if you haven't been personally abducted and operated upon. Alien abduction stories got a big boost with the publication of *Abduction: Human Encounters with Aliens* by a well-known Pulitzer Prize–winning Harvard psychiatrist, John Mack, who says he believes that these stories, however far-fetched, are actually true. Alien abduction is also a regular theme of allegedly nonfiction TV programs. Getting abducted by little gray men with large eyeballs is to the nineties what disco dancing in white suits was to the seventies.

We will stipulate that it could all be true. We don't know for sure. How can you disprove it? The aliens are doing it secretly, remember, so the absence of footprints, photographs, or direct alien confessions merely *corroborates* the scenario of a covert UFO operation.

But we can think of alternative explanations. Obviously some abduction stories are hoaxes—no one disputes that. Some are probably the result of madness. A few may be artifacts of therapy, the misapplication of hypnosis, or the implantation of false memories by pseudoscientific investigators. "Without a doubt, inadvertent cueing also plays a major role in UFO-abduction fantasies. The hypnotist unintentionally gives away to the person being regressed exactly what response is wanted," psychologist Robert Baker has written in *The Skeptical Inquirer*.

There's one explanation for UFO abduction that we find particularly intriguing. This is the theory that some abduction fantasies are a function of a sleeping disorder called sleep paralysis. It so happens that a key Why staffer has this very disorder, and, indeed, the symptoms match up with some of the symptoms of alien abduction.

The aliens usually strike at night while people are in bed; so too does sleep paralysis. The abductees report that their first sensation is apprehension, the sense that someone is in the room; that is what happens sometimes with sleep paralysis.

Sleep paralysis is a screwup of the brain's normal awake-asleep mechanism. Normally people lose muscle tone only when they are asleep. But if you have sleep paralysis this loss of muscle tone can kick in too early, before your brain is asleep, or persist after you've woken up. It's creepy! In fact, it's a lot like being zapped with a suspended-animation ray from the mother ship. You have to shake yourself out of it, no easy task. All the while you tend to have auditory hallucinations or dreamlike thoughts, usually with menacing overtones.

In his book *Communion*, Whitley Streiber describes waking up, being unable to move, seeing strange beings, then, incredibly, going back to sleep. Sounds just like sleep paralysis.

Our Why staffer has never imagined himself abducted. But he has felt, during these sleep paralysis attacks, that they were being done to him by someone else, some Other Being. It's all the more frustrating then to realize, when the attack goes away, that it is just one's own self that is doing this, that the Other Being is one's own brain.

Okay, so maybe that's not as interesting an explanation for alien abduction as the one that says aliens are really here and are trying to beam us aboard their spacecraft so they can do unseemly alien things to us. But you have to admit it's almost as weird.

Why is red red? Why is green green?

Roses are red—but what, precisely, do we mean by that? Let's not start tossing around words like "red" without coming up with some definitions! Why does red have that characteristic redness? Is the redness an artifact of the brain, varying from person to person, or does everyone see the very same red? Does scarlet appear scarlet to everyone, or do some people see crimson or cardinal?

This is a good topic for a late-night argument because the ludicrous position is in fact the correct one: There's no guarantee that people are "seeing" in their minds the same color when they talk about, say, "red" or "green." It's true that people with normal vision have the same basic color-registering cones and rods in their eyeballs, but the general quality we call *redness* is something that may be subjective. The redness in your brain may be what another person would call greenness.

You may have an absolute conviction that your red is what red really is, that yours is a truly red red, and yet you can't offer up a single word to describe your red that would confirm its redness. Colors can't be described. We can compare red to blood or fire or roses or whatever we want, but such descriptions are fundamentally circular. If you say red is the color of fresh blood, then you have to ask what the color of fresh blood is (red!).

The redness of red, the orangeosity of orange, the purplexion of purple are all rather mysterious from a scientific standpoint. Pain is another classic example. We all know pain. We can even give a verbal summary of different types of pain, like burning pain, throbbing pain, a dull aching pain, a piercing pain, whatever. But the painfulness of pain—the fact that it has this vivid characteristic, immediately recognized—is impossible to put into words. ("Ouch" is probably the best description.)

Scientists have a word for the subjective quality of mental experience, such as the painfulness of pain or the redness of red: qualia.

"It's very difficult to explain something scientifically when you can't describe what it is," says Francis Crick, the Nobel laureate (the Why staff has just about everyone this side of Einstein on a retainer at this point).

Ideally we could verify redness using brain scans. We could

scan the electrical patterns of different people to see if there's a specific pattern associated with red. The problem is, the brain scans of today are crude. They show overall patterns of brain activity, but can't possibly hone in on something as specific as registering a color. Looking for the "red" brain pattern with today's technology is like trying to find a needle in a haystack with a bulldozer.

Philosophers naturally love to argue about things like qualia. Some say redness is a real artifact of the universe. The "reductionists" dispute that: They say we invent redness, that it's just an artifact of our imagination.

That might sound daffy, but it's hard to ignore. After all, red is nothing more than light moving at a specific wavelength. The photons themselves aren't red. There's nothing red in the wave pattern. But somehow when the light hits our eye and registers in our gray matter, we see red. So where's the red? Out there in the universe? Or just in our heads?

Our best guess: Red is real. It's philosophy that's phony.

Why do even intelligent people rely on the "alphabet song" from kindergarten to remember the order of letters, particularly those in the "elemenopee" section?

Confess.

You still have trouble remembering the order of letters in the middle part of the alphabet, and in a crunch you hum that old classic that ends, "Now I've said my ABCs, tell me what you think of me."

You are secretly ashamed of this. You strongly suspect that someone like Stephen Hawking doesn't have to do this.

Are you dumb? No. You suffer from the serial order effect, sometimes known as the bowed serial order effect. This is a well-known effect of rote learning: If you memorize a series of words or letters or numbers, you are more likely to remember the items near the beginning and the end of the series. The alphabet, for example, is easy until about G, at which point it gets troublesome, until finally you reach your endgame, somewhere around the W, and cruise home on the XYZ.

"It's certainly not a consequence of stupidity on your part, it's just a consequence of the serial order effect," says John W. Moore, professor of psychology at the University of Massachusetts.

It's a standard technique of memorization to match items with visual or musical cues. You might even use physical cues: Punching out a phone number on a touch-tone phone might be more a reflexive action than a mental one. Try to dial that same number on a rotary dial phone and you could get befuddled.

The problem is, memorizing something through some secondary cue is not always the same thing as "knowing." This is why the alphabet song is slightly subversive. You memorize the alphabet in musical phrases, not as individual letters.

"It could be a crutch," says Moore. "It makes learning the alphabet easier if you're a child, but there are good theoretical reasons why later in life you would not want to retrieve a letter in a sequence by singing a musical phrase."

Not that life itself hangs in the balance, you understand. It's just that, to really know the alphabet, you should be able to go backward, from Z to A, with the same speed and certainty that you go forward. You can probably count down from one hundred fairly easily, for example. You know your numbers without any need for a song.

But you probably find it hard to go backward in the alphabet. And alas, you can't play the alphabet song backward. (We've discovered that if you do, it says "Child, go with Lucifer.")

THE MAILBAG

Mrs. Jack Trounce of Tacoma, Washington, says: "I suppose blind people dream, but do they imagine they see something or do they only dream in sounds?"

Dear Mrs. Jack: Blind people have dreams that essentially are no different from those of sighted people: It's the same quirky narrative, only with different types of imagery. If they were blinded before the age of five, they usually have no visual imagery, just auditory and kinesthetic. If they were blinded after that, particularly after the age of seven, they usually have visual imagery, at least for many years.

Dreams don't have to contain visual imagery to be vivid.

"Sighted people have a tendency to underestimate the information they get and use from their other senses," says Judy

Dixon, spokeswoman for the National Library Service for the Blind and Physically Handicapped.

Oral Miller, executive director of the American Council of the Blind, says that his dreams have as much fear, anticipation, joy, and excitement as those of a sighted person. As he puts it, "When you make love, do you always keep the lights on?"

History, Explained and Derided

Why are ancient towns buried under many layers of dirt, even though dirt is supposed to erode over time?

Until we researched this item, the Why staff's knowledge of archaeology was limited to the fact that the fabled Lost Ark of the Covenant is lost somewhere in a big government warehouse in Washington.

So naturally we were confused about ancient towns. It makes no sense that they're buried. Half the topsoil in Iowa has washed down the Mississippi into the Gulf of Mexico, and yet archaeologists are always digging up entire towns buried deep beneath the surface. At Jericho, the world's oldest known settlement, there are twelve distinct layers of construction going back almost ten thousand years. You have to wonder: Did the dirt just blow in and pile up like snowdrifts?

Here's your answer:

1. Adobe. Many ancient settlements were made out of sun-dried mud brick. This stuff tends to slowly erode over time. So it's the houses themselves that erode, not the surrounding landscape.

"Mud-constructed towns accumulate debris faster than do stone towns," says Gus Van Beek, a Smithsonian Institution archaeologist who has excavated ancient sites in Israel. He notes that mud bricks can't be salvaged, unlike stone blocks or heavy timbers. So homes just crumble in place, the mud is tamped down, and the once glorious home returns to the earth whence it came. A new home is built on top, and over many thousands of years you get that chocolate-layer-cake Jericho effect.

2. Street trash. They didn't have sewer systems or semi-weekly trash pickups by large groaning trucks. Towns were like giant mulch piles, and the street level slowly rose.

3. Alluviation. This is a word meaning "Pa! Lookit the dirt that got washed down into our yard!" It comes from highlands and fills up valleys. Bruce Smith, another Smithsonian archae-ologist, says ancient Native American communities can be found in the Little Tennessee River Valley under six or eight feet of alluvial sediment. The opposite also happens at higher sites: "You'll find a lot of stuff just sitting on the surface of the ground because the soil has been eroded away."

Now, that's our kind of archaeology. Hike along, admire the view, stub your toe on ancient pottery.

Why didn't the Black Death kill everyone in Europe in the fourteenth century, rather than just a third of the population?

There's nothing like a little light reading on the subject of bubonic plague to remind you of how nice it is to live in the Orkin era. For much of human history, people couldn't make solid plans for the weekend, both because "weekend" was not then a concept and because there always was the plague contingency—like, "We're going to the beach Saturday, unless we collapse and pustules form upon our flesh."

The reason plague didn't kill all the Europeans is both obvious and subtle. Some people never were exposed. Plague typically is spread from infected rats to humans by way of flea bites. It can also be spread by sneezing or coughing. The best solution was to get away from cities, to literally run to safer ground—*Fue cito, vade longe, redetarde* is the Latin warning: "Flee quickly, go far, return slowly."

Among those infected by the bacillus *Pasteurella pestis*, about 60 percent died, a rate that held fairly constant until the advent of modern treatment. Whether you die depends on how fast and how effectively your immune system reacts to the infection. The bacteria proliferate rapidly and can overrun the body within a matter of hours. Toxins produced by the bugs

The Black Death & his comic-relief sidekick,
moth-eaten yet lovable Roger Mortis.

cause "disseminated intravascular coagulation," says Susan
Lance, spokeswoman for the Centers for Disease Control Division of Vector-Borne Infectious Diseases. "That's kind of the
'Black Death' business. You get gangrene in your extremities
because the blood is clotted in the little capillaries and it turns
black."

The more subtle thing to understand is that plague, like any
infectious disease, has a delicate existence that requires a certain accommodation with the victims. It serves no guest to kill
the host. Darwinian logic says there have to be survivors, so
they can have lots of children who then can be decimated in a
later plague.

"Prolonged interaction between human host and infectious
organism, carried on across many generations and among suit-
ably numerous populations on each side, creates a pattern of
mutual adaptation which allows both to survive," says William
H. McNeill in his book *Plagues and Peoples*. "A disease organism that kills its host quickly creates a crisis for itself since a
new host must somehow be found often enough, and soon
enough, to keep its own chain of generations going."

Plague is thus a disease in constant crisis: It kills rapidly,
and those who are exposed but recover develop lifelong
immunity. Thus, in order to reach a stable, happy, parasitic
existence, bubonic plague has to play the role of vagabond,

hopping from port to port, always searching for a new community to infect.

That this happened in the 1300s in Europe was no accident: The rise of shipping, based in the Mediterranean, and the opening of the Strait of Gibraltar in 1291, created a transportation infrastructure capable of carrying plague throughout the continent. The disease arrived in the Crimea in 1346, having traveled across Asia by caravan route following a massive outbreak in China in 1331. By 1350 plague had raced from the Mediterranean through Scandinavia, and then it reappeared periodically over the centuries, though never at that early scale.

Diseases are most devastating to "virgin" populations, as the aboriginal peoples of North America learned when the Europeans introduced smallpox and other diseases after 1492.

How many Europeans died in the Black Death is essentially guesswork. The estimate of one-third is taken from English research showing that the population of England decreased between 20 and 45 percent. But some towns were wiped out entirely—thousands were depopulated and disappeared from the map. As a result, scapegoating became common. The French blamed the English. The Italians blamed the French. Everyone blamed Jews and lepers. Europeans descended into a moral and intellectual inferno, filled with morbid superstition, religious fanaticism, and a fetish for such instruments of persuasion as "the screw" and "the wheel."

And the strange thing is: They didn't even realize they were living in medieval times. They thought that was modern life. Let's all vow not to be so presumptuous.

Why did the Renaissance happen?

Europe got in one of the greatest ruts of all time, what we call the Dark Ages. Then, wham, Michelangelo's on his back, painting the ceiling of the Sistine Chapel. Explanation, anyone?

First, we have an obligation to acknowledge that the Renaissance wasn't an event per se. It was not a singular thing that happened. It was rather a gradual process in many places in Europe over a period of several centuries—an artistic, stylistic, intellectual evolution driven by political changes, religious schisms, voyages of discovery, etc.

Now that we have that paragraph out of the way we can give you the answer we prefer:

Aristotle.

He and his ilk—the ancient philosophers and poets and artists—were rediscovered in medieval Europe. The Renaissance was a surge of art and literature in the spirit of the ancients. Aristotle was unknown in Europe from about 500 to 1100 A.D. Luckily Arabic scholars preserved his texts. When he reemerged he was hailed as "The Philosopher" and was the most important intellectual figure of medieval Europe.

There was no single trigger of the Renaissance, but a few events and individuals were particularly important. In the mid-1300s, the Italian poet Petrarch found a number of classical works, including a collection of letters on Roman political life written by Cicero. Petrarch and his buddies became "humanists," interested in human history rather than just theology—they didn't care how many angels could dance on the head of a pin, they wanted to know if Cicero could limbo.

The humanists scoured monasteries for statues, coins, texts, anything they could dig up. Someone eventually found a copy of Aristotle's *Poetics* that had been preserved by Islamic scholars.

Robert Hollander, a professor of comparative literature at Princeton, notes that one of the early finds was in the year 1280, when a group of scholars found numerous classical texts in the monastery at Pomposa, near Venice.

"When they found the holdings of the monastery at Pomposa, that's when the Renaissance began," Hollander ventures playfully.

Of course, no one knew they were renaissancing. They just thought they had found some neat books. The word "Renaissance" was not used until the publication of Giorgio Vasari's book, *The Lives of the Most Excellent Painters, Sculptors and Architects,* in the sixteenth century.

Really big news always travels slowly.

Why are there no Puritans anymore?

There are so many churches in America, you'd think that at least one would have Puritan in the name and, out front, a yellow illuminated sign with plastic clip-on letters saying, "Come Friday to our Witch Fry."

But the Puritans are history, which means that for most of us they exist only in caricature: the dark clothes, the funny hats, the intense concern that, somewhere, someone might be having a good time.

In fact the Puritans have gotten a bad rap. Puritans were smart, bookish, deep-thinking. They didn't want religion served up to them by some corporate, hierarchical, pompous church; they wanted it pure.

They wanted the Church of England sanitized of all the remaining pageantry left over from Catholicism. They didn't like stained glass, for example. The Puritans were also called Precisionists, both names originating as epithets by other members of the Church of England who did not appreciate the picky, fussy, precise manner of these people. Some of the Puritans finally decided they couldn't take it any longer in England and so they came over here. The batch who landed at Plymouth we

call the Pilgrims; technically they were Separatists, not Puritans, but close enough. A group of Puritans landed in what is now Boston a dozen years later.

So what happened to them?

Basically they were betrayed by their kids. It happens to every generation. You bust your butt to achieve "regenerative grace," but your kids simply take it for granted. Second-generation and third-generation Americans were busy being capitalists, and they didn't have time to be Precisionists.

The children of Puritans often didn't even want to become full-fledged church members. Jon Butler, a historian at Yale (founded by Puritans, like Harvard), says that half the adults in Boston in 1649 were not churchgoers. Whether they didn't want to go to church or weren't allowed to for some strange reason is a matter of debate among academics.

Another reason the Puritans disappeared, at least by that name, is that Puritan congregations had an independent streak. They didn't want to be a big, fancy, convention-holding religious organization. They were always debating the finer points of Scripture, and when they had an intolerable disagreement they would split off into their own little ultra-Puritan minisect.

The term "Puritan" gradually fell out of favor, especially after the Salem witchcraft trials of 1692, which were a major public relations disaster, as you might imagine. But Puritans did survive, by a different name: Congregationalists. The Congregationalist church of today does not have many Puritan doctrines, but it does have some of the ecclesiastic structures, with church authority based in the specific congregation rather than coming from some powerful governing body elsewhere. (You might argue that the Baptists, who also have an independent streak, are heirs of the Puritans.)

Some Congregationalist churches in the early 1800s became Unitarian. And a few decades ago the Congregationalist church became part of the United Church of Christ. The Unitarian-Universalist Church and the United Church of Christ are among the most liberal, socially progressive religious denominations in America.

We don't want to make too big a deal about this, or exaggerate, but you can't help but conclude that the Puritans basically became hippies.

Why does no one care about the Revolutionary War, but people seem obsessed with the Civil War?

The only thing the Why staff remembers about the Revolutionary War is that George Washington crossed the Delaware and stood so precariously on the bow of the boat that he intimidated Cornwallis and Benedict Arnold and was thus able to defeat them at Valley Forge despite the cold. We also liked the part where Nathan Hale regretted that he had but one life to give for his country, and so offered up, as a bonus, his wife's.

Why is the Revolutionary War so underpublicized? Why are there hardly any Revolutionary War movies? It is, after all, the war that founded this country, the war that was an indisputable victory for us over the British and, let's face it, for good over evil.

Ah-ha! Therein lies the answer. The Revolutionary War is a victim of its own myth. So monochromatic is our memory of the Revolution that we have not allowed it to take on any interesting hues. The biggest error is that we arrogantly assume we were right and the British wrong and no other opinions need apply.

"We forgot that there was another side to this," says Fred Anderson, a historian at the University of Colorado.

Did you know, for example, that about half a million Americans in those days were in favor of the other side? They were "loyalists." Loyal to the king. The Revolutionary War was in many ways a civil war: The conflict was not just army against army but family against family, cousin against cousin.

"The only effective movie about the Revolution would be one that made us aware of the loyalists, that made us aware that it was a real civil war, in which families were divided, in which people took principled positions on both sides and were willing to shed one another's blood for these ideals," says Anderson.

After the British surrendered, many of the loyalists left for Canada. The ones who stayed in the United States had to keep their mouths shut. That was the price of peace: Loyalists couldn't mythologize their own roles in the war. Children grew up unaware that their parents had fought for the Crown. The myth of the Revolution thus grew as a one-sided battle of brave Americans versus tyrannical Britons.

By contrast, the losers of the Civil War vigorously promoted their own myth: the gallantry and heroism of the underdog. America's ongoing Civil War obsession is probably fed by Southerners more than Northerners.

Of course, there is another factor that makes the Civil War the greater conflict in American history: more blood. You want drama, you need lots of bodies strewed on cornfields. Only a few thousand Americans died during the entire Revolutionary War. There were years when hardly anything happened. Washington's great achievement was keeping the army together despite disease and starvation.

"The Revolution was a terrible war," says Anderson. "It was not glorious. It involved lots of suffering and little glory. It's one thing to reenact Pickett's Charge, it's another thing to just sit around and suffer for a winter and die of typhus."

Why did Napoleon always keep his hand tucked in his vest?

Whenever you think of Napoleon, you think: short man; kept hand in vest; came up short (as it were) during invasion of Russia; suffered from "Napoleonic complex"; Battle of Waterloo "was his Waterloo."

The traditional theory about the hand is that Napoleon had severe ulcers. His tummy hurt.

But here's another great theory about why he kept the hand in the vest: When posing, one always struggles to figure out what to do with one's hands. Ain't it the truth!

Napoleon was a chronic poser. He always was sitting for portraits, or riding into battle with everyone watching, or standing by some throne, and in these situations it is normal to be very self-conscious about the hands.

So why didn't he put his hands in his pants pockets like a regular Joe? Because he wore the kind of dorky pants that came only to the knees and had no pockets. They didn't invent pocketed pants until later. Apparently people didn't have wallets or car keys at that point. (How did men, you know, "adjust" themselves back then?)

The fact is, Napoleon probably didn't walk around with his hand in his vest. We think of that pose because it is the one in the famous painting *Napoleon in His Study* by Jacques-Louis "Give Me a Last Name" David, now hanging at the National

Zut Alors! Oú sont les clefs de ma voiture? ✱

✱ "Oh heck! Where are the keys of my car?"

Gallery of Art in Washington. It became commonplace to depict Napoleon that way, and the lore about the ulcers came later.

(Swift of mind that you are, you surely will want to know what Napoleon is doing with his other hand in the David portrait. The Why staff, breaking with tradition and actually leaving the bunker for once, trudged down to the gallery and took a look and saw that the Napster is holding a mysterious golden object, probably a seal, for putting his personal and pretentious stamp on decrees and letters and so forth. One hand in vest, one hand holding seal: The professional poser always does something with the hands.)

Florence Coman, the National Gallery's assistant curator of French painting, offers an intriguing reason why, in some Napoleon portraits, the Napoleonic hand was inserted into the Napoleonic vest: The painter may have had trouble painting hands.

"Some artists can't do that with any great facility, and somehow do whatever they can to mask their deficiency," she said.

For example, Henri Rousseau, the Postimpressionist painter, had trouble with both hands and feet. "He always, when he was painting feet, would show them masked by a lot of grass spears sticking up in front of them," she says.

Hands and feet don't look good in paintings or illustrations— there are too many things happening, a tangle of veins, bones, and knuckled digits, distracting from the simple curvilinear elegance of other body parts. We should note that other paintings by Jacques-Louis David at the National Gallery show figures with lovely hands, so the theory seems a bit thin in this particular case. But maybe other, lesser artists took the easy way out and invested a hand. It's the Mickey Mouse syndrome: Mickey's only got four fingers per hand because the illustrators couldn't make five look right.

So Napoleon's lucky. Someday people may think he had a fetish about scratching his tummy, but at least they don't go around asking, "Why did Napoleon only have four fingers on each hand?"

Why was whaling so profitable in the 1800s even though a single voyage required dozens of men and lasted four years and they had to sail all over the world chasing a creature that no one wanted to eat anyway?

Certain professions seem wildly improbable. Rice farming, for example—you picture people bending over in a paddy, plucking individual grains of rice from grassy stalks, using tweezers perhaps. Encyclopedia publishing is another mystery—so much copy to write and edit, and no tobacco ads to juice the bottom line.

And surely whaling, in the Moby Dick sense, seems ludicrous. It would have made sense, perhaps, if whaling were a variation of fishing because a whale has a fair bit of meat in it. Fact is, the booming American whaling industry of the early 1800s was based on the desire not for food but for energy. Sperm whales have an unusual anatomical feature: an oversized forehead filled with an oily substance called spermaceti that is excellent for burning in lamps. So whaling ships were like oil tankers, only loaded with barrels of whale gunk.

Could it really have been profitable? Indeed, and highly. New Bedford, Massachusetts, was the richest city in the coun-

try in its whaling heyday. Whaling historian Richard Kugler broke down the numbers for us:

First, it would cost you about $25,000 in the mid-1800s to build a boat, and it would last for dozens of voyages if you were lucky and it didn't get crushed in an ice floe somewhere. A similar sum would be needed for gear and provisions (sails, ropes, little sea biscuits, salted ham, etc.).

Then came your manpower cost. The secret here was that sailors weren't paid wages, but rather they worked for a percentage of the catch. The risk of the voyage was thus spread out among the workers. There were plenty of hapless souls and adventurers who thought nothing of jumping on a ship for a few years or even a lifetime, because time wasn't as valuable, wasn't as precious (nowadays if you asked a pal to go whaling he'd look at you funny and say, "What, you mean for the ENTIRE AFTERNOON?").

So you got your hardware and your manpower and you sailed away to the Arctic Ocean or whatnot and harpooned a bunch of whales. Herman Melville in *Moby Dick* reports: "A large whale's case [forehead] generally yields about five hundred gallons of sperm." Kugler says in the mid-1800s you could get $1.40 a gallon for that stuff—a lot of money in that time, not to mention more than what a gallon of crude oil or even refined petroleum costs today. The reason the whalers could get so much money was simply that Exxon didn't yet exist. Not until 1859 was oil discovered in the ground in commercially exploitable quantities, at which point the American whaling industry started to go into eclipse (it helped that sperm whales had been nearly driven to extinction).

Do a little math: The oil from a single large whale was worth about $700. (Why, it'd be immoral *not* to harpoon the dang thing!)

Kugler says a ship would typically bring back three thousand barrels of oil, with a barrel containing about 31.5 gallons. So that's about, what, upwards of $130,000 worth of oil brought into port. More than enough to pay off your initial $50,000 and keep your sailors in rum for a few weeks.

Why did John Wilkes Booth shoot Lincoln?

Here we go again! The last time we wrote an assassination item we were almost run out of the country for making the goofy assertion that Oswald, indeed, probably shot Kennedy (this is now known as the "lone nut" hypothesis because you have to be a nut, living alone, subsisting on canned food and hearing strange voices in your head, to believe that Oswald was even connected to the military coup that toppled JFK).

What makes the conspiracy theories about the Lincoln assassination unusual is that he was, in fact, killed in a conspiracy. (Or—this just now occurs to us—was it a lone nut who merely found a way to make it *look* like a conspiracy? Oh never mind.)

John Wilkes Booth and his cohorts had plotted to kidnap Lincoln from his carriage and take him to Confederate territory. That plan was aborted (the carriage didn't show up where expected, and everyone got spooked), and Booth decided to try something nastier. At about the same time that Booth shot Lincoln at Ford's Theatre, another conspirator knifed Secretary of State William Seward; a third conspirator got drunk or something and decided not to attack the vice president. (Trivia question: Who was sharing the presidential box that night with the Lincolns, and what were their fates? Answer to come.)

So it wasn't an Oswald-type situation. But how far did the conspiracy go? The evidence indicates that Booth was the ringleader and financier of his band of conspirators and that Booth alone masterminded the events of April 14, 1865. But there are, naturally, some more interesting theories floating around, including the recurring contention that the assassination was ordered by Secretary of War Edwin Stanton. (Oh, for the days when people had honest titles!) The U.S. government itself tried to link the murder to Jefferson Davis, president of the Confederacy.

But these larger conspiracies are wispy things, no more solid than a hologram. The assassination of Lincoln made little military or political sense. Robert E. Lee had surrendered five days earlier at Appomattox. So why did Booth do it? Was he seeking vengeance? Did he have some die-hard belief that the war wasn't lost? Why did this actor, of all the many people who hated Lincoln, decide to pull the trigger?

Here's a thought: Actors, like all creative people, tend to be egomaniacs. Acclaim is like cocaine: You get a little bit and you want a lot. John Wilkes Booth was one of the most successful actors in the country. His father and brother were famous actors too. He was handsome, smart, friendly. Women loved him. Yet he craved something more: fame and glory that would survive the ages.

The murder of Lincoln may have been nothing more than an act of Shakespearean drama, a bit of plagiarism of *Julius Caesar*. Booth didn't just shoot and run; he first jumped onto the stage and shouted, "Sic semper tyrannis"—"Thus always to tyrants."

"John wrote for himself in a crazed moment a part in a play that no playwright could have improved upon. He did it in a theater. It's not a coincidence. He shoots Lincoln, he jumps down upon the stage," argues Gene Smith, author of *American Gothic*, a biography of the Booth family. "It was an actor's dream . . . a starring role such as no actor before had ever had and none has had since."

Booth's own writings show his dramatic and narcissistic nature. The day of the assassination he wrote in his journal: "April 14, Friday, the Ides: . . . something decisive and great must be done. . . . Our country owed all her troubles to him, and God simply made me the instrument of his punishment."

Note that he doesn't say that Davis or Stanton or anyone else made him the instrument of this dastardly crime. Indeed,

Booth was shocked to find that even in the South, to where he had fled, he was seen as "a common cutthroat," as he wrote in his journal a week after the murder.

"With every man's hand against me, I am here in despair. And why? For doing what Brutus was honored for."

Even his death—shot through the neck on the porch of a burning tobacco barn—was theatrical. He asked with his dying breath to see his paralyzed hands. "Useless, useless," he said, and died. His infamy will survive the ages.

Trivia answer: Major Henry Rathbone and his fiancée, Clara Harris. Rathbone was knifed by Booth. Rathbone and Harris later married, but Rathbone, who always felt guilty for not saving the president, one day shot his wife to death and turned a knife on himself. He survived but lived out his years in a madhouse.

Why was the source of the Nile a mystery for so long?

When you make a list of the great rivers on the planet, right at the top, surpassing even the mighty Passaic, is the Nile. It's long, it's historic, and it flows due north, which, as anyone can see from looking at a globe, is directly uphill.

A simpleton might argue that the Amazon somehow is more impressive because of the vastness of its watershed and the biological diversity therein (simpletons use words like "therein" whenever possible). But the Nile is the artery of the planet's most ancient civilization. No Nile, no pyramids. The ancient Egyptians were the first to wonder where the Nile came from; it seemed to gush from nowhere, from the depths of a vast, parched desert. You could go upriver a thousand miles and see not a single tributary, feel not a drop of rain. During August, the dry season for the Egyptians, the Nile flooded.

Long after most of the planet had been explored, the source of the Nile remained a mystery. The quest for the source reached frenzied proportions in the mid-1800s, when the British Royal Geographic Society funded numerous highly publicized expeditions into the African interior. You have to wonder: Why wasn't the source found earlier? Why didn't someone just tromp upstream until they found the spring from which it spurted? Could that be so difficult?

Yes indeedy. For one thing, if you go up the White Nile (the longer, western branch) far enough, it practically disappears in a swamp. The swamp, in southern Sudan, is called the Sudd, and it's thoroughly nasty. In the wet season it's the size of England.

"It is not surprising that the ancients gave up the exploration of the Nile when they came to the countless windings and difficulties of the marshes; the river is like an entangled skein of thread," wrote Samuel White Baker, a British explorer, in *The Albert Nyanza, Great Basin of the Nile,* published in 1866.

(By the way we just noticed a lovely chapter subheading in "How I Found Livingstone" by Henry Morton Stanley: "I Sink to my Neck in the Ooze of the Rungwa.")

South of the Sudd, the Nile channel coheres again. But explorers faced other intimidating obstacles. Slave traders had brought terror to the interior. Western explorers who managed to overcome the cataracts, brutal heat, and malaria still had to deal with cutthroat slave traders and ivory hunters as well as powerful and not necessarily friendly tribal chieftains.

For example, guarding the headwaters of the Nile at Lake Victoria was Mutesa, King of Buganda, a nation of 3 million people. Mutesa was a formidable person.

"In the manner of Queen Victoria he did not look round

when he chose to sit down; a chair was automatically placed in readiness for him, except that in his case it was a page crouching on his hands and knees," wrote Alan Moorehead in *The White Nile*.

(Western accounts of African explorations are no doubt full of exaggerations, not to mention racist attitudes, so it's hard to know which exoticisms are real and which are imagined or invented. Certainly Moorehead's description of Rumanika, King of Karagwe, has a rather riveting Felliniesque quality: "He kept an extraordinary harem of wives who were so fat they could not stand upright, and instead groveled like seals about the floors of their huts.")

The final problem with the Nile is that it has no single source. The most prominent source is Lake Victoria, which itself has tributaries. Though known to the Arabs in the slave trade, the first European to see it was British explorer John Hanning Speke, on August 3, 1858. Four years later, on July 28, 1862, during a different expedition, Speke found the falls on the northern edge of the lake where the White Nile pours forth.

Though Speke was convinced he had found the source, there were skeptics back at the Royal Geographic Society, including Speke's rival in African exploration, Richard Francis Burton. They were supposed to debate the issue in front of society members, but the day before the debate Speke, engaged in a pleasant afternoon of sport shooting, accidentally blew himself away while climbing over a fence.

There's some kind of lesson there. Maybe it's just that even if you are such a humdinger of a man that you found the source of the Nile you still have to be careful with loaded firearms.

Why did they call it "D-day"?

The Pentagon confirms our worst fear: "D" stands for Day. That's right, it means Day-day, essentially. But of course no self-respecting soldier would ever use a term like Day-day because it sounds like baby talk. You can just imagine the generals in the command bunker saying "Boys, there's going to be a lot of bang-bang on Day-day, and so we all need to eat lots of din-din."

Our first thought was that D-day is a ridiculous term, but we've warmed to it. "D-day" is a way of referring to a date, known or unknown, when a military operation begins. It is not event-specific. The beauty of the term is that it allows you to refer to the next day as "D-plus-1" and the day after that as "D-plus-2." The day before D-day is "D-minus-1." Such terminology is economical, precise, quick. So too is the hour after H-hour known as "H-plus-1."

Think of the alternative. What would you call the day of an upcoming invasion? "The Day We Invade"? "Our Big Moment"? "Harvey"?

You certainly wouldn't want to refer to the day by the *date*. Imagine if the Allies, while plotting the Normandy invasion in 1944, used a term like "Operation: June 6." That would have been bad.

Karl Cocke, a historian with the U.S. Army Center of Military History, says the first known use of the term was Field Order Number 9, First Army, Army Expeditionary Forces, on September 7, 1918, which stated, "The First Army will attack at H-hour on D-day."

The fact is, the military uses the letter-hyphen-day construction for many purposes. M-day, for example, is the day mobilization for war begins. The term "M-plus-1" would mean one month after mobilization. There can be a "K-day," a "Z-day," whatever. But the letters D, H, and J are generally off-limits, used only to designate the commencement of a combat operation. Why the J? Because the J is used by the French.

Their term for D-day is, would you believe, "J-jour." Yes! Day-day again!

And you thought the French were so sophisticated.

Why didn't the Germans build the atomic bomb in World War II?

There are competing theories, but the one we like the most is that they made a mental error. A computational blunder. Imagine! The fate of civilization, turning on a misplaced digit, a rogue integer, a bit of slop in a back-of-the-envelope calculation.

The historical debate over the German bomb program centers on Werner Heisenberg, he of the famous Uncertainty Principle (which is something like "When in doubt, don't major in physics"). Although many of Germany's leading scientists fled the country soon after Hitler came to power in the

1930s, Heisenberg and many others remained, and they knew as much as their Allied counterparts about the frightening power locked within the atom. But they never came close to building a bomb. Why not?

Morality, perhaps. The American journalist Thomas Powers has argued in *Heisenberg's War: The Secret History of the German Bomb*, that Heisenberg had moral objections to the Nazi regime and intentionally suppressed the German bomb effort. His evidence is circumstantial. For example, in 1941 Heisenberg leaked word of the German bomb program to a colleague in the West, in gross violation of security.

In discussions with Albert Speer, Hitler's closest adviser, Heisenberg appeared to exaggerate the difficulty of building a bomb. When Speer asked him about rumors that an atomic bomb could catch the atmosphere on fire and burn up the entire planet, Heisenberg said he couldn't guarantee that wouldn't happen.

But Heisenberg repeatedly said in later years that he had no moral qualms with the bomb. He said it appeared too daunting during wartime conditions, with Germany under bombardment and resources stretched. So Powers' thesis requires one to believe that, to his dying day, Heisenberg covered up his own moral objections to the bomb, perhaps to avoid ridicule from countrymen.

We spoke to several veterans of the Manhattan Project and they all cited the official Heisenberg explanation: Germany didn't have the resources to build a bomb. They reject the Powers hypothesis.

Powers responds: "The reaction is a very sensitive, kind of touchy, prickly sort of reaction. The reason is not too hard to find. If Heisenberg refused to build a bomb for Hitler for moral reasons, then what were the Allied scientists' reasons for building a bomb that destroyed Hiroshima?"

Now let's look at one other explanation for Heisenberg's reluctance to build a bomb: He goofed.

"He was wrong in the physics of what it would take," Rudolph Peierls, an eighty-five-year-old physicist who played a key role in the Manhattan Project, told us.

To make a bomb, you need not just your average lump of uranium (atomic weight 238) but rather an isotope of uranium (such as U-235) that can rapidly destabilize if bombarded with neutrons. But no one had ever separated large quantities of an isotope of a heavy element like uranium. And initially, physicists on both sides of the Atlantic assumed that you'd need tons of it to make a bomb. Getting that much fissionable uranium seemed utopian.

But Peierls and a colleague sat down and labored over the equations and—surprise!—discovered that you really didn't need that much of this special uranium to make something really devastating. "We figured out that the critical mass was not very large, not the tons that one would have guessed intuitively, but kilograms," he says. "We also realized that such a chain reaction would release an enormous amount of energy."

Heisenberg, on the other hand, never liked to mess around much with those nasty physics equations, says Peierls, his former student. Heisenberg was a genius but maybe a little lazy. As they say, the Devil is in the details, and this Devil is one that Heisenberg—and, mercifully, Hitler—never found.

Why did ancient Greeks like Plato and Socrates have only one name?

You can search the history books forever and never find a single allusion to little Billy Socrates or his precocious playground sidekick, Leroy Plato. It's just Socrates and Plato and Aristotle and Sophocles and Aristophanes, each a one-name wonder. They might as well be brand names, like Xerox and Lysol and Jif.

The truth is, they had other names. In a formal setting Socrates might be referred to as "Socrates, son of Sophroniscus from Alopece" (except they didn't know how to speak English then and had to get by on Greek).

Most Indo-European languages use this naming system, with a given name followed by the father's name, says Kurt Raaflaub, codirector of the Center for Hellenic Studies in Washington, D.C. Even today, he says, people in the mountains of Switzerland, where he is from, would refer to him as "Kurt, son of Frederick."

We've heard that Plato was actually a nickname. His given name was Aristocles, after his paternal grandfather, but they called him Plato, from "platus," meaning broad, because he had such a broad forehead, broad shoulders, and a broad intellect.

The thing you need to remember is that these famous

Greeks could easily manage being on a first-name basis with their peers because they were snobby aristocrats, the country-club set of Athens.

Judy Hallett, a professor of classics at the University of Maryland, explains, "they were democratic within their elite circle."

Hmmm, sounds a lot like Washington, come to think of it.

THE MAILBAG

George and Grace Mattern of Phenix City, Alabama, ask, "At what point does something become ancient?"

Dear George and Grace: Anything that's been around a long time—a car, an animal companion, one of those thirty-seven-term Democratic congressmen—can be called "ancient" without violating the correct definition of the word. But if you want to know when the "ancient world" came to an end, that's tricky.

We passed your question on to Bernard Knox, director emeritus of the Center for Hellenic Studies in Washington, and he said, "The ancient world folds up sometime in the fifth century A.D."

An even more exact answer comes from *Webster's Third New International Dictionary*, which says the ancient world ended in A.D. 476, the fall of the western Roman Empire; "medieval" is defined as anything between about A.D. 500 and 1500.

Knox argues that any precise cutoff is too simplistic. There were about two centuries of transition, he says. "You just can't cut it that fine. Roughly speaking, I guess, Saint Augustine is about on the boundary—he's late fourth and early fifth century A.D. He's at the beginning of the Christian Middle Ages, but he's still very much of the ancient world."

That part of history always has been a mess. The emphasis on 476 ignores the earlier sacking of Rome in 410 and the later reestablishment of the western Roman Empire under the Emperor Justinian, not to mention the continuance of the eastern Roman Empire for another thousand years and the more fundamental problem of basing any historical cutoff on the actions of some alleged "barbarians" in one little corner of the globe.

We'd bet money that when the ancient world ended, no one remembered to tell the Chinese.

INVENTIONS THAT HAVEN'T BEEN INVENTED YET

(Or: Why Some Things Aren't)

Why hasn't anyone invented a ray gun, complete with "Stun" and "Kill" settings?

What makes the ray gun so magical a concept in science fiction is that it allows violence to be perpetrated cleanly, at a distance, and impermanently. No body parts fly. The enemy is just sort of . . . zapped. This is what we all want in a weapon: something that dispatches the enemy with efficiency, yet leaves our conscience clear. Unlike those messy, distasteful grenades.

Well, here's the headline: There are, in fact, ray guns of sorts. The Pentagon has for years been developing laser weapons, though nothing has yet been deployed. The main problem is that you can't create a powerful beam of light (or a beam of particles) unless you have a huge, bulky energy source.

"Right now the problem is in getting powerful enough ones that are portable enough to be useful," says Leland Atkinson, vice president of Gradient Lens Corporation in Rochester, New York. "To do something like they do on 'Star Trek' with their phasers, today you'd need a minivan."

Yet the Pentagon is undeterred. A laser weapon called the Stingray, developed by Martin Marietta Corporation, was tested by the military for possible use on Bradley fighting vehi-

The NRA, 2653 A.D.

cles. The Stingray can't actually kill anyone, but it can do something diabolical: It can blind the enemy.

In modern warfare a lot of fighting is done at night. A fighter pilot or tank commander staring through night-vision instruments is extremely vulnerable to a blast of laser light. In a fraction of a second a person can be permanently blinded.

Obviously there is an ethical question here. Some critics within the Pentagon think the use of such a weapon would be against international laws governing combat. But one army colonel in charge of the program has said, "Laser weapons are as moral, if not more moral, than systems which blow someone to bits."

As for putting a ray gun on a "Stun" setting, there's no such thing. A laser works by burning. If you turned down the volume, so to speak, you'd just end up making the enemy warm. Atkinson compared it to the use of a magnifying glass to aim sunlight at ants. "You either fry the ant or you don't. In between, I don't think the ant gets very stunned."

It's a vicious world. Too vicious. We should all vow to keep our phasers set on "Warm."

Why don't we all have our own jet packs so we can zoom around like Buck Rogers or Jonny Quest?

Y ou can imagine all sorts of problems if jet packs were widely used. Bad accidents involving overhead power lines, for example. Or the occasional catastrophic airburst, also known as "the fireworks effect."

Jet packs have been invented. In fact, we spoke to the man who holds the patent on the "jet vest." His name is Thomas Moore, and he was eighty-one when we spoke to him a couple of years ago. He received the patent in 1966 while working as an engineer at the U.S. Army's Redstone Arsenal in Huntsville, Alabama. He figured it could be used in certain military situations, like going from ship to shore, or jumping over barriers, but the military felt such devices were impractical. They cost a lot, and they weigh too much. A real jet vest, sad to say, isn't very spiffy.

"You can only fly for so long with the amount of weight you can conveniently put on your back," Moore said. "The weight of the fuel is quite a bit of the problem. You have to have an energetic fuel in order to do that." His own jet vest used hydrogen peroxide. It was tested with the aid of a tether, the better to guard against someone getting launched into the next state.

And it was tricky to fly. A jet pack looks like a snappy little gadget when it's Jonny Quest doing the flying, but in reality it's hard to maneuver because you have to worry about three dimensions of movement: pitch, roll, and yaw.

There have been other jet-packish devices designed over the years. Bell Aerospace built the Rocket Belt in the early 1960s, and a few years later produced the Jet Flying Belt. But the military never really cottoned to these gadgets. The tactical benefit never made up for the cost and hassle, and of course there remained the question of what would be a fair speed limit when flying over a school zone.

Ed Cornish, president of the World Future Society, makes an interesting point (and this allows us to come, as always, to the moral of the story): New gadgets require not just a scientific breakthrough and a technological breakthrough but also an economic breakthrough. Video phones, for example, have been around for decades, but they've always cost more than they're worth. Same with jet packs.

This is why we're skeptical about nuclear fusion power.

Supposedly this is the energy source of the future. The scientific principles are sound (to wit, the hydrogen bomb). In a few years it may even be technologically feasible to make a machine that creates more energy than it uses. But if building these fusion reactors costs too many billions of dollars, they'll fail the economic test. Because if you had to, you could always cook that hot dog over an open fire.

Why has no one yet invented a cyborg—a half-human, half-machine?

Y ou probably have to be under the age of eighteen, or have read a lot of comic books, or have watched the *Terminator* movies over and over again, to appreciate what a good question that is.

We already have the technology to change the human body. Pacemakers and defibrillators can steady a heartbeat. Bo Jackson has an artificial hip. The deaf can be made to hear, thanks to cochlear implants. An astonishing new generation of micromachines, with motors thinner than a human hair, has raised the possibility that someday machines will be small enough to travel in blood vessels and help repair damaged tissues.

An artificial hip or a cochlear implant is merely designed to replace or repair existing human body parts. But will machines ever be used to enhance already healthy bodies? How far can technology go?

Ed Cornish (see previous item) says that someday it might be possible to use computer chips to implant memory or knowledge in your brain. If you had to go to a meeting of geologists, you could buy a geology chip, insert it somehow, and suddenly have the geology vocabulary at the tip of your tongue.

"That hasn't happened, but it's the sort of thing we anticipate happening in the future," Cornish says.

You have to admit that's pretty snazzy. But we must say it's hard to see how a computer could interface with a brain— there's no slot for a floppy disk in your head, and even if there were, you might get confused at the geology conference and accidentally start uploading your unfinished screenplay.

But the Cornish example does point in the right direction: Cybernetic technology probably will enhance human intelligence and communication, rather than, say, make people stronger. The flaw with the Six Million Dollar Man concept is that it's easier to make people stronger and faster through genetic engineering and hormone treatments than through implantation of machinery. You don't need to do human engineering with gadgetry when you can do it with chemistry.

Moreover, the world increasingly does not care so much about the strength of people—power is supplied by machines. Technology alleviates human sweat. The really big money, the area where research will pay off, is in making people smarter, helping them communicate.

Gregory Stock, a biophysicist and author of *Metaman: The Merging of Humans and Machines into a Global Superorganism* (we are big believers in overstated book titles, incidentally), suggests that the cochlear implant idea might be extended, using fairly simple cellular phone technology, to allow people to receive telephone calls in their ears.

That's right: a whole new meaning to having ringing in your ear.

"It takes your breath away to think what's going to happen to us in one hundred years," he says.

Another idea: A voice-recognition computer chip, implanted in a tooth, allows you to communicate instantly with someone merely by saying his or her name.

"You could speak someone's name and access that person across the country," Stock says.

(The bad news: You sneeze and suddenly you're on the phone with the Achoo family.)

WHY KIDS "R"

Why can't we remember anything that happened to us prior to the age of, roughly, three?

Your basic two-year-old is no longer just a blubbering mass of protoplasm, but has become a talking, thinking, reasonably coherent, and often nondrooling creature. The child knows the names of people, can memorize songs, and may even remember what happened yesterday or last week. But the child will eventually forget all this. The memories will get purged, save for an image or two. Why?

Although this falls into the no-one-really-knows category, we heard an interesting theory from Robyn Fivush, a psychologist at Emory University. She says that our memories of past experiences are organized in our brain as narratives. Kids younger than about three don't yet know narrative conventions. They can't tell a story. They don't know how to set the scene. They don't understand time, place, character, plot.

So even though they have plenty of language, and perception, and even memory, they can't shape all this stuff into a story that has a point. (The Why staff is still struggling with this.)

"There has to be a notion of a rising action, a climax, a resolution. There has to be some kind of emotional meaning to the event," says Fivush.

In other words, our memories start at the age when we realize that what we're all trying to do in life is find the moral of the story.

Why are babies so precious when they're sleeping?

What a sweet question. Too bad we have to ruin it with one of our technical, mechanistic answers. ("It's simply the ionization of hydrogen atoms, nothing more.") The Why staff has long noticed that sleeping babies inspire universal adoration. All babies are cute, but sleeping babies are somehow entrancing, wondrous, painfully precious. Is there something about the baby's appearance while wrapped in the arms of Morpheus that is so remarkable, or is there something being triggered in our brain, some primal protectiveness instinct? How much is this an instinct at all versus a merely rational response to the sight of something so small and innocent achieving blissful sleep in a world of peril, pain, and the wailing of the damned?

For help we turned to auxiliary Why staffer Robert Wright, one of the best science writers around and the author of the new book *The Moral Animal.* Wright, who admits that he is basically Mr. Gene when it comes to these kinds of issues, said that maybe we're programmed to keep a close eye on sleeping babies since they are especially vulnerable at that moment, unable to cry and crawl away should peril approach in the form of, say, a tiger with a major craving for Bébé du Jour.

"The sensation of 'Oh, they're so cute' would be your genes saying you should be especially vigilant now, you should not stray far now," he said.

This might be a case where we are trying too hard to find a Darwinian explanation for something much simpler. When awake, babies have a tendency to be rather . . . demanding, shall we say. Okay, make that monstrous. They scream, whimper, whine, drool, spit, bite, and worse. Their eating habits are vile. Each child is its own EPA Superfund site.

But when they sleep . . . with those trusting little faces . . . they're just angels.

Awwwww . . .

Why do so many children's stories have animal protagonists? Why are there all these talking rabbits running around?

The other day we were reading the bedtime story *Goodnight Moon*—okay, we admit it, it was just the *Cliffs Notes* version—and we noticed something startling: The "quiet old lady whispering 'hush' " is actually a rabbit in human clothing! And sure enough, the "child" in the bed is also a bunny. Who do they think they're fooling? Rabbits don't live in human homes and wear pajamas to bed! It's zoologically indefensible.

Why are kids so animal-obsessed? Why do they love Bugs Bunny and Big Bird and Curious George and the Three Little Pigs and so forth?

It's not enough to say "because animals are so darn cute." There's got to be more to it than that. Another inadequate answer is: Because kids identify with animals. Sure, children anthropomorphize animals (and even inanimate objects, like balloons), but that doesn't explain why they would prefer an animal protagonist to a human protagonist. If they just wanted to identify with a character, you'd think a human child would be perfect.

The best answer is that animals, though childlike, are just a little bit different from real children, and this makes the dramatic events of a fairy tale or bedtime story or TV cartoon a little easier to handle. Your basic fairy tale confronts a fear in the child's life—separation from parents being the recurring story—and shows how the fear can be resolved. Or a story might deal with aggression, the wild instincts within every child. These tales can get pretty harrowing and violent, and it helps the child to follow the narrative from a little bit of a distance. The animal in, say, *The Runaway Bunny* is a surrogate for the child, but is clearly not a child, and so there's enough psychological distance to keep the story from being terrifying.

"They can get closer to it because it's a bunny and not a child," says Marc Nemiroff, a child psychologist in suburban Washington.

"Some children need the disguise or symbolism of animals to talk about their feelings," adds Irene Deitch, a psychologist at the College of Staten Island.

Nemiroff mentions one other reason why animals are useful in stories: They're neuter. The baby bunny going to sleep in *Goodnight Moon* is neither obviously a boy or a girl.

Our own pet theory (ahem) is that children love animals because children *are* animals. They recognize this about themselves. Adults are the ones who are confused.

Why are some toddlers extremely talkative but totally incomprehensible?

You've probably heard some eighteen-month-old critter say something like this: "Habba nooba seepie wooncom noo za Beast?" And you instinctively know that this means, "If I don't get to watch 'Beauty and the Beast' right now, I'm going to start slinging poop."

It is certainly true that children invent words that have meaning to the child but not to the nondiapered population. But that's not what this is. This is jargon babbling.

What's happening is, the kid is making sounds but not actually conveying words. The critter wants to be conversant but either has nothing to say or doesn't know how to say very much. So he or she mimics human sounds, including conversational intonations.

In fact, the child may presume that most of what we do, as adults, is babble meaninglessly. The child doesn't realize that speech has content.

Favorite Toddler Joke
* "Take my rubber
pants... please."

"You can think of it as part of the child's first theory of what people are doing with sounds," says Jacqueline Sachs, a psychologist at the University of Connecticut. "There might be a long string of babble syllables, and it will end with a nice falling intonation contour at the end. If you were listening across the room you'd think, my gosh, that little baby is already talking, but when you get closer you realize there aren't any words in there."

The strange thing is, we know plenty of adults who do jargon babbling. They are called "experts."

Why is childbirth so painful?

Human beings try so hard to be civilized, to maintain appearances, and yet when it comes time for birthin' babies we suddenly turn into . . . bugs, basically. Even with painkillers and epidurals and electronic monitoring it's still rather amazingly biological, a process as down and dirty as the fissioning of paramecia.

Theory: Puff, puff, phew.

Reality: *Eaaaarrrrgghh* (head spins 360 degrees).

So as we wait to evolve out of this mess let's figure out why it needs to be so painful. The generally accepted answer is that the pelvic structure that makes bipedalism possible also requires a narrow birth canal. There's not much clearance.

But still, you'd think that the forces of evolution would create some mechanism whereby childbirth wouldn't hurt so much. So now we raise another thought: Maybe pain is good. Wenda Travathan, author of *Human Birth: An Evolutionary Perspective*, speculates that the pain and temporary incapacity of childbirth inspires women to hang on to a male partner. "The pain of childbirth leads women to seek companionship," she says. Natural selection "to a point probably favored a certain amount of pain."

We will confess that this theory doesn't quite work for us. It leaves out the possibility that women could find sufficient companionship in other women. It also seems to suggest that men are so useless, so devoid of worth, that the only reason a woman would want one around the house is if she were on the verge of exploding.

But now let's go on to the next theory of painful childbirth: It doesn't hurt as bad as we think it does. Or, more exactly, we can't handle the pain, psychologically, because we are culturally obsessed with denying our own natures. We don't want childbirth to be natural. So we intervene with drugs and technology, turn birth into surgery, turn the mother into a disabled person. This is the general message of Robbie Davis-Floyd, an anthropologist at the University of Texas who is a vocal opponent of technologically manipulated childbirth.

"How you perceive pain is culturally mediated. Cultures who perceive childbirth as a natural process, as a natural part of life, tend to experience less pain in childbirth," she says.

She has written that hospital delivery is a "ritual enactment of the technocratic model of reality upon which our society is based." Hospitals break down the natural process of birth into identifiable parts and then reconstruct it as a mechanical process. This kind of birthing ritual reflects "our culture's deepest beliefs about the necessity for cultural control of natural processes, the untrustworthiness of nature, and the associated defectiveness of the female body. Modern birthing procedures also reinforce the validity of patriarchy, the superiority of science and technology, and the importance of institutions and machines . . ."

Davis-Floyd told us her two natural labors, the second of which was at home with midwives, were "extraordinarily painful, and I wouldn't have changed it."

We don't want to be snide here—not us, not ever—but we wonder if the proponents of natural childbirth also decline Novocain when having a cavity filled or a tooth pulled. Since time immemorial, women have been coming up with ways to dull the pain of childbirth. And it is largely thanks to technology and modern medicine that women don't commonly die in childbirth anymore. Intervention doesn't imply disrespect for nature, but rather a recognition that we are not precisely and perfectly designed creatures—as we've said before, evolution has some slop and wobble in it.

The holistic approach may work for some people, and more power to 'em, but if the Why staff ever goes into labor, we're going to ask for the stuff that makes you wake up when the kid can do yardwork.

FOOD AND BEVERAGE

Why is Middle America filled with soybean fields even though no one eats soybeans and tofu is the world's dullest food?

Soybeans are the Stealth Legume. They're in everything. Henry Ford once had a suit made out of soybeans and proposed the construction of a car out of soybean-derived plastic. (We're guessing that if you ever got stuck for days out in the desert, you could always just eat the car.)

A couple of years ago America grew about 61 million acres of soybeans, putting soybeans in third place behind the 78.5-million-acre corn crop and the 71.5-million-acre wheat crop. Corn and wheat are not mysterious plants. But soybeans truly are an enigma.

The secret of the soybean is threefold. First, it's cheap to grow. It doesn't need fertilizer. You just stick the seeds in the ground, pffft! you got beans a few months later. Second, soybeans are high in protein. That wouldn't ensure the plant's popularity were it not for the third secret: Soybeans are easily manipulated for a thousand uses.

When you harvest soybeans the first thing you do is, quite frankly, sell them and never think about them again. But someone else will take the soybeans, lick his lips, and extract lots of soybean oil from the seeds. That oil turns up everywhere at the supermarket except under the label Soybean Oil. It's used, among other places, in coffee creamers (that's some of the "nondairy" business you always hear about), mayonnaise, margarine, and salad dressings.

Most important, the soybean contains lecithin ("any of several waxy hygroscopic phospholipids that are widely distributed in animals and plants," says our dictionary), which is a great emulsifier. An emulsifier is something that makes two or more other things blend well. Without soybean lecithin to smooth everything out, mayonnaise would be a horror show. (Wasn't Reagan nicknamed "The Great Emulsifier"?)

The remaining fiber of the plant is usually turned into animal feed. We eventually consume that soybean protein in the form of beef or pork or chicken. Gripers may point out that a lot of protein is lost in the translation—that as a nation obsessed with eating meat we are wasting all this valuable vegetable protein by feeding it to animals. It is for these gripers that the torment known as tofu was invented.

The big soybean battle looms in the near future. Genetic engineering has made it possible to grow soybeans that are insect-resistant. There's a consumer backlash against genetically engineered foods, however. Some communities are passing laws to segregate such foods at the supermarket.

But Mike May, research director for the American Soybean Association, says that when genetically engineered soybeans hit the market they'll be throughout the store in one form or another. It is conceivable that any soybean controversy will be a boon to the canola plant, which also produces oil and meal and which is mostly grown in Canada and Europe.

Meanwhile the list of soybean uses, provided to us by the ASA, goes on and on: We see here that it can be an "anti-foam agent," an "anti-spattering agent," a "meat analog," a "pan grease extender," and a "sausage casing."

Man, you stuff some soybean sausage casings with some soybean meat analogs, you got a meal!

Why aren't seedless grapes biologically impossible?

Why aren't they extinct by now?

The answer is so easy, and so obvious, that we need to pause right here and offer a completely tangential insight into contemporary America: It is, increasingly, a seedless grape kind of place. Intolerant of the pits of existence. We insist that life be smooth, even-textured, uniform. Admit it, when you bite into a grape with a bitter little seed inside, you have a flashback to the days when people had to iron their bedsheets.

Now then: What you need to realize is that there are many ways to reproduce. The traditional way is sexually, the seed method. Every human being on Earth was produced this way.

But there's another trick that some plants and even a few lower animals use: regeneration. In this method, a small piece of tissue can regenerate into an entirely new, fully functioning organism.

If you're a horticulturist, you deal with this all the time and call it "taking cuttings." According to Harold Olmo, professor emeritus of viticulture at the University of California at Davis, the Thompson seedless grape variety widely consumed in America is the descendant of grapevines cultivated in Central Asia many centuries ago. Lost to history is the name of the savvy farmer who first noticed that a mutant grapevine had produced seedless grapes and who then took cuttings and kept the new species alive in perpetuity. In the Middle East, the seedless grape variety is called *kishmish*, Arabic for "hot water." That's because if you soak the grapes in a hot water/ash mixture, they develop cracks in the skins and can be more quickly dried in the sun to make raisins.

A couple of decades ago in California, a mutant Emperor grapevine produced some seedless grapes, and now there are seedless Emperor grapes. ("Seedless," by the way, is used loosely. Some seedless varieties have little wannabe seeds.)

So that's the story: Mutation and Propagation.

This whole process of regeneration deserves more attention than we can give it in this space. The biological dynamics are complicated: How does the tail half of a bisected flatworm know to grow a new head and not a new tail? There's also an evolutionary mystery: Why doesn't every species regenerate? Why do only humble life forms, the plants and worms and salamanders, have this bizarre talent?

Maybe the answer is that nature rewards humility. The larger forms of life—the creatures with the sharp teeth and the spines and the wings and the big brains—would become too powerful if they could withstand machine-gun fire and keep on living. If you nailed a grizzly with a bazooka and it just turned into sixteen new grizzlies, that'd complicate life for the entire food chain.

Why don't people think of alcohol as a drug?

You always hear about "drugs and alcohol." Why the "and"? What's the difference? The Why staff is not afraid to confront the ugly truth: A drink containing alcohol isn't just a benign "beverage." It's also a powerful, marvelous medicine. In the Why bunker we call it a "tonic." As in, "Chesterton thirsted for a tonic, and so did partake of the Pabst Blue Ribbon."

Obviously what we have with alcohol is a form of mass denial. It's addictive, it kills tens of thousands of people every year, and yet society declines to view it as a drug. The fact is, the economic cost of alcoholism and related problems exceeds that of all illicit drugs combined. Fetal alcohol syndrome is a major cause of birth defects.

Even people who don't drink much will have a taste here and there. Imagine if other drugs were like this: "I'm not into cocaine, but I do sometimes snort a line or two with dinner."

Tobacco now is clouded in shame, shame, shame. Increasingly, people scorn caffeine. Most drugs are simply illegal or available only by prescription. But alcohol not only is legal, it's advertised on TV; it's glorified. There are millions of young people who have joined that sodden fraternity, Tappa Kegga Beer.

Our question is: Are there pharmacological reasons for thinking of alcohol as distinct from other drugs? And are there historical and cultural reasons?

Not really, and yes, are the answers.

Alcohol is different from many drugs in that it's a naturally derived substance. Fermentation occurs in all sorts of organic materials. So it's not some evil compound synthesized in a lab. On the other hand, marijuana also is perfectly natural, as is morphine, and no one would dispute that those are drugs.

You might argue that alcohol is not a particularly potent drug, gram for gram. Usually it is consumed in solution. Wine usually is about 12 percent alcohol, roughly, and beer is about 4.5 percent. Many drugs, by contrast, are so powerful that they have to be combined with inert fillers simply to create a pill large enough to be picked up with your fingers. But since alcohol is washed down in tasty beverages, it's quite simple to give oneself a full dose of the stuff, or even an overdose (the most exalted New Year's Eve ritual is alcohol overdosing). Thus the gram-for-gram potency doesn't seem too relevant to the debate.

The real reason our society sanctions alcohol use is that it's part of our dietary heritage.

"For centuries it was an important part of the diet. It provided needed calories," says Patricia Tice, a curator at the Strong Museum in Rochester, New York, and author of *Altered States: Alcohol and Other Drugs*. She says, "Very few people recognize it as a drug because it's so deeply ingrained in our culture."

She notes that milk was an unreliable commodity in past centuries, and water often was dirty, the source of diseases. And, she says, "A cup of coffee in 1830 was about five times as expensive as a hot whiskey drink. It wasn't part of the average person's diet."

Until the Civil War you could pay taxes with liquor or hard cider instead of money. After the war, saloons, backed by large beer and whiskey companies, became common around the country—the easiest way to go into business was to open a bar.

The Anti-Saloon League soon started a grass-roots temperance movement that focused on alcohol as a drug associated with other vices, like prostitution and gambling. During World War I, many people thought it unpatriotic to drink beer, since it was made of grain that might otherwise have been used in the war effort and because many of the breweries had German names. That gave the final boost to Prohibition, but it was a failure because you can't legislate culture away.

Perhaps the repeal of Prohibition in 1933 not only legalized alcohol again but also legitimized it on the social front. Today the main societal prohibition is against drinking and driving, something the savvy partygoer avoids by simply giving up driving.

And by the way: Let's just decide right now that we are all going to pay our taxes this year with those half-empty Smirnoff bottles in the pantry.

Now This from the Booze Industry

After we wrote that alcohol is a drug we got a letter from Elizabeth Board, director of the public issues division, Distilled Spirits Council of the United States. She said, "The problem of saying that alcohol is a drug is that it sends the wrong message. Adults may be telling children to avoid drugs, but if the adults drink after telling children that alcohol is a drug, the children see adults and their guidance on drugs as hypocritical.

"Given that alcohol is a legal consumer product for adults, and that recent medical data indicate that moderate drinking may be associated with certain health benefits, it is irresponsible and misleading to categorize beverage alcohol with such substances as crack and heroin."

Dear Distilled Spirits Council: We deeply apologize for referring to beverage alcohol as a drug when we could have used the more accurate and economical phrase "legal consumer product." If we were in a more argumentative mood we'd point out that the status of a handgun as a "legal consumer product" doesn't make it any less capable of putting a hole in someone.

The Why staff has no objection to moderate, immoderate, or even coma-inducing levels of alcohol consumption. But we are greatly consternated by someone telling us that alcohol cannot be a drug because *if it were a drug that would mean parents are hypocrites*. Sorry, but we figured out a long time ago that Mommy and Daddy are not infallible. Besides, raising kids is hard enough; if we can't resort to hypocrisy once in a while we're finished.

Why isn't pork kosher?

The simple explanation is that God said so. In the Book of Leviticus, Chapter 11, God speaks to Moses and Aaron: "Any animal that has hoofs you may eat, provided it is cloven-footed and chews the cud." That means pigs (which have cloven hoofs but don't chew the cud) are unclean, as are camels (chew cud, hoofs not cloven), hares, and—He actually gets this specific—badgers.

What's going on here? Doesn't "chew the cud" sound like baseball slang, something the catcher would shout to the pitcher? ("Hum baby, hum baby, no stick, no stick, down the pipe, chew the cud, put some pepper on that ball . . .")

People have spent centuries floating theories about the origin of the Jewish dietary laws. Take your choice:

1. The theological answer. Purity and cleanliness are crucial to the idea of holiness in many religions, including Islam, which also bans the eating of pork. Pigs are nasty. "The aver-

sion to the pig, and it's not confined to the Jewish people, is an abhorrence to the mode of living. It lives in filth. It represents uncleanliness," says Rabbi David L. Blumenfeld of the United Synagogue of Conservative Judaism in New York. He adds that many religions "establish a daily sanctification of life. A sanctification of the person. What it is is a code of purity. Holiness is equal to purity."

2. The cultural answer. Jews wanted to preserve their identity and avoid assimilation, and strict and elaborate dietary laws served that purpose. There are even laws against eating with gentiles or eating food prepared by gentiles.

3. The hygienic answer. This is the one we've heard repeatedly over the years: The dietary laws were a way to avoid diseases. Pigs, for example, are subject to the disease trichinosis. The problem with this theory is that other animals also have diseases. Cows suffer from anthrax and brucellosis, diseases that were even more prevalent in ancient times.

4. The ecological answer. This comes from Marvin Harris, a University of Florida anthropologist and author of *Good to Eat* and many other books. Harris argues that these cultural eating taboos are elaborate ways to enforce long-term ecological goals. Pigs, he notes, require lots of water and shade and a high-protein diet. That doesn't mean they couldn't be raised— indeed, "there's a temptation to eat pigs," he says—but it does mean that they would have placed too many demands on the arid environment of the Middle East. For the same reason, he says, Babylonians and Egyptians developed taboos against pork. These cultures instead relied on "cud chewers." Those freakish extra stomachs allow a cow to eat grass, thistles, whatever. And goats can live in the trunk of your car.

Harris says that societies that rely on horses for transportation develop a belief that horse meat tastes bad. And in India, the cow is sacred because it births the bullocks that pull the plow. In time of famine, eating the cow would yield an obvious short-term benefit, but would create a long-term disaster. Simply explaining the long-term cost-benefit problem to a hungry person isn't likely to work—and thus is born the more persuasive religious taboo.

What does Rabbi Blumenfeld think of this last theory? "I would say that that's hogwash, pardon the pun," he said. He makes two good points: First, the cleanliness laws are incredibly elaborate and go way beyond the pig taboo. Second, there's no documented proof that any of these nontheological theories is true. The rabbinical literature is extensive, and there's not a word about avoiding trichinosis or combating the greenhouse effect or whatnot.

The true origin of the taboo probably can't be known for sure because it's prehistoric—it goes back to the first pages of the Bible. The Book of Genesis says that Noah brought some "unclean" animals with him on the Ark. Let's just say the ultimate answer got lost in The Wash.

Why do certain foods become inedible at the wrong temperature? Like why can't we eat hot ice cream?

We were eating some cream-intensive ice cream the other day, letting it soften to a perfect lubriciousness, and suddenly we came up with a brilliant question: If we write about this stuff, doesn't that mean we can put it on our expense account?

And second, why is it that if it warms up too much it becomes unbelievably disgusting? Why does temperature matter that much?

Now some of you may say, "Well, pea-brain, it has to be eaten cold because it's ICE cream. If it were warm, it wouldn't BE ice cream."

Right. It would be cream, with milk, sugar, and egg yolks added to make it completely disgusting. What we need to find out is precisely why temperature and texture are so darn important.

John Harrison, official tester for Dreyer's and Edy's brands of ice cream, pointed out that frozen ice cream has lots of air whipped into it, which is lost when the ice cream melts. But that's too simple. Fortunately we found Gail Vance Civille, president of Sensory Spectrum, a New Jersey firm that consults with companies about the taste and smell of their products.

Civille says that as food warms up, the molecules "volatilize." They become more mobile. Smells rocket into your nose. Sugars bathe your tongue. Most important, the fats loosen up and swish around, turning into a goopy, sloshy lard. When cold, that heavy cream has a nice mouth feel, but when warm it's like, well, like heavy cream.

"The fat is too obvious when it's melted," Civille says.

Another big problem: Ice cream can't melt in your mouth if

it's already melted. We like to feel the melting, to create it, to make it happen. We have an innate desire to keep the "action" in mastication.

"Control is a very, very big issue in food," Civille says. "People like to manipulate things, have things under control, and experience things. Part of the reason people like potato chips is that they can experience the rupturing and the moisture getting in. You're changing it. Babies don't like that, but adults like process in their food, and complicated process."

The fear of losing control of the food, she says, is "why people historically don't think they'll like oysters or cherry tomatoes. Because it might gush out of their mouth."

Why do people eat mushrooms even though they're a fungus?

You never feel a craving for fungi, have you ever noticed that? Mushrooms are not what you'd call a "mouthwatering" food. On what grounds do we eat these things? Shouldn't they be considered gross and unpalatable?

"We eat lots of fungi. We eat the yeast that we use to brew

beer," points out Mark Wach, director of agricultural products for Penwest Foods in Englewood, Colorado. He says there are as many types of fungi as there are types of plants (fungi aren't plants because they have no chlorophyll and feed off decaying matter).

"They're as diverse as any plant or animal would be," says this fungus apologist. Look at plants, he says: "You wouldn't eat poison oak or ivy, but you love lettuce."

Chefs say mushrooms are great at soaking up flavors from sauces and other foods. They're widely considered boring only because the standard button mushrooms sold in stores are not fully developed. Most of the mushroom's flavor comes from the spores and the gills, but you rarely find 'shrooms that are old enough to have them. One reason is that spores can carry diseases that hamper a commercial crop. But we'd guess the main reason is that fussy Americans don't like the look of those gills.

Why do bananas spoil if you put them in the refrigerator?

No no no, they don't spoil. The peels turn black. But the fruity part stays perfectly fresh.

The peels turn black because the cold temperature of the refrigerator kills the surface cells. "They're grown in the tropics, and when you put it at forty-two degrees, obviously it's going to kill some of those cells," says Ernie McCullough, a spokesman for Chiquita Brands International.

The prohibition against putting bananas in the fridge is mostly jingle-inspired, he says. The Chiquita Banana Song includes the lines "Bananas like the climate of the very, very tropical Equator/So you should never put bananas in the refrigerator."

Why does wine get better as it ages, unlike just about everything else in life?

We are students of the grape here in the Why bunker, and we'll let you in on the main secret to being a wine connoisseur: Buy jugs because you can reuse them as attractive flower vases. Trust us, James Bond does the same thing.

Now for the shocking truth: This wine-improves-with-age thing is basically a lie.

To improve with age, a wine has to be designed to improve with age, and most aren't. The ones that do improve with age—a certain elite group of red wines, basically—don't necessarily improve in a linear fashion. They "open" and "close" is how the experts put it. Ben Giliberti, *The Washington Post*'s wine critic, says there are "windows of opportunity" when the wine should be drunk. For example, right after wine is moved from barrel to bottle it might be delicious, but if you wait six months it could start to get skanky (not an official term; experts say "astringent") and you'd have to wait five years or so before it mellowed out again.

So then: Why do some reds improve with age? Because they are stocked with tannins. These are chemical compounds that come from the skins of the grape. Pete Downs, president of the American Society for Enology and Viticulture, compares the tannins in wine to individual Tinkertoys (do you think he's talking down to us?). At first, he says, they're all scattered and don't do much for the wine. But gradually they join up in longer molecular structures that give a great wine, like a '61 Lafite, a wonderfully complex taste (we drink it over ice, for that Deep Down Body Thirst).

When small compounds join up to make larger ones, that's called polymerization. Next time you drink wine and want to sound smart, say, "Ah, nicely polymerized." Some chemical reactions take longer than others; ethyl alcohol and tartaric acid need as long as thirteen years to reach equilibrium, says Vernon Singleton, a viticulturist at the University of California at Davis. "I've spent thirty years trying to make sense out of it," he adds.

Now then: Isn't there a way to age wine more quickly? Some technological gimmick?

Singleton says there is: You can heat the wine at 120 degrees, provided that you take care of certain variables, such as removing all the oxygen from the bottle. But it's a risky business, he says, because you might heat it too long and start degrading the wine. And besides, he says, no reputable winemaker would risk the wrath of the consumers by cheating on the aging process.

We plan to put some in the microwave as soon as we get home.

Why does a can of Diet Coke float in water, while a can of regular Coke sinks?

We heard about this from reader Mary Callahan of Washington, who heard about it in a speech by Maxine Singer, a chemist, and sure enough, when we called the people at Coca-Cola USA, they said it's true. Of course, we have a policy in the Why bunker of experimentally verifying everything we hear, so we obtained two specimens of soda of the specified Coca-Cola brand, one "Diet" and one "Classic," and immersed them in the sink in the men's room.

Not since Galileo dropped weights off the Leaning Tower of Pisa has an experiment proved so brilliant. Yes, the Diet Coke bobs right to the surface. Definitely the more buoyant of the two. We must note, though, that the Classic didn't exactly sink. It seemed to have trouble making up its mind whether it could float. (No doubt both cans were buoyed by the air pocket inside.)

The explanation from Coca-Cola: Diet Coke contains aspartame (NutraSweet), which is less dense than sugar and also much sweeter, so less is needed. We would imagine that the second half of that is what really matters here. Aspartame is two hundred times sweeter than sugar; if it takes nine teaspoons of sugar (sucrose or high-fructose corn syrup) to sweeten a Coke, then it takes less than a twentieth of a teaspoon of aspartame. Check out the ingredient label: There's less sweetener in a Diet Coke than there is caramel coloring.

So the gobs of dissolved sugar make Classic denser than either water or Diet Coke. But if you drop both cans off a building simultaneously, they hit the ground at the same time. This time, we'll take Galileo's word for it.

Why do we presume that human meat tastes worse than, say, cow meat or pig meat?

There we go again—being tasteless!

Don't be so sure that anthropophagy (cannibalism) is merely the habit of exotic Stone Age tribes and the occasional American psycho. A thousand years ago in France and Germany, professional killers would attack travelers, butcher them, and sell the meat in markets as "two-legged mutton," according to *The Consuming Passions: The Anthropology of Eat-*

ing, by Peter Farb and George Armelagos. (This is the kind of anecdote about which you can say in defense, "Seriously, I read it in a *book*.")

Armelagos, an anthropologist at the University of Florida, told us that there's no reason to assume that human meat tastes bad. Indeed, it probably doesn't have a whole lot of flavor because humans are so lean. The fat is what creates much of the flavor we like in meat.

"Humans probably aren't marbled as well as cow meat," says Armelagos.

What's a humanburger taste like? "Someone would probably say that it tastes like chicken," he said.

Admittedly, people don't refrain from eating human flesh simply because they think it would be unpalatable. There are ethical and religious reasons not to eat the stuff. But the morality of the matter is mixed up with an interesting gut-level reaction: It seems so gross! The flip side to this purely psychological bias is that eating other animals doesn't seem gross at all, at least to most of us. We are nauseated by the mere thought of consuming one of our own kind, and yet we think nothing of literally grinding up other critters and frying them in a pan.

You have to wonder if the phobia is a precondition for the philia.

Although we don't do "What" questions as a general rule, we were struck by this one today while eating a wonderfully healthy lunch (we favor yogurt, carrot sticks, celery, and a double order of onion rings):

What does yogurt turn into when it spoils?

We've always been suspicious of yogurt. Like maybe we should be disgusted by it. Like maybe it is not technically edible but we have been brainwashed to think it is. Naturally we called the National Yogurt Association in McLean, Virginia, and the veep of regulatory and technical affairs, Bob Garfield, told us that if you leave yogurt around long enough it will eventually turn into cottage cheese. Not really! What he said was:

"Yogurt is protected because it's a low-acid food. Unlike regular milk products, it has lower acidity so it doesn't spoil as much."

He said if you abandon yogurt in an unrefrigerated place, it will gradually spoil and the "whey" will separate from the rest of the yogurt, giving you lots of that watery stuff on top, not to mention probably some mold and other charming substances. He explained that yogurt is created by the adding of "cultures" to skim milk. A "culture" is a nice way of saying "a whole bunch of bacteria."

But they are nice bacteria, unlike the "spoilage bacteria" that can turn milk into a putrid substance. The yogurt bacteria, such as *Lactobacillus bulgaricus* and *Streptococcus thermophilus*, don't break down the milk the way bad bacteria do.

"There are good and bad bacteria in this universe," Garfield reminds us. He notes, "You can drink spoiled milk, but certainly the smell and taste are not good. The spoilage bacteria are different from the cultures."

We asked whether the cultured bacteria might mutate and turn your cup of Dannon fruit-on-the-bottom strawberry yogurt into something that could star in a movie with a title like *It Came from the Bayou*.

"They won't mutate," he assured us. "They're made under laboratory conditions."

So there you go. Just talking about this makes us want to strap on the feed bag and chow down on some serious bacteria cultures, preferably an entire bacteria civilization.

Why does soup take longer to heat up in the microwave than meat loaf?

L et's not worry about how microwave ovens work. You can just assume that they pick up gamma rays from the Andromeda galaxy.

What matters is that some things take longer to heat up than other things, and this phenomenon doesn't seem to follow any logical system. The heating speeds of various substances seem utterly arbitrary; you have to learn through trial and error, which is why everyone's microwave oven always looks as though at some point in the recent past a rabbit exploded in there.

Here are the main factors in the heating of food in a microwave, according to Bob Schiffmann, a physical chemist in New York City.

1. The amount of the food. This is the one concession to logic. Twice as much food takes twice as long to heat.

2. Specific heat. This refers to how much energy it takes to heat a substance. The higher the specific heat, the harder it is to heat something. Soup takes a long time to heat because it is mostly water, and water, as loyal readers of the Why books know by now, has the highest specific heat of just about anything on Earth. It sets the standard: Water's specific heat is 1, meaning it takes one calorie of energy to heat one gram of water one degree Centigrade. Fats and oils—the kind of thing you get in meat loaf—heat up about twice as fast as water.

3. Density. Things that are compact, that aren't filled with little air pockets, heat quickly.

4. The X-factor. For example, ice heats up extremely slowly because the water molecules are locked in a rigid crystalline structure and are transparent to the microwaves. Salty substances heat up faster the hotter they get because a secondary heating process kicks in ("ionic conduction"—never mind). Same with plastic tubs—they heat slowly at first, but as they

soften, they go into a different mode, "runaway heating." Put a little plastic tub of macaroni and cheese in the microwave, says Schiffmann, and "the next thing you know you'll have a mound of macaroni and cheese and a puddle of polyethylene."

Why do some drinking fountains shoot water from two holes instead of one?

You have noticed this your entire life and probably just accepted it without question. Here, finally, is the explanation:

One hole shoots out hydrogen. The other shoots out oxygen. The two streams come together and form H_2O.

Okay, that's a lie, but we enjoyed it.

The two-hole water fountain is made by Halsey-Taylor, one of the giants of the industry. The design causes the two streams of water to converge at the apex of the arc of water and supposedly creates a fuller, wider, broader, rounder, more watery drink.

Perhaps more important, the two streams aerate the water as it rises toward your mouth, and aerated water tastes better. It's not quite as tinny and stale.

A technological misstep:
the 34-hole fountain.

We are guessing that someday, to appeal to water snobs, a bottle of Evian will come with two holes in the top.

Why do beer companies brag that their products are "cold-filtered" or "beechwood aged" or "dry-brewed" or "genuine draft" even though no one knows what these terms mean?

In the old days, when we were small children, a "draught" beer came out of a tap and words had specific meanings. Today, there is beer sold in bottles and cans that purports to be "draft" beer. We are thrilled at the de-Britishizing of the word, but you have to admit that the total subversion of the word's meaning is a strong reminder that we live very close to the End of Time.

Obviously, the main reason beer companies use these terms is that customers respond favorably to them and buy more beer. This is called "marketing." The fact is that all beer is cold filtered. "Cold filtered" refers to a type of filtering in which a fine screening removes not only all particulates but even microbes.

Some New Euphemisms
1. Michelobotomized
2. Schlitz-faced
3. Sadder Budweiser
4. Pabst-smeared

"The term 'cold-filtered' is a little bit of a glorification of a process that sounds better from a marketing communications standpoint than 'ultra-fine microscopic screening' or some other term," says Tom Sharbaugh, the candid vice president for brand management at Anheuser-Busch.

This filtering process also allows a canned or bottled beer to claim to be "draft" beer. The filtering is so careful and the conditions so sterile—"aseptic filling" is the industry term for a clean operation—that nasty bacteria are eliminated. That means the beer doesn't have to be pasteurized. (Pasteurization involves briefly heating the beer to a high temperature, which kills not only bacteria but also some of the flavor.)

The old-fashioned "draught" beer wasn't pasteurized, either. So that's why this new stuff can claim to be "draft," even though this creates problems, such as what you call a "Miller Genuine Draft" that comes from a tapped keg. A Miller Genuine Draft draft?

But don't be cynical about marketing. It is through brilliant marketing that the beer industry makes the profits that can be funneled in the form of advertising to the TV networks that broadcast the major professional sporting events that provide the jobs for athletes not yet old enough or fat enough to appear in beer commercials.

Why is nonalcoholic beer blander than alcoholic beer even though alcohol has no taste?

The last thing we'd want to do is denigrate or ridicule nonalcoholic beer just because, if you're a guy, it makes the hair fall out of your chest.

The weird thing is, nonalcoholic beer doesn't taste nearly as robust and flavorful as regular beer even though the only ingredient that's officially missing is itself flavorless. Why?

"The flavor of beer is developed while the yeast makes alcohol," answers Joseph Owades, director of the Center for Brewing Studies in San Francisco.

The yeast converts sugar to a number of things: alcohol, carbon dioxide, and various flavor compounds (what a whiskey maker would call "congeners"). There's no easy way to make flavorful beer without also creating alcohol.

So brewmasters have several tricks for making nonalcoholic

beer. The easy way is to stop the fermentation early in the brewing process. You end up with sweet beer with a smidgen of alcohol (if you read the label closely, you'll see there is a little bit of alcohol in nonalcoholic beer). Another way is to make regular beer and then remove the alcohol. You can do this by distilling it, but that removes some of the flavor compounds as well. The most promising method, says Owades, is "dialysis," in which alcohol is separated from the beer through a membrane that only alcohol can penetrate. But Owades says the perfect membrane has yet to be invented. (Imagine owning that patent.)

Chicago brewer Ron Siebel makes another point: Alcohol alone might be tasteless, but it does affect the "mouth feel" of a beer. The alcohol makes a beer taste smoother.

In any case, there's nothing quite like coming home from a hard day's work and bolting down a cold, frosty glass of nonalcoholic beer—followed by a soy burger and some fat-free ice cream (invented by the same person who came up with the idea of "phone sex").

THE GLORIOUS TEMPLE THAT IS THE HUMAN BODY

Why do we get pimples, and why do dermatologists insist we shouldn't pop them?

Humans are among the few creatures on the planet that get acne. It's gross and it's unfair. On the other hand, we have large brains, and thus unlike dogs we don't find it amusing to roll around in poop. It all evens out eventually.

About 85 percent of the population gets acne to some degree between the ages of twelve and twenty-five. Simply washing your face a lot won't prevent acne. "If washing faces really helped get rid of acne, we would be home washing our faces instead of going to the doctor," says dermatologist Mervyn Elgart of George Washington University Medical School.

Teenagers with raging hormones get enlarged sebaceous glands (among other things). These glands make (WARNING: discussion of nonsolid and nondry substances immediately to follow) an oily substance called sebum that coats the inside walls of hair follicles and makes the skin cells shed rapidly and stick together.

Humans don't have much hair, compared with other animals, and many of our hair follicles have only the most puny, invisible, vestigial hairs in them, and thus there's nothing much to keep the follicles open as all this glop is piling up in there. So the follicle gets clogged with broken-down skin cells and dried oil and bacteria. (FYI, the blackness of a blackhead isn't caused by dirt, but rather by oxidized skin cells. When a clerk at a department store rubs a cotton ball on your face and it comes up black, that's not necessarily because your face is dirty. It could just be dead skin cells, which are dark.)

When the follicle gets stopped up, the body starts reacting. It senses the presence of bacteria. White blood cells charge to the rescue. They envelop the bacteria using a process called phagocytosis, from the Greek for "scarfing down a mess o' germs." The white blood cells, in destroying the bacteria, release enzymes that have as a side effect the destruction of the walls of the hair canal and inflammation.

"The body is trying to fight off the bacteria and in that process you are getting some destructive inflammation," says Alan Shalita, dermatologist at the State University of New York at Brooklyn.

So why does popping a zit make it get better?

"If you remove the core of material," says Shalita, "you are removing what is essentially a foreign body."

But don't pop. So say dermatologists. If you're not careful you can squeeze those inflammatory enzymes and nasty bacteria and supergross dead skin cells and ultramega-disgusting dried-up oil nodules back into the tissues surrounding the lesion. Hence more inflammation, major facial acne disasters, and possibly the need for, yes, amputation of the head.

"I always tell people not to squeeze pimples. That's the party line," says Elgart.

The dermatologist says you should instead (surprise, surprise) see a dermatologist.

But then he 'fesses up: "Most of us stand in front of the mirror and we squeeze anyway."

Why do we have wisdom teeth, even though they're useless and often need to be yanked out?

The problem with the human body is not simply that it tends to get overweight. No, the real problem is that it's kind of silly. There is hair in weird places. The knees are too big, and you probably don't need all those fingers. The appendix is a joke, the spleen a mystery. Men have those absurd nipples. Clearly the basic human body was designed by someone who had already taken a better job at another firm.

The wisdom teeth are interesting because they represent a freeze-frame of human evolution. The "third molars," as they are more precisely known, are left over from a day when humans didn't know how to cook—like several hundred thousand years ago. Cooking makes food softer; upon the mastery of fire the large human jaw became an anachronism. The wisdom teeth, so called because they emerge last, when you're old and wise, are slowly being crowded out of the mouth.

"What's happened in human evolution is we've tended to shorten the dental arcade," says A. W. Crompton, a professor of biology at Harvard. "We're not using our mouths as aggressively as our ancestors probably did. They were probably partially carnivorous, and they were taking pretty vicious bites of things to kill them."

As long as we're discussing annoying body parts, what's the deal with armpit hair? Does that have a purpose too?

Of course. David Givens, an anthropologist with the American Anthropological Association, says armpit hair and other kinds of body hair are specifically designed to accentuate your scent. The armpit contains apocrine glands, which release heavily scented sweat. Odor is a communication device; it has a sexual function and, in moments of conflict, gives an extra punch to your aggression. No doubt it was a caveman, sensing an imminent attack, who first said, "I smell trouble."

"The hair is a way of increasing the surface area in those regions, to help the scent to be broadcast more," Givens says. "These days people don't rely so much on apocrine odor in sexuality."

It's only in relatively modern times that we've declared war on our bodies and decided that we should smell like the first floor of Saks Fifth Avenue. Or, failing that, like nothing at all. The new trend is to be utterly unscented, to smell like empty space. That'll be the new brand of cologne: Air by Calvin Klein.

Why doesn't the hair on your arms grow as long as the hair on your head?

They've done experiments in which they've transferred arm hair to someone's scalp. Guess what happens. Right. People walk up to you and say, "Excuse me, but you appear to have arm hair growing on your head."

Head hair and arm hair are the same thing. Both are types of "terminal hair," as opposed to "lanugo hair," also known as "vellus hair," which is the almost invisible, pigmentless hair that covers most of your body and is left over from the days when we dragged our knuckles on the ground except for the odd moment when we reached up to scratch our underarms.

There's no major difference between head hair and arm hair, except that arm hair has a shorter growing cycle (called the "anagen" of the hair). It'll grow for a few weeks or months and then stop growing. The hair will sit in the follicle for a while, then fall out. Head hair, on the other hand, can grow for years and years. At any given moment, 80 to 85 percent of the hair on your head is in the growing phase, while the rest is just sitting there waiting to fall out.

In short, head hair grows longer than arm hair because head hair grows for a longer time.

All this is genetically determined and varies from person to person. Some people have hair that will grow until it reaches the ground, while others can't grow it longer than about shoulder length.

We should note that hair is, in fact, skin. Same thing. Hair is made out of keratin.

"Keratin is the major structural protein of the skin," says Alan Moshell, a dermatologist at the National Institutes of Health. "Hair is a modification of skin. So is nail. So is whiskers in dogs and cats and feathers in chickens. They're all skin modification."

We had always assumed hair was something totally different. Thread, maybe.

Why is the toenail on the little toe so hard?

And deformed! The deformity is the result of bad footwear, says James Michelson, an orthopedic surgeon at Johns Hopkins University Hospital in Baltimore. Women in particular suffer from these bent-over digits. The condition is called "onychogryphosis." (You know it even *looks* like it should be called onychogryphosis.)

And the hardness of the toenail? "The reason the small one seems stronger is that it's smaller," Michelson says. The big toenail is actually thicker, but because it's wider it doesn't seem as hard.

This Little Piggy had
Onychogryphosis

Do you need that little toe? No. "You can amputate the fifth toe and you can walk completely normally." But you don't want to amputate the first toe, the "thumb of the foot" as the Why staff likes to call it. "The big toe is important in ambulation; it acts as a stabilizer," says Michelson (and yes, when we interviewed him we heard the semicolon).

The big toe, we'd add, is not just a stabilizer. It's also an important stubbing instrument. It lets you know where the chair legs are in a darkened room.

Why doesn't the heart get tired the way other muscles do?

You would think the heart would get tired from all that thudding. Even when you sleep, the heart keeps pounding, never gets a breather, never gets to just shut down for a few minutes, never gets to signal for the backup system to take over. The heart does its job so peacefully that you usually can't feel it. Even if you climb some stairs, your thigh muscles will get tired before your heart does.

Is your heart made of some kind of superstrong muscle?

Yeah, actually. Cardiac muscle is different from skeletal

muscle. The mitochondria—the little engines within a cell that convert food to energy—make up 30 to 35 percent of the volume of the cells of heart muscle. In skeletal muscle the mitochondria take up only 1 or 2 percent of the volume. The result is your heart muscle doesn't get taxed as easily.

"In a regular cell at some point fatigue sets in because the mitochondria in the cell can't keep up with the energy demands, whereas in a heart cell there's no problem doing that because of the huge volume of mitochondria," says Larry Stephenson, a heart surgeon and professor at Wayne State University.

Second, heart muscle contracts differently. This gets rather technical and boring—yes, that's *in contrast* to other things we write—and so we will summarize the situation by saying that the little fibers of heart muscle contract more slowly than skeletal muscle, less frantically. Your heart keeps a nice, smooth beat. (For now.)

Why do so many people have lousy vision? Why hasn't evolution given us better eyesight?

S eems to us this whole evolution business has been pretty much a waste of time—we've been mutating for millions of years and we *still* need glasses.

The way evolution is supposed to work is like this: Two hunter-gatherers go looking for some wild game. One guy has keen vision, and he's able to discern which critter is the slowest afoot. He dashes out of the bushes and gathers the animal in his customary fashion (if we're not mistaken, the usual technique in prehistoric times was a swift, disabling bite to the throat).

But the other hunter-gatherer has lousy eyesight, and all he sees is a bunch of fuzzy shapes, and so he starves, and his genes aren't passed on, and good eyesight is thus "selected."

So why do so many people need corrective eyewear?

Three reasons:

1. Modern society is a strain. The hunter-gatherers didn't have to stare at computer terminals all day, they didn't read books, and they didn't scrutinize the agate listings in the sports section. Children who read books suffer worse vision problems than those who don't. But as optometrist Michael D. Jones of

Athens, Tennessee, points out, "I would much rather my child be nearsighted and be a good reader."

2. It doesn't really matter. Poor vision from birth, or blindness, certainly doesn't preclude survival, because the other senses become keener. And there is also a peculiar correlation between myopia and certain kinds of intelligence, which is why smart, nerdy kids often have thick glasses.

3. Presbyopia. At about the age of forty, almost every human being starts to have trouble with near vision. This is because the unusual tissue that makes up the lens of your eye has never been sloughed off or replaced, like most tissue. It's been there since you were an embryo. The tissue gradually becomes less elastic and you lose your autofocus abilities. By the age of forty it has hardened up to the point where you have to have reading glasses. The astonishing thing is that presbyopia at forty is essentially universal. No one gets spared. It's like a timer going off.

"It would be amazing if someone could develop a drug to keep the lens elastic," says Daniel Poth, a Reston, Virginia optometrist. "That would eliminate bifocals."

Natural selection didn't affect presbyopia because, during most of the time humans have been evolving, hardly anyone lived to the age of forty anyway. As we always say, anyone over forty is really just a freak of nature.

Why don't doctors get sick from treating so many infectious patients?

You're feeling awful, so you go see the doctor. You can barely keep your chin off your chest. The doctor walks in; she's the definition of vitality. You cough and wheeze and feel like crawling under the examination table and staying there until your body turns to mulch. The doctor cracks a joke and exudes animal vigor. You weakly raise your hand and ask permission to die now.

Shouldn't doctors be sickly? Shouldn't they be wiped out from handling so many germy people?

Historically, it was the other way around. Doctors were major vectors of disease. (Yes, vector is a great word. Babies should be named Vector. Funny *and* scientifically accurate.).

Before the germ theory gained acceptance about a century

ago, doctors "went from the morgue to the operating room to the delivery room and back again, without ever washing their hands or instruments or changing clothes," says Edward McSweegan, an expert in nosocomial (hospital acquired) infections at the National Institute of Allergy and Infectious Diseases. "Most surgeons couldn't conceive of themselves as sources of infection and contamination. They were the healers, not the lepers, in their minds."

Today, doctors are the ones who are in danger. And they do, in fact, get sick. There is no documented evidence that they have abnormally strong immune systems or anything like that. There's currently a serious problem with doctors and nurses contracting tuberculosis and hepatitis B from patients.

But in general doctors don't get sick any more often than the rest of us. Why not? Because most infectious diseases aren't really that infectious—they're not spread by tiny airborne droplets the way measles and tuberculosis are. Rather, for most nasty things it is the hands that are the big menace. Hands are dirty. That's why doctors are always over at the sink.

"Most physicians are reasonably compulsive about hand washing, and that probably prevents most bacterial and viral infections," says Richard P. Wenzel, a physician in Iowa City who is a specialist in infectious diseases.

So the next time a doctor washes her hands after touching you, remember, it doesn't necessarily mean that you're unusually repulsive.

This reminds us of another question that has nagged us for years:

Why, in past centuries, did people go weeks or months between baths?

There was a time when a bath once a year was not considered unreasonable. People were basically giant gobs of grease.

Why did people live like this? For a good reason: They thought that water was a health hazard. They thought it spread the plague. Bathing was literally considered a dangerous activity because it opened up the pores and exposed them to "pestiferous vapors," as they say.

"The skin was seen as porous, and countless openings

seemed to threaten, since the surfaces were weak and the frontiers uncertain . . . heat and water created openings, the plague had only to slip through," writes Georges Vigarello in *Concepts of Cleanliness: Changing Attitudes in France Since the Middle Ages*.

People did bathe, but only after taking many precautions, including immediate wrapping of the skin in cloth afterward and plenty of bed rest.

Instead of bathing frequently, people would clean their faces and hands—no water involved here—by wiping them with clean white cloth. They also took great care with their clothing: So long as their exterior created an appearance of decency, it didn't matter if they smelled like a stable underneath.

Why is a short nap so rejuvenating?

There have been many power nappers through the ages: Leonardo da Vinci, Thomas Edison, Winston Churchill, Bob Hope, the Why staff, Norman Schwarzkopf. (We know, we know, in a list of great American heroes "Bob Hope" jumps out at you as incongruous.)

Naps may seem quaint and kindergartenish, but in fact they are a matter of intense scientific scrutiny. Sleep remains a mysterious behavior since it exposes the sleeper to peril and has no easily understood neurological benefit. We know only that most every creature sleeps. What's new is the realization that humans also have a natural inclination to nap. We're supposed to nap. That midafternoon lull you experience is genetically programmed; it's not just because your life is tedious or your professor uses the words "dichotomy" and "eschatology" too often.

Not napping is what's unnatural. Only in work-obsessed societies, such as the United States, do people forgo the daily nap.

"Right now if you get caught napping in your office you're considered a joke, if not a failure. We've got to do something to turn that perception around," says David Dinges, author of *Sleep and Alertness: Chronobiological, Behavioral and Medical Aspects of Napping*. (The title alone makes you want to lie down.)

Dinges and his colleagues think that there's an epidemic of drowsiness-related accidents. As many as 40 percent of automobile accidents are due to inattention, he says. Many of those big eighteen-wheelers jackknifed on the highway got that way simply because the truckers pushed too hard too long and fell asleep. Even a short nap of seven minutes or so can cure that sleepiness. Dinges says people in some professions should use "prophylactic napping." Airline pilots, for example.

No one yet knows precisely why a nap works so well. We know that when you get sleepy your brain patterns become more variable, slower. "Microsleeps," brief moments when your brain exhibits the patterns we associate with being asleep, intrude into your wakefulness.

The next time you are at a boring dinner party and someone accuses you of nodding off, just say, "Excuse me. Prophylactic microsleep."

Why do your digits get shriveled up in the bathtub?

There's nothing more sensual and decadent than a long, leisurely, steamy soak in the tub, especially if you have both a propeller-powered plastic submarine *and* a sub-hunting, depth-charge-dropping surface vessel. The bad thing is that within about ten minutes you start turning into Prune Person.

Here's the headline: Your fingers and toes don't shrivel, they expand. Your digits get larger when you take a bath. You literally gain weight.

What's happening is the dead outer layer of your skin (the *stratum corneum*, for those of you who insist on everything in Latin; we hesitate to report that the *stratum corneum* also is known more informally as the "horny layer" because, we're told, it has hornlike characteristics) is being hydrated. When things get hydrated they expand because the water molecules are wedging themselves between the fibers or tissues. Your skin buckles and swells and folds in the same way wall-to-wall carpeting would wrinkle if it got soaked.

You may have noticed that the "shriveling" of your flesh in the tub doesn't happen as often or as much as it once did, back when you were a tyke. The reason is kids have more resilient skin. Their flesh expands more.

Or maybe you've just stopped bathing.

Why don't you ever get carsick when you drive?

Most of our research about carsickness had been conducted in the bent position until just the other day, when we got hold of "What Is Motion Sickness?," a report in the Annals of the New York Academy of Sciences that said, rather shockingly:

"The symptoms of motion sickness have been experienced at least since the invention of oceangoing vessels. It seems extraordinary that several millenniums later, the fundamental nature of the disorder is still not understood. In particular, it is not clear why it exists at all."

Not clear why?!! Perhaps we will simply have to step forward, on behalf of science, and deliver our own redoubtable explanation.

First, some obvious points. When you drive a car, you're in control; you know when it will stop and swerve and turn, and so you can anticipate these movements. "That's easier to handle than when it just happens to you passively," says Edwin Monsell of Henry Ford Hospital in Detroit.

But there's more to it than that. If you really want to find someone who has the time and the money to study puking-related phenomena in depth, you have to go to the federal government. At NASA's Ames Research Center, at Moffett Field, California, there's something called the Vestibular Research Facility. It's there to figure out why astronauts get sick in space.

The science director, David Tomko, told us that the key factor in motion sickness is where you're looking. You get sick because your eyes aren't stable. Normally your eyes can stand a certain amount of jostling—you could run through the veld with a spear, chasing antelope, and your vestibular system would keep your eyes focused on the animal. You don't get motion sickness from hunting, jogging, or playing basketball.

Likewise, it's safe to sit in the driver's seat and look straight ahead; you are jostled, but your eyes can adjust. But if you look out the side window at things whirling by, or try to read a book that's vibrating in your hand, your eyes can't adjust fast enough and there's "slippage" in your vision.

But now comes the hard part: When the vestibular system gets overstimulated, why does that make you want to talk to Ralph on the big white phone?

No one knows. One theory is that motion sickness is like pain: It forces you to stop unnatural or unhealthy behavior. (After all, it does rapidly persuade you to stop reading in the car.)

A theory we really love—because it reinforces our long-standing belief that evolution is sloppy—is that you get sick because your brain thinks you've been poisoned. You experience symptoms—blurry vision, loss of balance—that are similar to those of poisoning. So the brain sends out the signal that you should purge the contents of your stomach.

But perhaps for now the best theory is simply that our vestibular system is designed to keep us upright, focused, and balanced. Excessive rocking and rolling and bobbing and weaving is reckless and dangerous and our vestibular system makes sure we stop by creating motion sickness. Certainly we were never designed to do anything so dangerous as drive at sixty-five miles an hour down a road.

"We did not evolve riding in cars and planes," says Tomko. "Evolution has not conditioned us for funny combinations of angular and linear acceleration that are passively applied to you."

If man were meant to drive, he'd have wheels. Something like that.

Why do we itch?

First we should report a fact you may not know: When a mosquito sucks your blood, she (yes, she; the females are the bloodsuckers) gets so bloated that it is hard for her to fly away. What does she do? Right. She gets rid of some ballast. A little urination action. We tell you this only so that you can get really mad the next time you're bitten.

Now then: An itch is hard to define. It's kind of like pain. But it doesn't hurt. It's just bothersome, sometimes intensely so. It sends a signal to your brain saying: Scratch me. In fact, that is pretty much the scientific definition of an itch.

"Itch evokes a desire to scratch. Whereas pain hurts," says Robert LaMotte, a Yale neurobiologist who is an expert on the physiology of itching. Unlike an itch, a pain "evokes an avoidance reaction. You try to avoid touching the part that hurts."

Itching can be caused by many things, like a rash, a bite, a

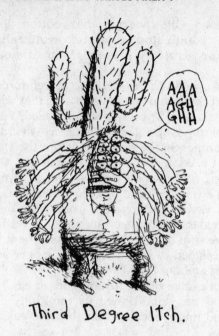

Third Degree Itch.

serious metabolic illness like kidney disease, or even a light pricking from a piano wire. For a long time people thought an itch was just a modified form of pain, perhaps some lesser version of it. LaMotte rejects that idea.

An itch, he notes, can be intense, even debilitating. It's clearly a different type of sensation with its own physiological mechanics.

He has studied nerves up close. What he's found is that there are many different types of stimulation-registering nerve fibers, called nociceptors. Some nociceptors respond to painful stimuli. Others respond to both pain and itch-producing stimuli. But the itch signal has its own pathway through the spinal cord. "Those nociceptors that respond to itch are connected to an itch-producing circuit in the central nervous system," he says.

If an itchy stimulus is joined by a painful stimulus, the itch will disappear, because the itch signal is blocked or repressed by the pain. And that's why you scratch: you scratch yourself to create enough pain to overwhelm that itchy feeling.

If you have a little poison ivy inflammation, you can aim a blow dryer at it, just enough heat to hurt a bit without actually burning yourself, and the itch will go away.

The strange thing is that itching has been largely ignored by the scientific community. That's not because it's not a serious issue: The problem is that you can't interview animals. You can't ask them if something hurts or itches.

"It's a subjective sensation that's hard to measure in experimental animals," says LaMotte.

In any case, we don't really like the idea of scientists doing things to make animals feel itchy. That seems a bit diabolical. But if they have to do such experiments, we know exactly which species most deserves to be the test subject. Yeah. Dang skeeters.

Why didn't the old manual typewriters cause repetitive stress injuries the way new computer keyboards do?

We are embarrassed to admit that the Why column is banged out on a computer keyboard with the assistance of a Daisy Wrist Rest, which helps protect our dainty little hands from that new malady everyone's talking about, carpal tunnel syndrome.

You ever notice that they're always inventing new diseases? And that people immediately line up to say that they've got a bad case of whatever that is? And that no one in the past seems to have suffered in such a way? Why is pain and whining such a growth industry?

Anyway, this typewriter thing is particularly weird because people seem to be injuring their hands even though typing is easier than ever before. Here's the explanation: Carpal tunnel syndrome occurs *because* typing has become so much easier.

More precisely, in the old days you had to do a lot of things with your hands when you typed on a manual typewriter. In addition to the wild flailing of the fingers you also had to return the carriage with a motion as though you were slapping the typewriter across the cheek. At the end of each page you had to pull out the paper, roll up another sheet, and line everything up again. Plus you were always halting the whole show so that you could dab correction fluid on every other word because you never learned to type in the first place.

Typing was a workout.

Now, with computers, the page never ends. You make corrections with keystrokes. You just tap away, tappety-tap till the cows come home, and meanwhile the tendons in your carpal tunnel in the wrist are slowly swelling and putting pressure on the nerve in there so that you start getting pins-and-needles feelings in your digits, numbness, nerve damage, and finally—and this part we're just presuming—death.

Though even that is better than dealing with correction fluid.

Since we're mostly made of water, why don't we slosh around more?

You always hear that our bodies are three-fourths water, or even 97 percent water, or some such incredible statistic. So why aren't we sloshier? Shouldn't we just spread all over the floor? Why don't football players, when they collide, make a splash?

The first thing you have to realize is that some people are more watery than others. Lean, muscular people have more water in them than fat, porky people because there's lots of water in muscles and not much in fatty tissues (fat and water don't mix). And our water content is in constant flux. People constantly exude fluids. (Exudation is our middle name.) You lose about a pint of water a day just exhaling, the air carrying away water from your lungs. You can sweat away as much as ten pints a day.

Your water content also varies with age, but outside the womb it's never as high as three fourths of your body weight. A fetus is about 90 percent water, a newborn about 70 percent water, and a mature adult about 60 percent water, according to the Federation of American Societies for Experimental Biology.

You could argue that we're mostly made of oxygen atoms. Our handy biology textbook says 65 percent of a human being is composed of the element oxygen. Another 17.5 percent is carbon, 10.2 percent hydrogen, with some calcium and nitrogen and phosphorus making up most of the rest. (Some of us have lead in certain places.)

Jeffrey Rosenstein, a George Washington University anatomist, says, "We're not a water, we're a gel." This is because a lot of the water in our bodies combines with other elements to form complex compounds, such as proteins, carbohydrates, and lipids. Something like a carbohydrate doesn't really contain "water" as we traditionally think of it.

Individual cells are like gel caps. The goop is contained. Between the cells is more goop. The larger goopy areas are kept in place by, among other things, firm collagen tissues, which in turn are held in place by the skeleton. "The reason we don't slop apart is that all these cells are attached to your bony framework," says Rosenstein.

So now you see why we have bones. Otherwise we'd quiver and tremble like Jell-O.

Why don't identical twins have identical fingerprints?

The strange thing about identical twins is not the fact that they're identical, but that they're not, actually, identical. (Another victory for concise writing.) Sure, sometimes they freak you out with that dress-alike Doublemint look, but eventually you can tell which one is Gilbert and which one is Philbert.

"Identical twins are identical only in the sense that they have identical genomes," says Thomas Bouchard, a psychologist at the University of Minnesota who is famous for his work on twins separated at birth and raised apart (e.g., Al Gore and Clark Kent).

So if their genomes (genetic codes) are the same—notwithstanding the occasional spontaneous genetic mutation—why aren't they truly identical? Bouchard answers, "There is what is called developmental noise."

Developmental noise! An important phrase. (Guns N' Roses is developmental noise for teenagers.) The term refers to anything in the environment that affects the way the genetic instructions are translated into an actual living thing. For example, twin embryos don't have equal blood supplies; one embryo grows larger, and so by birth there is a pronounced difference in the weight of the twins.

Developmental noise probably has an effect at an even more basic level—the translation of the DNA code into a biological construction project that results in, say, a fingerprint. The fingerprints of identical twins are quite similar, enough to be an indication that twins are identical and not fraternal. But there are subtle differences that are observable even when they are still embryos.

The DNA is a precise set of instructions, but the secretion of growth factors and hormones and so forth is a matter of approximation, notes Paul Berg, professor of biochemistry at Stanford and author of *Genes and Genomes*. What the genes say is not as important as how they are "read," he says. "Minor variations in the environment of two cells could easily influence how the identical genes in those two cells are read out," he explains.

It's kind of like whispering "fire hose" into someone's ear and asking him to pass it down the line: A dozen people later, the phrase has turned into "nose hairs."

Why is the throat designed to handle both breathing and eating even though it means we might choke?

Who designed this mess? Is it just a terrible mistake or some kind of cruel joke? Every time you swallow something you know you have to get that piece of food safely past the opening to your windpipe. Feeding children is a white-knuckle affair.

There's a great new book that explains our stupidly constructed eating and breathing apparatuses: *Why We Get Sick: The New Science of Darwinian Medicine* by Randolph M. Nesse and George C. Williams. They say the problem is an "evolutionary legacy" that had its origins in a worm.

The worm, Nesse says, was a type of "larval tunicate" (as was what we had for dinner last night in the Why bunker). The worm lived eons ago. It was the original mouth-breather, you might say. It fed on microorganisms strained from water. It didn't need a respiratory system because it was so small. Dissolved gases just diffused into its tissues.

As the creature evolved and grew larger, a primitive gill-like respiratory system developed in the forward end of the digestive system. This structure was no problem for a small creature. It only grew problematic for later vertebrates—but by then it was too late to go back and start over with separate pipes. Fish, dogs, people: We all have the same problem.

Nesse told us, "It's really a maldesign. There's no reason it has to be this way. The only reason it's that way is that evolution cannot do fresh starts." The problem would have been solved if our ancestors had developed nostrils below the mouth, on the neck. But they needed their nostrils up high, to stick out of the water while most of the body was submerged. At the same time the windpipe developed forward of the esophagus. So the breathing and eating systems have no choice but to intersect. When you breathe, air comes down the nasopharynx into the back of the throat and has to skip across to the windpipe (trachea) not far below the front of your neck.

The opening to the windpipe is called (as you know) the glottis. When you swallow, a little flap of skin, called the epiglottis, automatically covers the glottis; it's a reflex. As a backup you have a choking reflex, which expels anything that goes down the wrong pipe.

So it's not like we're completely without intelligently designed anatomical features. The body has a good attitude: It does the best it can with what it's got.

Why do we get a runny nose when we get a cold?

We've been in the Why business so long now we no longer make mere statements—we make pronouncements. And one of the pronouncements we've been making of late is that a cold virus doesn't cause a runny nose, but rather the brain commands the nose to run as a mechanism for ridding the nasal passages of the virus.

The one problem with this logical, scientific, and faintly reassuring pronouncement is that it's wrong. Our sources now tell us that the runny nose is not an efficient way to get rid of a virus.

In fact—here's the awful truth—the runny nose is something of a trick conjured up by the virus itself for its own dastardly purposes. The runny nose is usually a way of getting rid of particles that fly up your nose, like pepper or pollen. The virus has exploited this mechanism. It triggers the release of inflammatory chemicals that make your nose congested. It does this because it can use the fluid as a transportation mechanism—it literally can ride the stuff all through your head and chest and then out into the world where it can invade the lives *of other innocents*. Meanwhile, most of the virus remains securely fixed inside the cells of your nose and won't budge no matter how often you reach for the hankie.

"The nose was maybe not designed to handle cold viruses but to handle these other things, and the cold virus may take advantage of some of these natural processes," says Jack Gwaltney, professor of internal medicine at the University of Virginia. "Everything our bodies do for us is not necessarily good."

We may be highly evolved, but so is the little thing that causes the common cold.

ENCYCLOPEDIA AERONAUTICA:
Why Flying's Not Crazy

Why is it safer to fly in an airplane thirty thousand feet above the ground than to drive across town in an automobile?

Whenever we board a large metallic device designed to carry us six or seven miles off the surface of the planet, we always make a point to remain serene, calm, logical. We think: Flying is statistically safe. We think: The pilots know what they're doing. We think: Um, gee, what do they mean, "Seats can be used as flotation devices"?

Basically the only way you can get through an airline flight is through the suspension of your normal animal instinct for self-preservation. You have to recite figures: In a recent year 41,150 Americans died in auto accidents and only 49 died in major commercial airline accidents.

But let's explore that. Why don't planes crash more often? Why do they almost never malfunction during flight? There are lots of reasons, but this is the one we find most reassuring:

1. Simplicity. There is, first of all, simplicity in the principles of flight. Due to the shape of the wing, lift overcomes gravity. What you need is a reliable source of thrust, and here's where simplicity comes in again: A jet engine is much simpler than a car engine. Your car has lots of moving parts. A jet engine has only one moving part, a turbine.

When planes switched from piston-powered engines to jet engines in the 1960s they immediately became more reliable by a factor of ten. The latest jet engines almost never fail, which is why more and more planes have just two engines instead of three or four. Two-engine planes now are approved for transatlantic flight. And yes, these twin-engine planes can fly on just one engine; at high speed the tail acts like the keel of a sailboat and keeps the plane flying straight.

Because you are so clever you probably are thinking: So why doesn't my stupid car have one of these simple turbine engines? In fact, Chrysler considered using turbines on cars in the 1960s. But, among other problems, a turbine isn't good for stop-and-go travel. "Gas turbines work well at constant speeds. You don't drive at constant speed in a car," says Robert van der Linden, a curator at the National Air and Space Museum.

Here are some other reassuring things you can say to the jittery, sedative-popping passenger next to you:

2. Commercial air safety, unlike ticket pricing, never was deregulated.

3. A plane is a device in the control of a professional pilot; a car often is in the control of a drunken idiot.

4. Redundancies. There are more engines than are absolutely necessary. There's also a backup hydraulic system to control the wing flaps and landing gear.

5. Economics. Crashes are horrifying and spectacular, and so for the industry to remain economically viable, it has to have virtually no crashes at all. Thus there's a basic, capitalistic imperative to make flying so safe that normal, sane people are willing to go through with it even though it is rather terrifying.

6. Say, "Don't worry, I just read something in a book about how planes never crash. So this one can't crash because that would be just too weird of a coincidence."

Why do the safety instructions on airplanes tell you to put on your own oxygen mask before assisting any children next to you?

We thought of several possible reasons:
1. The life of a child isn't as valuable as that of an adult.

2. Children, because they are biologically smaller units, don't need as much oxygen as adults.

3. If you start fumbling with the child's mask first, you'll probably pass out, and neither you nor the child will be conscious to see what actually happens during a "water landing."

The third answer is (basically) correct, according to our sources at the Federal Aviation Administration and the National Transportation Safety Board. "The reason for that is that if you run into any trouble at all putting the mask on the child, there's a good chance that you'll pass out and you won't be able to help either yourself or the child," says FAA spokesman Fred Farrar. "The child is not going to be able to do anything for you," says NTSB spokesman Ted Lopatkiewicz.

The experts refer to something called TUC—Time of Useful Consciousness. This is the period after decompression in which you can still function well enough to mess with something like an oxygen mask. According to "The Pilot: An Air Breathing Mammal," a 1984 article by Stanley Mohler in a journal called *Flight Crew*, your TUC is essentially indefinite if you have a sudden loss of cabin pressure at 15,000 feet altitude, but at 20,000 feet "all unacclimatized persons become torpid, experience an increase in stuporousness and lose useful consciousness in ten minutes." (We have the same reaction to watching "This Week with David Brinkley.")

Your TUC then drops to thirty seconds at 30,000 feet and fifteen seconds at 40,000.

The chart doesn't say, but we're guessing that at 100,000 feet you simply explode.

Why is it possible for airplanes to fly upside down?

For years we had been mightily impressed with ourselves for understanding how a plane used Bernoulli's principle to achieve lift: The shape of the wing causes air to move faster across the top of the wing than across the bottom. This means lower air pressure above the wing and higher below, and thus lift.

But what about planes that fly upside down, like stunt planes? Isn't that a rather gaping hole in our explanation? Isn't it logical that the moment a plane flipped over, it would be sucked to the ground? Shouldn't we just admit, once and for all, that we're actually really dumb and merely pretending to be a smart person who is pretending to be dumb?

The answer is, planes can fly upside down by tilting the nose upward. This, in turn, tilts the wings at a higher angle off the horizontal. See, wings aren't exactly horizontal in normal flight. They may have about four degrees of upward tilt. If you flip the plane upside down, the wings will need about eight degrees of upward tilt to achieve the same amount of lift.

The bottom line is, flying's not that tricky. You don't need a fancy airfoil.

"A barn door will fly through the air," says John Anderson, a professor of aerospace engineering at the University of Maryland. "You can generate lift and fly it through the air, but it generates a lot of drag. It's not an efficient aerodynamic configuration."

A cow, for example, would be hard-pressed to get airborne. And once up there, the gas mileage would be terrible.

Anderson says a plane can fly upside down indefinitely, but with the wing tilted at the higher angle there's more drag created and thus more thrust necessary to keep the plane in the air. The fuel will run out faster. The pilot may get disoriented.

And you really wouldn't want to go into the lavatories.

Why don't the tires on planes blow out when the plane lands?

Our great fear when flying is not that the plane will crash, but that it will get a flat tire on impact, forcing another annoying delay while the pilot gets out and fiddles with a jack the size of an elephant.

The Federal Aviation Administration assures us that plane tires, like all commercial aviation parts, meet rigid FAA standards for wonderfulness. But they do blow out sometimes. The reason this is nothing to worry about is that they are designed to have blowouts if they get too hot—there's a small rubber plug built into the tire so that when the air pressure gets too high the plug will pop out and the tire will deflate in a gradual and orderly fashion.

If you go on a long drive in a car, air pressure builds in the tires and they are more vulnerable to blowouts. But planes only use their tires briefly, and the tires can dissipate heat when the plane is in the air or sitting for an hour between the gate and the runway, waiting for permission to take off.

Why do some planes leave contrails in the sky but not others?

This is the kind of thing a child will sometimes ask. What we always do is crouch down so we're on the same level as the child and then explain in clear, simple sentences that the white stuff in the sky is the smoke billowing from fires raging aboard the plane. Kids love it!

You may want to try a different, more accurate approach: The white stuff is ice. It's condensed water vapor at high altitudes, eight miles up or so, where the air is really cold, way below freezing.

As you know, a jet's turbine engine sucks in air through a large opening on the front, then spews out the exhaust through a small opening on the back side. As water vapor gets squeezed through the engine it gets denser. As it emerges into the cold air behind the plane it goes through a transition called sublimation, in which it changes directly from vapor to ice without ever being a liquid. How very sublime!

A plane at a low altitude can have a liquid water trail behind the engine, but it's not a contrail per se because it dissipates too quickly. A real, proper contrail stretches across the sky.

Multiple factors are in play: temperature, humidity, wind. The type of jet engine doesn't matter, we're told by Boeing.

Of course, you won't remember any of this next time a child asks you about it. Go with smoke.

Why didn't supersonic airline flights catch on?

We called British Airways to find out what a round-trip jaunt to London on the Concorde would cost, and they told us, in a flat tone of voice that suggests years of training so as to avoid cracking up, $7,800. We offered to stay over a Saturday night. They still wouldn't budge.

So there's part of your answer. Supersonic flights didn't catch on because most people, rather than parting with $7,800, would sooner attach chunks of raw bleeding meat to their limbs and swim across the Atlantic.

The Concorde, though a technological triumph, is old. It's 1960s technology. It holds only about one hundred passengers because it's a thin, sleek plane. And it has a range of only about three thousand miles. Even that distance requires 200,000 pounds of fuel, half the weight of the entire plane. Adding significantly more fuel isn't possible because the plane would be too heavy.

With so few passengers the Concorde has a high operating cost per "passenger mile." And the short range means it can't fly the increasingly popular Pacific routes, which require a range of closer to six thousand miles.

But here's the headline: Supersonic travel is about to have a renaissance, though it will still be limited to transoceanic flights. Numerous U.S. and European aircraft makers have already come up with designs for planes that can fly up to Mach 2.4, about 1,600 miles an hour. NASA has been helping with research. The burgeoning Pacific market is driving the effort. Right now it takes ten hours to fly between Los Angeles and Tokyo, but with supersonic planes it would take only four. And a supersonic plane could do two round trips a day, making such a plane a better investment for an airline.

Randy Harrison, a spokesman for Boeing, says his company's High Speed Civil Transport project has come up with a design that has a delta-shaped wing configuration (not wide from tip to tip but with lots of surface area) and is 311 feet long, compared with only 231 feet for the Boeing 747. He says the plane could fly as soon as the year 2005.

Harrison promises it won't be too expensive. There will be three classes of travel, he says, not just one.

There are two problems: First, plane exhaust can damage the ozone layer at the altitude where supersonics cruise, around sixty thousand feet. Second, the new generation of supersonic planes need to be quiet as they come in and out of airports at subsonic speeds. Ideally the engineers will also find a way to dampen the noise from the sonic boom. Lou Williams, director of high-speed research at NASA, says engineers want to find a way to make the shock wave from a supersonic plane less organized so the noise is not so explosive and startling.

"What we're trying to do in terms of softening the noise is turn it from a shotgun into a thump," Williams says.

In other words, not so much a sonic boom as a sonic thud.

Why did the Germans have the daffy idea of filling the *Hindenburg* with highly flammable hydrogen instead of much safer helium?

Because we all believe that our good luck will hold. And because there aren't oil wells in Germany.

You see, early in the century, before oil was discovered in the Middle East, America dominated the oil and gas industry. One of the things you can get out of certain natural gas fields is helium, which is nonflammable. America essentially cornered the market on the stuff. To this day, most of the world's commercial helium comes from only five fields: two in Texas, one in Oklahoma, one that spans the Kansas-Colorado border, and a giant field that runs from Texas through Oklahoma to Kansas.

The Helium Control Act of 1927 forbade the export of the gas because there was fear that other nations would build helium-filled bombers (in those days, people were still a little paranoid about the new technology of flight).

In the 1930s, when the Germans were clamoring for us to sell them helium—the *Hindenburg* was actually designed to hold helium rather than hydrogen—the ban may have been enforced for selfish economic motives. We had heavier-than-air commercial aircraft companies, aspiring to dominate transatlantic air travel. The Germans, meanwhile, had perfected lighter-than-air travel with their zeppelins. Selling the Germans helium might have undermined American companies such as Pan Am, writes Harold Dick in *The Golden Age of the Great Passenger Airships Graf Zeppelin and Hindenburg.*

The Germans managed to avoid disaster for a long time. They were way ahead of everyone else in blimp technology, dating back to Count von Zeppelin's first airship, a 420-footer that flew in 1900. The Germans knew that hydrogen was dangerous, but they took the risk. For one thing, the Nazis loved the propaganda value of the huge airships in the 1930s (as did Goodyear, we might add).

Hydrogen also has advantages. It's cheap. Electricity passed through water can create hydrogen gas. Moreover, hydrogen is lighter than helium. A thousand cubic feet of hydrogen weighs 5.61 pounds, compared with 11.14 pounds for helium and 80.72 pounds for regular old air.

So although the Germans took the risk of their zeppelins' burning up, they also enjoyed the benefits of extra lift, one reason the 803-foot *Hindenburg* was able to have such luxurious and spacious passenger quarters. (For those of you who have always wondered, the passenger quarters were inside the hull of the ship, not dangling from the bottom. The zeppelins were not just big balloons; they were rigid structures containing numerous inflatable gas cells.)

The *Hindenburg* fire at Lakehurst, New Jersey, on May 6, 1937, was apparently caused by static electricity igniting a hydrogen leak. It was a freak accident. But there have always been rumors that the fire was the result of sabotage. We vote for that theory because "static electricity" is in the Boring Answer Hall of Fame.

Why did Lindbergh succeed where others failed?

You know the story: Someone named Orteig puts up $25,000 for the first nonstop flight from New York to Paris or vice versa. Big fuss. Daredevil pilots crash, burn, disappear over Atlantic, lots of exciting stuff. Young guy named Charles Lindbergh comes out of nowhere, nails it. Instant massive hero. How'd he do it?

The simple answer is, he presumed success. He didn't load

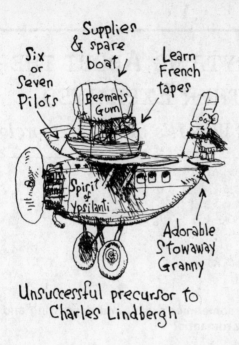

Supplies & spare boat

Six or Seven Pilots

Learn French tapes

Beeman's Gum

Spirit of Ypsilanti

Adorable Stowaway Granny

Unsuccessful precursor to Charles Lindbergh

his plane with precautions. There was, most noticeably, no copilot to spell him if he got tired or sleepy (the Orteig Prize didn't require a solo flight). He took no radio because he knew if he crashed in the Atlantic he'd probably die before anyone found him. He had only one engine rather than the usual two. He literally didn't weigh himself down with fear.

So there's today's inspiring trivia nugget: To get far in life, never countenance failure. Though marrying someone rich is also a good technique.

Everything About the Weather Explained,

Except Why It's Called Meteorology

Why is rain sometimes dreary and depressing and sometimes wonderfully romantic?

Rain is an umbrella term, if you will, for many distinct forms of precipitation: the drizzle, the shower, the sprinkle, the downpour, the cloudburst, the deluge, and, of course, the raining of the cats and the dogs. We define rain in terms of intensity, volume, duration.

But wait a second—what about the mood of a rainfall? Why are some kinds of rain annoying and some enchanting? One day you'll recite that famous poem, "Rain, Rain, Go Away, Come Again Some Other Day," and another day you'll experience the entire Gene Kelly effect and start splashing around in puddles and swinging from lampposts. Of course they don't make lampposts like they used to, but that's another issue.

Here's one scientific factoid: If the air pressure falls and the humidity rises, as happens on a typical muggy day in August, we retain more water in our bodies and that causes a sluggish personality. This is for real. The experts call it a "flat affect," but we know it as the blahs.

The kind of rain that people really love is associated with thunderstorms. The lightning puts ozone in the air, and ozone, in modest, sub–Los Angeles quantities, has been shown to be a euphoriant. Negative ions in the air alter your brain chemistry, exciting your neurons. Your brain feels sharp, focused, you do well on tests, you find your own comments really amusing and clever, you catch your image in a mirror and say, "Hey, Good Lookin'."

There's also a scientific equation that tells us how long we can endure rain, or heat, or snow before we get totally annoyed. The equation was created by Michael Persinger, a professor of neuroscience at Laurentian University. He takes *the square of the frequency of rainfall* and divides it by *the duration of rainfall*.

So let's say it rains half the day today, and then tomorrow it rains for half the day again. The frequency is 1 because it is raining every day, and the duration is .5 because it rains half the day. That's 1 squared, which is 1, divided by .5, which equals 2. So according to Persinger, by the end of the second day (this is what the 2 represents) you should reach maximum unhappiness, that point when you simply curl into a fetal position and whimper.

But if it rains every *other* day for half a day, that's 2 squared (4) divided by .5, which is 8. So we can stand that kind of intermittent rain for 8 days before bitterness prevails.

Let's interject right here that this stuff seems a bit digitalized for a world that's still operating in analog.

But maybe in this case we don't need such a scientific answer.

Chances are, our reaction to rain mostly reflects our previous mood. Rain is an all-purpose metaphor. It can be The Flood, or it can be sustenance. "The selfish heart is all chapped by drought. It is a cistern that holds no water," Miss Carrie Dennen wrote in her little book *The Rain*, published in 1883.

We may see ourselves as cleansed by the rain, nourished, quenched, or we may feel ourselves splattered, submerged, drowned.

Rain is rain; we invent the rest.

Why can't we bomb hurricanes or find some other way to snuff them out before they hit us?

The most common question the Why staff receives is: "Do you just make them questions up or what?" The intimation is that there would be something illegitimate, something undemocratic, were we to concoct a question from our own imagination rather than answer only the inquiries of readers.

The answer is, we're all one big team. Collaborators in curiosity. For example, this question is a simplification of the following, written by a certain Ferdinand E. of Alexandria, Virginia:

"Hurricane Andrew. I GUESS 600 miles to 1,000 in diameter. An eddy around an eye. Would bombs (concussion) dropped along a diameter (or radius) placed by height and distance and timed for maximum effect, altitude ignited, disrupt the eddy enough to destroy the energy of the storm and thus kill it? In mid-Atlantic?"

Dear Ferdinand: You don't mean "altitude ignited," you mean "airburst." And the answer is no. Richard Pasch, a hurricane specialist at the National Hurricane Center in Coral Gables, Florida, told us, "They [hurricanes] are too big and powerful. The energy released in a hurricane is really staggering even compared to that released in a nuclear explosion." A hurricane has the energy equivalent of something like 500,000 atomic bombs, he said.

So if you can't bomb a hurricane, what can you do? Answer: Seed it. That was the idea behind Project Storm Fury, an effort by the federal government, including the navy and air force, to mitigate the effects of hurricanes. The project ran from 1962 to 1983 and had debatable success.

Here was the concept: A general indicator of the intensity of a hurricane is the diameter of the eye. The tighter the eye, the stronger the storm. If you could somehow get the eye to widen, the power of the storm would decrease. So that's what researchers did: They tried to create a new "eye wall," farther out, that would replace the existing eye. They flew planes into hurricanes and dropped crystals of silver iodide, which triggered the condensation of water vapor and formed a new eye wall outside the existing eye.

Did it work? Maybe. Hugh Willoughby, a research meteorologist at the Atlantic Oceanographic and Meteorological Laboratory in Miami, says that of the eight hurricanes seeded, half appeared to form new eye walls and weaken (the last one was Hurricane Debbie in 1969). But he says these sort of changes in the diameter of the eye happen all the time through natural forces, and it's hard to say what was caused by nature and what was caused by Project Storm Fury.

Then there were the legal worries.

"The political people and the lawyers got really jumpy about this experiment. They were afraid of bad publicity, lawsuits," Willoughby says.

Think about it. What would happen if the experimenters accidentally made a storm worse? Or if they somehow made it veer away from one city and into another? The most likely scenario is that any success in weakening storms would backfire: The public would come to expect more of the same. Hurricanes would become wards of the state; if they didn't behave, we'd have to appoint a presidential commission to investigate what went wrong, who should be fired, why the system didn't work.

Maybe it's just as well that the government is out of the hurricane-mitigation business. There's something a bit arrogant about presuming that we can control what has long been considered an Act of God. (Though, at this rate, He might be wise to obtain counsel.)

Why don't storm clouds run out of rain? Why do they keep dumping rain for hours and even days as they slowly move across the country?

Get this straight: Rain is just a symptom. Even a cloud is just a symptom. Clouds are caused by uplifting air. It's kind of like a runny nose: The runny nose is not the thing, it is but a symptom of the thing, which is why you keep on having a runny nose long after you are certain you should have run out of material with which your nose could run.

Storm clouds and storm fronts keep replenishing themselves as they roll along. Inside your basic thunderhead, moist air is rising rapidly, maybe even thirty meters per second. As it does, it cools. Cooler air can't hold as much water vapor, so the water condenses and rain falls.

But here's the tricky part: The rain usually falls *behind* the storm. So the storm acts like a wave, rolling across the land: Air rises at the front edge, rain falls at the back. This is why it sometimes "looks stormy" for several minutes before the rain actually starts pelting you.

We're told that a storm that rains back down its updraft will kill itself. Surely there are metaphoric possibilities in that.

Why doesn't fog feel uncomfortably humid?

Fog has a relative humidity of 100 percent. Precisely. On the nose. Bingo. Exactamundo. So why doesn't fog feel gross, like "humidity"? Why, in fact, does fog sometimes feel good, kind of refreshing and sweet, while "humidity" feels like you may have to gouge out your eyeballs merely as a distraction?

You know, of course, that fog and humidity are water-related climatic phenomena. What's the diff?

For one thing, fog is liquid water suspended in the air, while

The fog comes in on...
a freak low-pressure system off the Gulf.
the red-eye from L.A.
big white nurse shoes

Mr. Carl Sandburg

relative humidity refers to how much water vapor—a gas—is in the air relative to how much the air could hold. When we say it's humid, we mean that there's a lot of water vapor in the air. It gets tricky because, in fact, the very unpleasant, muggy, suffocating ninety-degree days of summer often have a relative humidity of only 50 percent or so, which sounds kind of low. The reason that number is low is that hot air can handle a vast amount of water vapor. Cool air can't.

That's why you get fog, because the cool air can't handle the water vapor and it condenses into a liquid. Foggy air at forty-five degrees has a lot less water in it than sticky, gummy, goopy air at ninety degrees, even though the "relative humidity" is 100 percent in the cool fog and maybe only 50 percent in the hot humid air.

As for why fog doesn't make you uncomfortable, that's so simple we'd be too embarrassed to write about it were we not desperate for material. If you're dressed well, a cool fog doesn't bother you. But if you're hot and sweaty, humid air is a nightmare because the sweat can't easily evaporate into the already saturated air. You just stand there soaking, a globule of fluidity, sopping wet, a loser.

So remember, everything depends on the temperature of the air. We are tempted to say that it's not the humidity—it's the heat.

Why does the planet sometimes have these strange climatological spasms called Ice Ages?

We realize this item might not be perfectly suited to the "Weather" chapter. An Ice Age seems like more than just a type of weather. Think about how you'd feel if you picked up the newspaper and saw, in the corner, under "Today's Weather," "Clear, cold, turning to Ice Age. Forty percent chance of glaciers."

The origin of Ice Ages is one of those topics that seemed solved back when we were all in elementary school (or, for you younger readers out there, back when you were just a pink dot in a do-it-yourself pregnancy test). But as science has marched forward, things have gotten more uncertain. Let's tell you the moral of the story right away because in a minute we might forget: Nature is complicated.

The traditional theory is that Ice Ages are an astronomical artifact, the result of fluctuations in the Earth's orbit and axial tilt. The Earth has an elliptical, not circular, orbit around the sun. That orbital ellipse gets more or less circular in a 100,000-year cycle; when the orbit is most elliptical, the seasonal change is more intense in one hemisphere and more moderate in the other. So you might get really cold winters for a few thousand years in the Northern Hemisphere, and that juices the glaciers.

The axial tilt, meanwhile, varies from about 21.5 degrees to 24.5 degrees and back again every 41,000 years. When the tilt is greatest, the winters are colder.

If only that were the end of the story. But there's more. Oceans get involved. New evidence indicates that the ocean circulates differently during glacial periods. Even though astronomical factors create the general environment for an Ice Age, the trigger may be a catastrophic, sudden change in flow in the dark, abyssal regions of the ocean.

There is a remarkable thing that happens in the North Atlantic around the latitude of Iceland. Winds blow surface water to one side, causing deeper, warmer water to rise. At the surface, this water cools and throws off a massive amount of heat, which moderates the winters in Europe. (You may have thought only the Gulf Stream did this.) This cooled water then sinks to the abyss and migrates down through the Atlantic and the Horn of Africa to distant oceans.

It's like a pump, operating on an almost global scale. And if this big pump shuts down for some reason (there are all kinds of theories how this could happen), the change in oceanic circulation might create another Ice Age.

One last theory: It may be that climate varies for no good reason at all. We all know how quirky the weather can be. Ice Ages may be nothing more than a larger version of that same chaotic process.

Meanwhile, new research shows we live in a time of unusual climate stability.

"Variability is very weak compared to what has been observed in the past. We're very lucky. Maybe that's why we're here," says Andrew Weaver, a climate dynamicist at the University of Victoria.

But don't worry: We are doing our best to destabilize the situation. Just keep driving down the road with the AC cranked, and maybe someday there will be, if not an ice sheet over Manhattan, at least some massive sand dunes.

Why are there so many kinds of clouds?

As any schoolkid can tell you, the major species (or "genera") of clouds are: cumulus, stratus, nimbus, altosaxus, rhombus, doofus, stratodoofus, bungus, and cumulobungus. Amazingly we tend to forget these words as we get older.

But cirrusly, our sources tell us that there are only two types of clouds:

Layer.

Convective.

All the clouds you see are one or the other. Layer clouds are, as you'd guess, the flat, sheetlike clouds that form at a specific altitude, while convective clouds are the puffy, globular ones. You might also divide them this way: There are clouds where the wind is in control (layer clouds) and clouds where the cloud is in control (convective clouds).

An Invective Cloud
(only seen in cartoons.)

For example, your basic, pretty, horse-tail-like cirrus cloud takes on that shape because the wind up there is blowing it in a swirling pattern. A cirrus cloud is made of ice crystals, not liquid water. It's so thin the moon can shine right through it, often with colorful rings as the light reflects off the ice. Cirrocumulus, altostratus, altocumulus, and stratus are also layer clouds, shaped by various wind and evaporation patterns.

The common white cumulus cloud, by contrast, is a roiling bubble of turbulence, shaped by its own internal dynamics. It forms when warm, moist air rises rapidly and cools so that the water vapor condenses. A cumulus cloud has fairly well defined borders because along the edge of this warm bubble of air the tiny drops of liquid water are evaporating quickly.

The truth is, you probably won't remember that the two types of clouds are layer and convective mainly because "convective" is one of those words that you can't quite summon during a crucial moment during dinner conversation and thus are forced to use "conductive" instead. Our advice: Just say that the two types of cloud are ice and liquid. Which also happens to be true, conveniently.

Why do tornadoes happen? And why do they seem to happen most often in Dorothy-and-Toto country?

This is one of those questions that children ask (because tornadoes are so neat) but that adults find boring because they already know that tornadoes are caused by "some kind of scientific weather phenomenon involving wind."

The main thing you need to know about tornadoes is that the air is going upward even though the funnel descends from the cloud and touches down. Also you should not worry about them too much: Even in places like Kansas and Oklahoma, they are fairly rare in any given county, and more property damage occurs annually from straight wind than from twisters.

To make a tornado, you have to start with a layer of warm, moist air near the ground. Above that, you need a layer of cool, dry air. And above both of those, at about thirty thousand feet, you need the jet stream.

These conditions exist frequently in the Midwest and Great Plains because the prevailing weather patterns bring humid air northward from the Gulf of Mexico, while, higher up, colder and drier air blows in from the Far West. Still, that's not enough to create the kind of tornado that sucked Dorothy's house all the way to Munchkinland. You also need an instigating force—some pressure from a cold front, perhaps. When two air masses come together, they squeeze the warm air upward the same way you squeeze a zit. A thunderstorm forms. Inside the storm, warm air continues to rise in a column, accelerating upward and finally reaching the jet stream, which carries the air away. Meanwhile, the layer of cool air mixes with and evaporates much of the water of the thunderstorm, which causes that air to become colder still and sink toward the ground.

So you have an updraft and downdraft side by side, and this leads to a "spinning of the air" at about ten thousand feet, says Grant Darkow, a professor of atmospheric science at the University of Missouri. The precise cause of this high-velocity spinning is something scientists still are studying, he says. This vortex slowly descends from the cloud and, if it touches down to earth, officially becomes a tornado.

In other words, it's some kind of scientific weather phenomenon involving wind.

THE MAILBAG

James and Marie Elise Underwood of Morganza, Maryland, ask, "Why are raindrops sometimes heavy, fat drops that splat across the windshield, yet other times fine, small drops that, even in a heavy rain, seem to fall lightly?"

Dear Jimmy and Marie: We've always wondered if rain has ever come down so hard that it was fatal. Because we think killed-by-rain would be a really poetic way to go.

The big heavy raindrops usually come from thunderheads, those tall cumulus clouds common in summer. The wind currents force the droplets up and down and they grow bigger and bigger, with the biggest drops being about the size of a pea—a fifth of an inch across—according to Allan Eustis, a meteorologist with the National Weather Service.

The larger the drop, the greater its terminal velocity. This is not because gravity "pulls" it harder. It's because air pressure has more effect on a small drop. It can't cut through the atmosphere as well.

A pea-sized drop can reach a terminal velocity of about thirty feet per second. It hits your windshield with all that force because it's big and fast, like a pro football linebacker.

The smaller drops tend to form in horizontally organized, layered clouds, without all the convection and turbulence and drama. A typical raindrop is 0.06 inches, or about one seventeenth of an inch, across. At that size it can't go much faster than about thirteen feet per second. It just pitter-patters.

Eustis points out that raindrops aren't teardrop-shaped. They have flattened bottoms because of the air pressure.

"They kind of look like hamburger buns," he says.

Eustis says that if the drops are less than 0.02 inches in diameter, the precipitation is no longer considered rain. By definition it's drizzle. (Before you tell anyone it's drizzling outside, please verify the droplet diameter.)

THE ANIMATED AND SOMETIMES REPULSIVE GOOP WE CALL "LIFE"

Why didn't life ever get a toehold on Venus or Mars even though it pops up in all kinds of unlikely places on Earth?

New Jersey, for example. Surely that's harsher than your average crater on Mars.

There's a feast-or-famine quality to life in our solar system. Our planet is literally crawling with it, from deep-sea vents to subterranean rock in Antarctica. Meanwhile, every other planet and moon in the solar system is severely dead, a hopeless wasteland.

Life on Earth is ubiquitous because it's adaptive. With enough time it can get comfortable anywhere. We also should remember that the proverbial primordial soup (or is it the primordial proverbial soup?) wasn't a harsh environment at all. It was rich in complex molecules, warm, dynamic—pretty cushy if you were a young amino acid in a hurry.

Originally things were pretty nice on Venus and Mars too.

"Venus, Earth, and Mars probably started off with fairly similar climates," says Chris McKay, a NASA research scientist at Moffett Field, California.

But Venus never had a chance. It's too close to the sun. The heat boiled off the water. "Life as we know it requires liquid water," says planetary scientist David Paige of UCLA. To make matters worse, solar radiation broke down the evaporated water molecules in the Venusian upper atmosphere and the hydrogen escaped into space.

The carbon dioxide molecule is made of sturdier stuff. It accumulated in Venus's atmosphere, where it trapped solar radiation. Hence, a runaway greenhouse effect. Hence, surface temperatures of nine hundred degrees F. Hence, no bunnies.

Mars is the big mystery. About 3.5 billion years ago it was warm and wet and liquid water flowed across the surface. There could have been life! So why did Mars go belly-up? Size, probably. Mars is not nearly as large as Earth. Without a lot of gravity, it had a hard time keeping its atmosphere from evaporating into space.

Most important, it lacked tectonic forces. On Earth, we have colliding tectonic plates, which seems like your typical boring geology factoid but is something that turns out to be crucial to a living planet. The carbon in the atmosphere dissolves in water and forms calcium carbonate, piling up on the bottom of lakes and the ocean floor. But some of the Earth's crust gets subducted under adjacent plates, is heated, and finally is spewed out from volcanoes, with the vaporized carbon rejoining the atmosphere.

Without this kind of tectonic dynamism, Mars couldn't recycle its carbon. The atmospheric carbon dioxide chemically reacted with surface elements. Gradually the carbon dioxide in the air diminished. The greenhouse effect lessened. Mars got colder, and finally the surface water evaporated or froze.

An interesting asterisk to this depressing tale: Because Mars is small, it may have lived fast, so to speak. On Earth, life evolved verrrrrrry slowly. McKay, the NASA scientist, argues that the Martian atmosphere could have become oxygen-rich more quickly than Earth's, and thus life might have evolved rapidly into oxygen-demanding multicellular organisms. "It could have had the buildup of multicellular organisms, dinosaurs, people, everything," he says.

There could have been Martians! And they could have died gasping!

Today Mars is a complete disaster. There may be liquid water under the surface of Mars, but there are not likely to be Martian mole people. And although there are scenarios in which life may have formed in the mild upper atmosphere of Venus or in liquid water under the frozen surface of the Jovian moon Europa or beneath the hazy cloud cover of the Saturnian moon Titan, that's probably wishful thinking. Cold, dead, and desolate are the norms in this universe.

The way we see it, life is lucky to be alive.

Why is "biodiversity" so important? Why can't we survive indefinitely with just a few useful species, such as pigs, potatoes, and pine trees?

Sure, it's sad when a species goes extinct. We'd weep like anyone else if, say, zebras were erased from the picture. But would it matter in a purely utilitarian sense? Do we really need the planet to be overrun with upward of 10 million different species? Who needs all those doggone beetles?

It sounds like a facetious question, but let's be hard-nosed scientists about this. What level of speciation is necessary for the indefinite continuation of life on Earth? A million? A hundred thousand?

Suppose we reduced the number to a few hundred. The planet would be like a farm. We could even do some genetic engineering so that instead of pigs we just had giant wads of bacon wandering around.

Yes, it's a disturbing vision, but that's what we're basically doing at the moment, eradicating species at a rate not seen on the planet since the age of the dinosaurs. We are simultaneously trying to control and harvest many of the species that remain. We are replacing rain forests with eucalyptus groves. Can we do this indefinitely?

The answer is yes. Theoretically it would be possible to turn the Earth into a giant farm. But in a practical sense, it would be too much work.

"You could turn the world into a garden with a small number of species, but you would require huge amounts of monitoring and maintenance," says E. O. Wilson, the Harvard biologist and author of *The Diversity of Life*.

"It can be a terrible burden on humanity to have to monitor everything and have to work frantically to keep things working—things that were working perfectly well when we allowed natural ecosystems to exist."

We've all heard of the "food chain," but that diagram is too simple. Ecosystems are like a fabric, and no one knows which threads are holding the thing together. Scientists use an architectural metaphor: They talk about "keystone species," the plants or animals whose extinction could cause an ecosystem to fall apart.

For example, sea otters once proliferated along the California coast. We killed them. It turns out that they had kept the sea urchin population under control. When the urchin population exploded, the whole ecosystem went out of whack, leading to the disappearance of the offshore kelp forest, which had been a grazing area for whales, which had enough problems before any of this started.

"When you simplify ecosystems, it reduces the network of predators and prey items and they go out of kilter," says Michael Robinson, director of the National Zoo.

He notes that arctic climates, which are relatively simple ecosystems, are also highly unstable. We all know about the "lemming years," when the lemming population explodes to the point that the locals need to put up special road signs saying "Slippery When Visceral." The same thing happens with snowshoe hares. One day everything's cool and then SKLURK! there are 9 billion hares making a run on snowshoes down at the mall.

The lesson is, complex ecosystems are more stable than simple ones. So we're begging for trouble if we "simplify" the environment. And we haven't even talked about the aesthetic and philosophical objections to the winnowing of species. (Like, it would be wrong.)

One theory we like comes from conservationist Russ Mittermeier. He speculates that, as humans proliferate and the number of other species diminishes, we will become a "primary food species." Naturally, lions and tigers and bears won't be able to eat us because we own bazookas, but the microbes will go to town. Already we've seen a worldwide resurgence of malaria, cholera, polio, and tuberculosis.

Humans: Smart, funny, and packed with essential vitamins and iron.

Why do scientists always say that life is carbon-based? Why isn't it a lot more accurate to say that it's water-based?

As you know, "carbon-based" is the answer to the age-old question, "What kind of woman does Bob Packwood find attractive?"

The big hoo-ha about carbon is in honor of its utility in forming elaborate molecules. If you want to do something as grandiose as construct a living thing, you can't do it with a few dribs of hydrogen and a few drabs of helium. You need the big stuff: carbon. A brawny element.

And carbon by itself—pure carbon, graphite, soot, whatever—isn't enough either. The secret is to come up with a menagerie of diverse molecules, and carbon's perfect for that job. Carbon has a gift for being the integral element within lots of cool molecules, including those vital amino acids.

"Carbon is very special in its ability to make an extraordinary diversity of molecules, and to make molecules that can in turn combine to make more complex structures, such as the double helix," says David Stevenson, a planetary scientist at Caltech who studies the origins of life.

We are, in a sense, water-based also. But water is operating on a grander scale than carbon. Water, as a unique solvent, is the medium in which all the other molecules form. Water's like the dance floor where these materials meet and shake their groove thang, as it were.

Now that we've got your rapt attention (chemistry: the subject readers crave!), let us tell you about how the Earth was once frozen. That's right, the Earth was once an ice ball. Actually, this is not a confirmed fact, but it is a neat theory, emerging from a NASA-funded study of the origins of life. (NASA wants to know how likely it is that life exists out in space, so first we have to figure out why on earth it's on Earth.)

Here's the deal: It has long been assumed that life formed about 4 billion years ago in the ocean. But there have been some major kinks in that scenario. The sun was dimmer back then and provided only about 70 percent of the radiant energy that Earth receives from the sun today. The ocean easily could have been frozen under those conditions.

But scientists have had trouble stomaching the idea of a frozen ocean back then because the icy surface would have reflected so much of the sun's energy back into space that the ocean would still be frozen even today. They did the calculations and concluded: Frozen then, frozen now. Hence, it couldn't have been frozen then.

Instead, they theorized that there was a lot of carbon dioxide in the atmosphere, creating a "greenhouse effect" to keep the planet warm.

But—there's always another but—carbon dioxide is bad news for the chemistry of life. The planet's carbon gets locked into that CO_2 molecule: It can't break free to form the more complex molecules needed for the development of living organisms.

So here's the new scenario, as described to us by Jeffrey Bada, a marine chemist at the University of California at San Diego: There wasn't a thick CO_2 atmosphere. No greenhouse effect. Forget that nonsense! The ocean was frozen. But the ice was only about three hundred meters thick. There was lots of liquid water underneath, molecularly enriched by volcanic activity. An early form of life (the RNA molecule) formed under that ice sheet.

Then why isn't the ocean still frozen? Because at some point an asteroid pummeled the Earth with such awesome power that it melted all the ice. The Earth, basking under a hotter sun, snapped out of its ice funk. And the sunshine inspired those boring RNA molecules to start photosynthesizing and turn into something more interesting, like trilobites.

One implication of this theory is that if there's another planet with Earth-like conditions (lots of water, etc.) there still may not be any living organisms. "You may have to have some very carefully timed events," says Bada.

That's the bad thing about researching the amazing transformation of an unliving world into a living one: It begins to look like so unlikely an event you have to question whether we're even here.

Why do creatures get more complicated as they evolve, instead of getting simpler?

It's not because "complicated" is better than "simple"— That's not true in animals any more than it's true in VCRs. This has actually been the subject of much research and theorizing among biologists. No one can deny that life is more

Lyle Lovett haircut

Lots more brains

16 fingers

Airbag in Nose

Built in clock

Musical pancreas

More Legroom

Adjustable knees

The next Big step in Homo Sapiens

complicated now than it was a few eons ago. You just can't get around the fact that once upon a time there was nothing but scum, oozing along rocks and floating in seawater. Billions of years later, your average blob of scum has an accountant and a lawyer. So the question is, what drives this march toward complexity? Does evolution have some built-in bias for larger, brainier, more gadget-enhanced creatures?

Probably not. There's a simpler (ahem) explanation: Life mutates and evolves at random in both directions, toward simplicity and toward complexity. There's a bottom limit on how simple things can get—you can't get much more basic than scum—but there's no upper limit.

"If you look at the largest animals or the largest plants over geologic time, slowly the upper limits have been increasing," says John Bonner, a professor of biology at Princeton and author of *The Evolution of Complexity*.

Some types of parasites have lost parts of their anatomy over time, he notes. Rotifers, a small invertebrate creature, apparently evolved from larger ancestors. And common duckweed has fewer cell types than the plants from which it is descended.

Bonner says, "There must be some instances where brains get smaller as well."

Maybe he should do an experiment of people watching old episodes of "Gilligan's Island."

Why hasn't evolution wiped out hereditary diseases?

There are a lot of strange genes persisting in the collective genetic pool of the human species. The gene that makes you grow up to be a loud, bullying radio talk show host: adaptation or mutation? The gene that makes certain people drive at an excruciatingly slow speed in the passing lane of a busy highway: a Darwinian paradox?

The general truism is that genetic diversity is good. It makes sure there are many avenues of survival for the species. But how could anyone possibly explain away the horrible genetic defects that cause disease or crippling disabilities? Shouldn't those genes drive themselves to extinction over time?

The answer is rather startling: Genetic defects, however brutal to the individual, have subtle benefits to the larger population.

To understand this, you have to remember that genes come in pairs. You inherit one copy from your father and one from your mother. Many people carry just one copy of a defective gene, and they remain healthy. Relatively few people inherit two copies of that defective gene; if they do, they will develop the disease.

If you have just one copy of the mutant gene (if you are "heterozygous" for that gene rather than "homozygous"), you may still be physically affected, only in a beneficial way. The best-known example of this is sickle-cell anemia in Africans. Someone with two copies of the gene will often die. But someone with one copy of the defective gene will remain healthy and have a boosted resistance to the malaria parasite.

Another example is cystic fibrosis, the most common fatal genetic disorder of Caucasians. A new study shows that these heterozygous carriers of CF have additional resistance to cholera. Cystic fibrosis retards the body's ability to secrete salts and fluids. But if you have just one copy of that gene, you will have the ability to retain fluids better if exposed to the cholera bacillus, which normally can cause fatal cases of diarrhea.

"Cholera was one of the leading causes of infant mortality in the Middle Ages in Northern European populations," says Sherif Gabriel, a researcher with the Cystic Fibrosis Research and Treatment Center in Chapel Hill, North Carolina.

A March 1991 article in *Discover* magazine by Jared Diamond explained the cruel logic of Tay-Sachs, which is found throughout the world but is particularly prevalent in Jews of Eastern European descent. Tay-Sachs is a terrible killer of children, with one aspect of the disease being excessive accumulation of fats in the body's tissues. But carriers of just one copy of the gene seem to have had protection, somehow, against tuberculosis.

TB was prevalent in the Jewish ghettos in times past, so there was selective pressure in favor of any gene that fought off TB, even though homozygote (two-copy) carriers of the gene died in infancy.

One lesson of this is that genes are not simply transmitted from person to person. They are transmitted in populations. We may ideologically worship the right of the individual, but Nature likes a crowd.

Why are old-fashioned diseases like tuberculosis and malaria making a comeback?

Bacteria are back! For a while there, we had assumed that "infections" were a mere nuisance, a little-kids' problem, easily remedied with antibiotics, a quick shot of Bactine, a splash of vodka, whatever. Those pathetic little bacteria, we figured, were no match for modern science. Our complacency was backed by the federal government—the U.S. surgeon general boldly proclaimed in 1969 that it was time to "close the book on infectious diseases."

But we were stupid. We were arrogant. We were hubristic (a word that means "stupid and arrogant"). The bugs outsmarted us. They *adapted*.

Indeed, the reemergence of bacteria is a fairly dramatic confirmation of what Charles Darwin was talking about.

"For twenty years, we didn't think infections were important. We thought we had conquered them. We thought we could put them aside and work on heart disease and cancer. Of course, the microbes flow in the stream of evolution. They have tremendous genetic versatility; they can develop resistance to almost any antibiotic we throw at them," says Richard Krause, a microbiologist and immunologist at the National Institutes of Health.

"Microbes occupied the globe for two billion years before there were higher organisms, and they learned all the tricks of the trade in how to survive," Krause says.

Antibiotics typically prevent the bacteria from constructing cell walls so that they literally disintegrate and die. But bacteria have a secret weapon: mutation. About one in a million bacteria will mutate in such a way as to be resistant to a specific antibiotic. For this reason, doctors often prescribe more than one drug to treat an infection; the body's natural immune system helps out as well.

Still, new strains of germs emerge. A hundred years ago, people died of strep throat. Penicillin changed that. But about five years ago, a new form of strep throat emerged. One victim was Jim Henson, creator of the Muppets. And now there is an epidemic of drug-resistant tuberculosis. It is particularly a problem in urban, poverty-stricken areas and among people whose immune systems are already weakened by the AIDS virus. The TB bacteria itself is nearly ubiquitous; researchers say that about 1.75 billion people have some level of TB infection (though the vast majority won't get sick because they have strong immunity).

How is tuberculosis spread? In the air. "The major risk behavior for acquiring tuberculosis infection is breathing," says Barry Bloom, a microbiologist at Albert Einstein College of Medicine.

Yikes! Should we stay indoors? Hide under the bed? Or is the bed dangerous too? Bloom says there's hardly any chance that you could get TB (much less the drug-resistant kind) from, say, riding a bus. The big threat is to health care workers who handle a lot of sick patients.

But the long-term problem won't go away. Someone once said that a bacterium's only ambition in life is to become bacteria.

NUMBERS

Why do we use Arabic numerals instead of Roman numerals?

Many of you probably don't realize you use Arabic numerals. Some of you may think this explains why you have so much trouble with math—the numbers are in a different language! How can you divide 73 by 13 when the numbers aren't even English?

Actually, we don't use Arabic numerals. We use Hindu numerals. Western nations call them Arabic because Europe got the numerals from the Islamic world, which got them from the Hindus. (People used to pay less attention to the subtleties of multiculturalism.)

The switch from Roman to Arabic numerals took place in the Middle Ages, propelled by a book in the thirteenth century by the mathematician Leonardo Fibonacci in which he discussed the merits of the Hindu-Arabic numeral system. Islamic mathematics was not a far-off, exotic concept at that point because for much of the Middle Ages the Muslims had ruled Spain, Sicily, and North Africa, and when they were finally driven out by Europeans they left behind mathematical treatises. We tend to forget that Islam was a more powerful culture, and more scientifically advanced, than European civilization in the centuries after the fall of the Western Roman Empire.

"If you had landed from Mars in the year 800 A.D. and wanted to go to the center of mathematical learning on Earth, you'd go to Baghdad," says Bill Dunham, author of a book, *The Mathematical Universe.*

Many accountants in the Middle Ages retained Roman numerals instead of switching. The reason is that addition and subtraction can often be quite easy in the Roman system. Let's say you want to subtract 16 from 68. In the Arabic system, you plop the 68 on top of the 16, subtract 6 from 8, and 1 from 6, to get your answer, 52. But in the Roman system you'd just whack an X and a V and an I from LXVIII to get LII. It's subtraction by meat cleaver.

But Arabic numerals are more graceful in other ways. Their main advantage is that they have a "place" system, in which the value of a numeral is determined by its position. This is one reason why it's so much easier to write 1994 than MCMXCIV. In the Roman system, the numerals are intransigent. An X is always 10, a C is always 100, and so on. (XC is 90, but the X still represents 10 and the C still represents 100.)

The Hindus also invented a 0, one of the great inventions of all time. No one knows who came up with this idea. Originally the 0 was probably just a place holder, for use between, say, a 5 and a 7 in the number 507. Eventually it grew to be the number we know and love so much now, one unit less than 1, the number that most perfectly represents the social skills of the average Why staffer.

Our advice to everyone is to revert, whenever possible, to cuneiform numerals. These were invented by the Sumerians and Chaldeans about five thousand years ago and were devised on a base 60 system (as opposed to our base 10 system). They used little wedges as symbols, and the direction the wedge pointed determined the number.

For extra credit you might want to try the Egyptian system in use about four thousand years ago, in which 100 was represented by a chain, 1,000 by a lotus flower, 10,000 by a pointed finger, 100,000 by a tadpole, and 1 million by a man with his arms outstretched.

Admit it: What math needs these days is fewer irrational numbers like pi or the square root of 2 and more tadpoles.

Why are SATs scored on a scale of 200 to 800? Why can't you get less than 200?

As you know, your worth as a human being is precisely measured by the SAT. If you get a 520 verbal and your best friend gets a 510 verbal, then you are obviously a better person than your best friend.

So it's good that you can't get a zero on the SAT. That might create a slight self-esteem situation. In fact, that's one of the reasons the SAT uses the 200 to 800 scale—there was concern that a zero score would imply that the student knew nothing whatsoever, was utterly brainless. As it is, a score of 200 merely implies .hat the student is an appalling academic disaster.

"Also, an 800 doesn't mean you know everything. It's just the top reported score," says Jim Braswell, senior examiner in mathematics for Educational Testing Service, the company that designs the test.

Braswell says the creators of the SAT scale wanted to avoid existing grading scales, notably the IQ scale, in which 100 is the mean, and the standard 0-to-100 examination scale.

What students never see is their raw score. The highest raw score you can get on the verbal test is 85 because there are 85 questions. The lowest score you can get is negative 21. You lose a quarter point for each wrong answer.

But it would be hard to get every question wrong because it's multiple choice. In fact, says Braswell, when a student once got the lowest possible raw score on the Preliminary SAT—every question incorrectly answered—the examiners got suspicious. Sure enough, it turns out the student was a whiz kid, just trying to be funny, to appear ostentatiously stupid.

Why does the stock market go up and down for no apparent reason?

Famous anecdote: Someone once asked millionaire J. P. Morgan what the stock market would do in the near future.

"It will fluctuate," Morgan said.

Maybe he said it with a certain flair. In any case, it's a famous anecdote in financial circles. Stockbrokers tell that story and are so wracked with mirth they double over and turn red and their toupees fall off. The reason is, Morgan's answer summarizes the market's reflexive quivering, a jitteriness that if not entirely absurd is usually rather meaningless.

A stock trader might protest that the market goes up and down in a logical manner—say, in response to economic news or to information about a decline in a company's earnings.

That's rubbish. The market goes up and down in part because that's how traders make money. They buy low and sell high. If the market didn't fluctuate they'd go out of business. They *create* the market by bidding up prices, then selling into a decline.

"There's a vested interest on the part of lawyers to have more lawsuits, and there's a vested interest on the part of traders to have more volatility," says Daniel Turov, a prominent investment adviser in Oak Ridge, Tennessee.

Yale Hirsch, publisher of *Stock Trader's Almanac*, says a given stock price will go up and down "independent of anything. It has nothing to do with the company's business." The market, he says, "is a live thing. It's crawling with humans who want to make more money."

Smart investors, and many successful stock traders, don't worry about skimming the market on a daily basis. But some traders are on a hair trigger because they may be holding 100,000 shares of Microsoft and can make or lose big money if the price goes up or down twelve cents a share.

So let's say the Commerce Department releases some new figure showing a 2.3 percent increase in durable goods orders. The trader doesn't think, "Is this good?" The trader thinks, "Will this make the market go up or down?" And so the trader watches the other traders, and everyone stands around with a wet finger in the air, and then suddenly they all start screaming in unison.

James W. Gottfurcht, a clinical psychologist who writes about finance, says traders exhibit the classic fight-or-flight reaction that is part of every human being's psychology. The trading pit is a high-stress environment, adrenaline is pumping, decisions must be made on the quick—fight or flight—and in such a state a person is easily influenced, says Gottfurcht.

Compounding this is the proliferation of information. News is coming over all sorts of wires. Something happens in Japan or Germany, and everyone jumps. "There's an overstimulation. It's a global economy," Gottfurcht says.

Turov, who worked for years on the floor of the New York Stock Exchange, says, "The closer you are to the center of what's happening, the greater the tendency there is to be influenced by all those people around you. So you get changes in sentiment much more quickly. You have things taking place in an hour that used to take place in a day."

And in case you had any doubt: Never buy a stock upon reading good news about the company's performance. Because by the time you get the official news, the professionals will have already bid up the price. They know the rule: Buy on the rumor, sell on the news.

Why are there no trillionaires? And why hasn't anyone figured out a way to get rich enough to buy the entire world?

The closest thing to a trillionaire is the Sultan of Brunei, who has 165 Rolls-Royces and a net worth estimated at $37 billion. He's the world's richest person. We would love to know what gives him the most pleasure: the money, the Rollses, or the right to be called "Sultan."

First let's deal with the fundamental issue of why, in the world governed by free enterprise, no one could own everything. Even if you owned all the machines in all the factories, and owned all the land and all the bridges, there'd be one thing you couldn't own: the labor of other people. You can own the things that labor produces, but you have to pay for the labor, and that adds up. In fact, labor accounts for about 75 percent of the measurable output of a competitive economy, says Laurence Kotlikoff, professor of economics at Boston University.

"Even if you owned all the capital in the world, you'd still only receive about a quarter of the total income," he says.

Sorry to dash your hopes.

Now, as for why no one's a trillionaire:

1. Death. People die before they make that much, and then their wealth is spread out among heirs. The John D. Rockefeller fortune is still out there, bigger than ever, but more spread out, and so being a Rockefeller isn't what it used to be— you find them selling pencils on the corner, practically.

2. Government policy. The progressive income tax and antitrust laws were direct responses to the obscene fortunes of the robber barons. "The moment you become too big, you be-

come a target and society starts changing the rules to limit your power," says Barry Bosworth, an economist at the Brookings Institution.

3. Sentiment. The grossly rich often lose their zest for making more money. There is a limit on how much one can actually consume in terms of cars and vacations and caviar. They decide that wealth isn't the only thing in life. There's also self-aggrandizement. Hence, philanthropists.

But the main reason no one's a trillionaire is:

4. Market forces. Take the Sultan of Brunei. He can't raise his oil prices because there are other oil producers. If he and the other producers form a cartel, they might raise prices, but OPEC discovered that this doesn't work in the long run because it creates an incentive for conservation and the creation of alternative fuels.

Let's say you want to invest your money. The stock market, over time, has provided a return of about 7 percent a year in real dollars. Good, but hardly good enough to turn a billion into a trillion.

So that means you have to find some new idea or product. But great ideas can be copied. Introduce a new computer gizmo and within six months everyone else will have his own version, slightly modified to avoid patent infringement.

We on the Why staff have decided to be content with the goal of becoming mere millionaires. A few pathetic million, that's all we ask. And a couple of yachts. And one of the larger prairies, out west, with bison.

Monkeys, Hamlet, and Infinity

The Why staff has developed an obsession over a truism, and we have to deal with it before we can return to our normal format.

The truism is: If an infinite number of monkeys pound randomly on an infinite number of typewriters, one of them will write *Hamlet*.

There are slight variations on this. You might have just a few monkeys and an infinite amount of time. For that matter, the truism works if you have just one monkey, so long as the monkey is given an infinite amount of time to tickle the keyboard.

(To cite one fine use of the truism: *Washington Post* columnist Richard Cohen wrote a few years ago, "If an infinite number of monkeys, given an infinite amount of time, could produce 'Hamlet,' then two of them could, in a night's work, come up with 'The Morton Downey Jr. Show.' ")

We decided the truism needed to be checked out. We found that the truism is, in fact, true, but with an asterisk.

First, you have to realize that the mathematical basis of the truism is irrefutable. If a single monkey is put in front of a typewriter (we are presuming that the monkey has some innate desire to type and never grows old or gets tired or runs out of typing paper), there is a very small but nonzero probability that he will knock out *Hamlet* his first try. The more chances the monkey gets, the greater the probability of writing *Hamlet*. As the number of chances rises to infinity, the probability of writing *Hamlet* increases to one—a certainty.

You should also recognize a disturbing corollary of the truism: Not only will the monkey eventually write *Hamlet*, he'll even write the lesser Shakespearean plays and all the works of Marlowe, Shaw, and O'Neill, and he'll write *Moby Dick* and *Soul on Ice*, and he'll write that letter your mother sent you last week in which she talked about the beetles in her garden, and he'll write the Great American Novel that will be composed in the year 2078 by an as-yet-unliving person.

The monkey, by chance, eventually will write everything that can be written using a typewriter keyboard. (We'll cut him some slack on italicizing certain stage directions.)

An article in *New Scientist* magazine in 1984 criticized the monkey truism on the grounds that there's not enough energy in the universe to allow a monkey to hit the keyboard enough times (10 to the power of 150 keystrokes) to come up with even so much as the line "There are more things in heaven and earth, Horatio, Than are dreamt of in your philosophy." But we don't share that objection because this is just a thought experiment, not a real experiment.

Here's our beef: The same randomness that causes the monkey to write *Hamlet* should leave open the very slim possibility that the monkey will *not* write *Hamlet*.

Let's say the monkey, by chance, is in the middle of pounding out *Hamlet* and is right at the point where Hamlet is holding Yorick's skull, and the monkey types, "Alas, poor Yorick. I knew him."

What will he type next? The text says, "I knew him, Horatio," but people often misquote the line as, "I knew him well." Sure, chances are that at some point during the infinite reaches of time the monkey will write, "I knew him, Horatio," but—here's the rub—it wouldn't violate any law of physics or math for the monkey to screw up the line every time, forever.

It also wouldn't violate any laws of physics or math for someone flipping a coin to flip tails, and only tails, forever. Every flip, just as every keystroke, is an independent act and can have any result.

So maybe we shouldn't say the monkey "will" type *Hamlet*.

This, admittedly, is a hair-splitting point, though not totally inappropriate given the already absurd nature of the truism. Listen to this, from James Cargile, professor of philosophy at the University of Virginia:

"Something could have a probability of zero and nonetheless happen, or a probability of one and not happen."

His colleague at U-Va., Paul Humphreys, helped us understand this paradox. Take an infinite number of monkeys and let them type. The first monkey might hit *Hamlet* after 2 billion years, the second after two weeks, and the third might never (as we've shown) type *Hamlet* at all.

At that point, the ratio of monkeys who will type *Hamlet* to the total number of monkeys is two to three. The fourth monkey will type *Hamlet* after 900 quadrillion years. So the ratio of *Hamlet*-typing monkeys to the total number of monkeys rises to three to four. The fifth types *Hamlet* after a period of time so vast that the imagining of it would cause your brain to explode, but it still manages to write *Hamlet*. The ratio is now four to five. This continues on down the line of monkeys. Occasionally a monkey fails to write *Hamlet*—but at the same time, the ratio of monkeys who do type *Hamlet* to the total number of monkeys gets infinitely close to one.

And a number that is "infinitely close to one" is, in fact, one. A mathematician will say that these are simply two ways of expressing the same number. You might raise some philosophical objections, but on the chalkboard it's undisputed. But even though there is this probability of one that a monkey will write *Hamlet*, we've already shown that the second monkey in the group didn't manage to write *Hamlet* despite pounding away until the cows came home.

So the bottom line is: There's a probability of one that a

monkey with an infinite amount of time will write *Hamlet*, even though you can't absolutely rule out the possibility that he might never write anything better than *Titus Andronicus*.

We're glad we could clear this up.

(For the record, the preceding was typed in two hours. Pretty much randomly.)

Why did it take 350 years to prove Fermat's Last Theorem?

Like most people you probably dabbled a little over the years with your own proof to Fermat's Last Theorem—jotting down a few sines and cosines and logarithms on the back of a napkin, running the odd polynomial equation through your mind during a shower, and so on. And what did you get? Nothing but frustration. Agony. In a fit of pique you Cuisinarted the calculator. Who hasn't done that at least once?

Thus you were fascinated when Princeton mathematician Andrew Wiles announced that he had found a proof for Fermat's Last Theorem, more than three centuries after Fermat's demise. Pardon us for restating the obvious, but F.L.T. says that if "n" represents any positive whole number larger than 2, there is no solution to the equation "x to the nth power plus y to the nth power equals z to the nth power."

The reason that seemed so marvelous a theorem is that it is simple, by math standards, and yet not at all obviously true. For one thing, if "n" is 2, then there are lots of solutions to the equation. Do it yourself: 3 squared plus 4 squared equals 5 squared (9 plus 16 equals 25). And 6 squared plus 8 squared equals 10 squared (36 plus 64 equals 100). But 3 cubed plus 4 cubed doesn't equal 5 cubed! Two cubes added together *never* equal a third cube.

Pierre de Fermat jotted a note to himself in a book margin saying that he had found "an admirable proof of this theorem, but the margin is too narrow to contain it." No one knows to this day if Fermat was lying, deluding himself, or telling the truth. But there are lots of math geniuses and no one, until Wiles, had found a proof.

Here's why it took so long: There is no "admirable" proof. There's no single Aha! solution. It's not like other mathematicians forgot to "carry the one" or anything like that. Wiles's proof runs two hundred pages. More than marginalia, indeed! Whatever Fermat was thinking of when he said he had a proof, we know he wasn't thinking of what Wiles came up with. Wiles invented several new math concepts as part of his proof.

Moreover, Wiles had to build on the incremental gains of others. The most important leap in recent times occurred when a mathematician showed that something called Taniyama's Conjecture implied the truth of Fermat's Last Theorem. But no one had a proof to Taniyama's Conjecture either. So Wiles, wily guy that he is, managed to prove T.C. and thus proved F.L.T.

Last we checked, five "referees" were examining Wiles's work to see if it is completely sound. The Why staff brilliantly made no attempt even to read it since that kind of math is in a language that we don't speak and even most mathematicians find impenetrable. Wiles himself spent many months trying to deal with a portion of his proof that might possibly be flawed.

"Whatever happens, he's made a fantastic advance," says Wiles's colleague at Princeton, John Conway.

Conway points out that a proof is not the same thing as a calculation. A calculation can be done with a computer, but a computer can't usually prove a proof or a theorem. For example, Fermat noted that every number is the sum of the squares of four other numbers. Take the number 5. That's the sum of the square of 2, the square of 1, the square of 0 and the square of 0. Simple, right? But how do you prove that it is always true? You need a conceptual framework that shows that it must always be so.

Or how about this conjecture: A times B is always the same as B times A. You can plug in some numbers and see that it does work out (3 times 5 is 15, and 5 times 3 is 15), but how do you prove that it's true for all numbers? Conway suggests that perhaps you would argue that the equation represents dots shaped in a rectangle; by reversing the factors you are essentially turning the rectangle ninety degrees. Same number of dots, different orientation.

What's the point of all this? The point is, math is not just about number manipulation, it's also about ideas, concepts, visions of the universe. So the next time someone tells you that 2 plus 2 is 4, you should lift one eyebrow and say, "Yeah? Prove it."

Why is negative 2 times negative 2 equal to positive 4?

We always were bugged by the equation $-2 \times -2 = 4$ because it made no sense. What does it even mean? When we tell kids about math we try to make them understand that an equation is a statement, a declaration, not just a gaggle of numbers that serve only their own internal logic. But this one seems to be a logic-defier.

Mercifully, Frank Wilczek, a theoretical physicist at the Institute for Advanced Study, put us out of our misery. He explained: The term "−1" is a kind of instruction. It tells you to go backward on a number line. Thus if you are at 4 and are told to add −1 you know to take a step back to 3.

It's a bit trickier to understand why −2 times −2 is equal to 4. First, you have to realize that −2 times 2 is equal to −4. The equation is telling you that when you are moving into the negative numbers and go twice as far "forward" you end up twice as deep down that rat hole. But -2×-2 means that, just as you are getting ready to jump from 0 to −2, you decide instead to move twice as far in the opposite direction—to positive 4.

One way this was explained to us was in terms of a tank of water. Let's say you drain water from a tank and film the water running out. Then you play the film backward. This is a negative times a negative. The film, when you see it, shows water filling the tank.

But keep one thing in mind: Even when two negatives make a positive, that doesn't mean two wrongs make a right.

THE MAILBAG

Robert Hershey of Washington, D.C., has his own description of why −2 times −2 equals 4. He says, imagine that you ride the subway and buy a fare card at the beginning of the week for $10. The ride to work costs a buck, the ride back a buck. That subtracts $2 from the card every day. At the end of the week, after five round trips, the machine keeps your card. You could say that's −2 times 5, which equals −10.

But what about Thanksgiving week? On Wednesday afternoon, the machine gives you your card back, and you don't have to go to work the next two days. So that's −2 times −2, which equals positive 4—and so your card still has four bucks on it.

Why do people who are seven feet tall look as though they are eight feet tall?

We recall the time we spent a few hours following around Wilt Chamberlain, whose hips seemed to be at shoulder height. He was startlingly large. He also didn't like people making a big deal about his height. He definitely wasn't someone to whom you would inquire about how the weather was up there.

But here's the strange thing about height: Wilt Chamberlain, at seven feet tall, is only about 17 percent taller than an ordinary six-foot man. So why does that 17 percent superiority register so dramatically?

The answer is that we are not reacting to the raw footage of the person but rather to the rarity of his height. We are reacting to the deviation from the mean. That 17 percent figure is irrelevant; the important statistic is how many seven-footers there are in the population.

The National Center for Health Statistics is the agency that keeps tabs on everyone's height. (They're the ones who come into your house with a tape measure and make you stand against the kitchen door.) The agency tells us that the mean height for American men ages eighteen to seventy-four is five feet nine inches. Definitely a mean statistic.

We need to talk for a minute about standard deviations. The world would be a better place if we could simply define a "standard deviation" as any interaction between consenting adults that does not lead directly to the production of offspring. Unfortunately "standard deviation" is a statistical concept. The equation for things with a "normal distribution" states that about 68 percent of those things are within one standard deviation, 95 percent within two standard deviations, and 99.7 percent within three standard deviations.

One standard deviation for adult men is 2.8 inches. In other words, 68 percent of the population is between about five feet six inches and six feet tall, that is to say, within one standard deviation of the mean.

We can't tell you the height you'd have to be to be more than three standard deviations from the mean height. The Center for Health Statistics doesn't even keep track of people taller than six feet four.

But we'll wager that when you see a seven-footer you immediately and instinctively register the fact that this person is more than three standard deviations from the mean, even though you have no conscious understanding of what a standard deviation is.

(Note to Wilt: Rest assured that he who winds up with the most standard deviations wins.)

THE GAMES WE PLAY

Why are the cloverleaf-shaped symbols on playing cards called "clubs," even though they ought to be called "clovers"?

All summer long you've probably been whiling away the hours playing cards. Deep in the back of your mind—back near the hippocampus, if you can imagine something that remote—you were no doubt bothered by the suit we call clubs.

Those little symbols are not clubs. There is nothing clublike about them. They are shaped like cloverleafs. You cannot deny this reality. They are not clubs, they are clovers! Yet you continue to live in your own little dreamworld, happily dealing the cards as though the whole thing isn't a pathetic sham, a lie, a fraud.

Here's what happened. The English got confused. Hundreds of years ago, during the Renaissance, the English adopted the French cloverleaf design on playing cards. The French have never been confused about this. They call clubs clovers, though of course they use the French word for clovers, which is *trèfles*.

Now comes the big and rather inexplicable mistake of the English. Although they used the French design, they used the Spanish word for that suit. The Spanish word was "basto," meaning club. The reason the Spanish named this suit clubs is that in their iconography they literally show a club, an actual cudgel, a big knobby wooden thing, like what cavemen would use to bonk each other over the head. We've seen some of these

Spanish cards, and the clubs is truly a brutal-looking suit, much more impressive than the wimpy vegetal cluster we find on our cards.

The lesson in all this is that you can't appropriate various words and symbols from other languages and glop them all together as though they will blend smoothly and coherently. French and Spanish don't mix. It's like poker and milk.

One of these days we'll have to deal with another problem. Hearts are not actually heart-shaped. You go into someone's chest, and the thing you find is not some neatly symmetrical thing with two lobes at the top and a point at the bottom. The real thing is much, much blobbier than the thing you see on playing cards.

Maybe it's time for someone to design a decent deck of cards, a deck with integrity, a deck with some internal logic. Instead of clovers, we need cudgels. Instead of hearts, blobs.

Why does the Queen in the game of chess have so much power, while the King can only stumble around one square at a time?

In chess the King is a wimp. He is always cringing and trembling and whimpering on the sidelines, saying, "Oh dear!" and "Get away from me, you dreadful Rook!"

The Queen, meanwhile, is racing around the board, lopping off heads, gnawing on noses, sinking her arms elbow deep in human entrails, chugging beers, belching—you know, doing *guy* stuff.

Chess is a medieval game—it goes back at least to the seventh century—and you'd think it would be the Queen who would be pampered and protected and sequestered in the corner.

Here's the deal: For a long time the Queen didn't even exist. In India, where the game probably was invented, the piece next to the King was a Minister. He had little power—he could only move one square at a time, and only diagonally.

The game evolved from century to century and from country to country. The Arabs called the Minister a "wise man." When the game reached Europe the wise man became the Queen, but she still had limited movement.

Indeed, there was something a bit puritanical, possibly sexist, dare we say, in the description of the Queen's powers in the early European rules, as reported by H.J.R. Murray in *A History of Chess*: "The Queen goes one square aslant: She is to guard the King, is not to leave him, is to cover him from checks and mates when these are said to him, and to go farther afield and help him win when the game is well opened."

Obviously the Queen can leave the King's side but "is not to" do so. Is this strategy or social instruction?

The problem with the medieval game was that it was slow. To speed up the game, the powers of the Queen and the Bishop (an elephant in the India version) were expanded. Another rule change allowed a Pawn to turn into a Queen if it reached the other side of the board, but that caused a bit of a stir because, as Murray reports, "by it becoming a Queen when the original Queen was still upon the board, the moral sense of some players was outraged."

Why are sumo wrestlers so fat?

Because it's a gravity-based sport.

Every kind of wrestling has its own strategy. In Greco-Roman wrestling, you can win by controlling your opponent, pinning him to the canvas, escaping an attempted pin, and executing various other point-earning moves. In TV wrestling, you can win by biting your opponent's nose or distracting him while your "manager" or some wrestler who just happens to be in the audience sneaks up and clobbers him with a chair.

A sumo match is won, typically, by throwing your opponent out of the ring entirely. You also can win by making any part of his body other than his feet—even his hair bun—touch the dirt-covered floor.

A sumo match features several minutes of grunting and stamping without any actual contact between the wrestlers. Then, suddenly, they rush together—ka-splat!—flesh smacking flesh. A wrestler using the popular tactic called *tsuridashi* will grab his opponent by the waist sash, lift him in the air, and carry him from the 4.55-meter diameter ring (the *dohyo*). Another fun move is called *tsukitaoshi*—basically running straight into your opponent with blind ferocity and bouncing him into the first row. It's against the rules to punch, pull hair, gouge eyes, choke, kick the face or chest, or "seize the part of the band covering the vital organs," as one sumo brochure puts it.

KONISHIKI vs. GODZILLA

So, obviously, there is a great advantage to being heavy. The heavier you are, the more you have inertia on your side.

Now you might ask: Why do they have to be so *flabby*? After all, sumo wrestlers, with an average weight of three hundred pounds, are not much heavier than the average pro football lineman, who doesn't look nearly as fat and certainly never would be caught running around in a big-butt-exposing loincloth.

The answer has to do with leverage: Sumo wrestlers are six feet tall on average, several inches shorter than most football players. Thus their mass is more focused; they are essentially spheric. Spheres are stable because their center of gravity never changes, no matter how they roll or squirm.

Why are some bobsled teams faster than others, even though they're all basically just canned meat sliding down a chute?

Admit it. You fantasize, to this day, about winning a gold medal at the Olympics, even though you are technically an old fat person with no talent. The odd thing about these fantasies is that they have to have some very slight degree

of plausibility. You probably don't think about winning the gold medal in weightlifting, or winning anything in a swimming pool. But you figure the ninety-meter ski jump doesn't look so hard.

And what about bobsledding? Couldn't someone be, like, one of the middle guys in the four-man bobsled? Aren't we all fairly talented at sitting? Unfortunately, it's more complicated than that. The best bobsled teams know how to shave small fractions of time off their run. The difference between a gold medal and no medal at all is usually less than one second. That makes it all the more important that the teams find ways to go ever so marginally faster. There are three ways to do it:

1. The push. This is the part where physical strength, speed, and agility come into play. Everyone pushes. It's why you probably couldn't be one of the middle people—you aren't sufficiently fast, strong, and lithe. The U.S. team tried using Herschel Walker, the football player, but the tactic bombed. Walker could push, but he wasn't so great at jumping into the sled. Don't expect to see any more part-time bobsledders on the U.S. team.

2. The design of the sled. Bobsledding is like the soapbox derby: You get to make your own vehicle.

3. Steering. Yes, a bobsled has to be steered. Only one person is the driver. After the push, the other people in the sled

are just cargo. The driver has to figure out precisely how to take the curves.

The secret is: Not too high on the curve. Not too low. Not too much steering, not too little.

In fact it's like a complicated mathematics equation. We spoke to Mont Hubbard, a mechanical engineer at the University of California at Davis who has designed a bobsled simulator that allows bobsledders to figure out the fastest way to steer down the run. He explains that steering involves friction. The runners under the sled bite into the ice. So you don't want to steer too much because you'll slow down the sled. But if you don't steer at all, and just go with the flow so to speak, the sled will ride up high on the curve. That will make the distance the sled has to travel ever so slightly longer. A foot here, a foot there make a huge difference.

"A terrible driver can kill the best push," Hubbard claims.

Complicating matters is that each curve has to be treated differently. For example, you don't want to go through the first curve as quickly as possible. The reason is that the quickest way to get through the curve is to steer low, taking the shortest route. But because this route requires lots of steering, with the attendant biting of ice, your exit velocity out of the curve will be slower than if you didn't make it through so fast. You lose speed by not spending enough time in the curve. Zounds! It's very complicated.

By the time you reach the last curve, your tactics should have changed. By then you can steer a lot, taking the shortcut, losing velocity, because the run is almost over and the cost of losing some steam is more than made up for by the shorter distance you travel.

The bottom line is: You personally have as much chance of winning the gold in the bobsled as you do in synchronized swimming.

Why do baseball players hit foul balls all over the place, but never foul the ball back into their face?

The whole point of attending a baseball game in person, rather than watching it in the much greater comfort of home, is that you might catch a foul ball. Indeed, the players are instructed by the team owners to foul off lots of pitches to boost attendance. This is why the third-base coach is always grabbing himself and patting down his own body as though he's not sure he still exists in the physical world; he's giving the batter the secret signal to foul the next pitch back to a certain section of the stadium.

Anyway, several times a game a player will foul the ball into his shin or ankle, at which point the announcers make the astute observation that this really smarts. But never does the ball rebound off the bat and into the face of the batter, or his chest, or anywhere else above his knees.

Robert Adair, a professor of physics at Yale and the author of *The Physics of Baseball*, explained that as a general rule the ball bounces off the bat at a right angle. Because the bat is extended from shoulder height, there's almost no way to get it in position so that a perpendicular line from the bat will intersect the batter's body above the knees.

"The only way you could do it is if you tried a freak bunt," Adair said. If the batter held the bat vertically, rather than horizontally, he could manage to deflect the pitch back into his face.

It has happened. A few years ago Mark Whiten, an outfielder for the Cleveland Indians, somehow managed (presumably by tilting the bat toward the vertical) to bunt the ball back into his face in a game against the Toronto Blue Jays.

That really smarts.

Why did Michael Jordan average fewer than eighteen points a game in college?

Michael Jordan, the world's greatest basketball player, averaged a meager 17.7 points a game in three years at the University of North Carolina. Not once did he score as many as forty points in a single game. Why not? Because, to be fair to the opposition, he played on his knees.

Just a theory! Actually, he did everything his coach, Dean Smith, wanted him to do. Like pass the ball a lot. Move it around. Teamwork. Why drive-and-dunk in a spectacular fashion when you can be a wonderful passer? It's the Tar Heel style. And it explains why "Dean Smith" is the punch line to the famous sports joke "Who was the last person to hold Michael Jordan to under twenty points in a game?"

The folks at UNC defend themselves.

"Coach Smith's philosophy is that it is a team game. If one guy takes forty-five shots, you're not going to be a very successful team," says Rick Brewer, the sports information director. "We were a much better basketball team with him passing the ball, playing defense, and of course shooting."

Not everyone agrees. Jim Naughton, a former *Washington Post* reporter and author of *Taking to the Air: The Rise of Michael Jordan*, says that Dean Smith teams are sometimes underachievers, in part because "nobody has developed a big enough ego. You want a couple of guys who say, 'Give me the ball, I'm going to win the game for us.'"

Jordan won quite a few games, and as a freshman in 1982 he made the last shot to beat Georgetown, 63–62, and win the national championship. But there were other stars at North Carolina during the Jordan years—James Worthy, Sam Perkins, Brad Daugherty, Kenny Smith—and even though Jordan won several national Player of the Year awards he wasn't what he later became, a phenomenon, an icon.

He wasn't even the first draft choice out of college. The pro ball orthodoxy in 1984 was that a team needed a big man, a seven-footer, to win a championship. So the Houston Rockets picked Hakeem Olajuwon (who proved to be a superstar) and the Portland Trailblazers picked Sam Bowie (um, a very nice person, no doubt). Chicago then picked Jordan, but the team executives were kind of blue. They wanted a center, not some scrawny guard!

Jordan became the game's best player in part because Chicago in the mid-eighties was such a lousy team, says Sam Smith, author of *The Jordan Rules*. Jordan had to do everything, and he averaged well over thirty points a game. But Naughton makes a final point: Jordan also got better. His outside shot improved. The fact is, he worked hard.

That's the problem with being a superstar: People think it's just magic.

Why are baseball games stopped in the rain but not football games?

Baseball has no right calling itself a "sport" when it continues to cancel games simply because of inclement flooding. Football games, by contrast, are never rained out.

Indeed, the Minnesota Vikings, before they had a domed stadium, played almost exclusively in blizzards. The snow was so deep some players had their own drifts. It was so cold, when they'd huddle up to call a play, they'd build a fire. These were *men*.

Meanwhile, baseball players go mincing back to the dugout at the first sign of a dark cloud, practically. Why the big attitudinal dissimilarity between the two sports, climate-wise? (Okay, that's a badly written sentence, but who cares? This is the sports section.)

The proximate reason is that baseball simply cannot be played worth a dang in heavy rain. It is a finesse game with small margins of error. It's not that the slipping and sliding make the game frustrating so much as it makes the game dangerous.

For example, the mound will get muddy and the pitcher can't get good footing. That, combined with the slippery ball, will make it hard to find the strike zone and easy to throw a beanball. Another problem is that these huge sluggers can't hold on to the slippery bat. It could easily go flying into the stands.

The ultimate reason baseball games get rained out is that it's not a logistical disaster. A major-league baseball team plays almost every day, 162 games a season, so it's no big deal to postpone a game. A pro football team plays only sixteen games, hence the need to keep playing despite rain, snow, sleet, earthquakes, volcanoes, and extremely bad officiating.

Why, for the thousandth time, is there no national championship tournament in college football?

Big-time college football, unlike every other major team sport, has no national champion, just a vote-getter. A poll-winner. The college football championship is a heuristic rather than analog calculation, you might say.

Every sports fan understands that the obstacle to a playoff is the existence of the bowls. But there's more to it than that: What you have to realize is that a play-off is in the interest of no one involved in this process except the sports fans themselves.

The bowls certainly are the main opponents of a play-off; no one has come up with a play-off scheme that doesn't diminish the role of the bowls. Keep in mind that the bowls aren't just a game, they're a weeklong orgy of parties, parades, prayer breakfasts, and the like, so none of them wants to be just a quarterfinal or semifinal contest in some larger play-off.

The schools already make a lot of money off the bowl games, as do the TV networks and, indirectly, the TV advertisers. The National Collegiate Athletic Association can't simply order a play-off; the schools, by a two-thirds vote, have to approve one, and to date the schools have remained loyal to the bowls.

And what about the players? Many probably would love to participate in a play-off, but they are, let's remember, college students. Most of them aren't even paid! The players already are ruthlessly exploited, and extending the season with several levels of play-offs would worsen the situation. (Though we are not so naive as to think that, under the right circumstances, they wouldn't be exploited even more.)

Finally, there are the sportswriters. Every year, many of them write about what a shame it is that there's no play-off. But don't be fooled. They secretly love the controversy that's generated by the polls, the uncertainty, the indeterminacy. Gives them something to write about in a pinch.

Only you sports fans want a play-off. And you're nobody. Get back on the couch and hush up.

Why are hockey players fighting all the time?

The answer is: You'd fight, too, if you were a hockey player. Seriously, that's part of the real answer. It's such a hard game! You almost never score. You spend the whole time slipping and sliding around a frozen rink, using a stick to slap at a tiny hard puck. You keep missing. (We've watched hockey on TV, squinting to follow the movements of these spinning, flopping, crashing beings, and we've concluded that sometimes they don't use a puck at all. It's a kind of elaborate mime.)

"Hockey has been called the game of mistakes. There's a lot of frustration that comes about. A lot of the fights are the product of this frustration," says Stan Fischler, author of sixty-five books on hockey (now that's an expert! It's great to quote a

'spert who's not just another associate professor of refrigerated recreation or whatnot).

Another factor is the physicality of the game. You are constantly getting slammed against the boards in what is politely called a "body check," as though it's just a gentle pat on the rump. It's true that there is a lot of body contact in some other sports too, notably football and basketball, but only in hockey are the players armed with weapons, e.g., sticks.

Fighting has always existed in hockey but didn't become a serious problem until 1967, Fischler says. That was the year the National Hockey League expanded from six to twelve teams, and the sudden need for new players opened the door to some who were basically just goons. Goons are players who exist solely to perpetrate a fight. The Philadelphia Flyers were notorious for their thuggery, says Fischler. He says coach Fred Shero used to tell his players, "I want you to go into the corners in ill-humor."

The existence of goons created the need for even more goons. Fischler compares it to the nuclear arms race. Every team needed at least one goon to protect its "skill players" from the goons on the other side.

So thuggery became a kind of ritual. You get two opposing goons on the ice, you know you're going to get a fight. The problem is, Madison Avenue doesn't like all the fighting, and the advertising revenue of hockey games has suffered. Recently the problem may have reached its ugliest point when the league's biggest star, Mario Lemieux, suffered a broken hand when an opponent flagrantly poleaxed him. Lemieux was knocked out of the play-offs.

The culprit, Adam Graves, was sent to the penalty box. For two minutes. He played the next game and then finally was suspended for the duration of the season.

The NHL claims it is cracking down. New rules have toughened the penalties for fighting, particularly for "premeditated" fights. (Note to goons: If you slug another player in the face repeatedly, mashing his features into an unrecognizable pulp, make sure it is a spontaneous behavior.)

Why are snowshoes shaped like tennis racquets?

The classic snowshoe design is called a "bear-paw." A typical bear-paw snowshoe (of course it must be made of wood—none of this plastic stuff) will be about twelve or maybe fourteen inches across at the widest part, tapering toward the rear. The design allows you to walk without clacking your shoes together. The tapered end of one shoe can ride up next to the wide part of the other shoe; they fit around one another, like a yin-yang symbol.

If the shoes weren't shaped like tennis racquets, they'd have to be wider, maybe twenty inches across, in order to bear your weight on top of the snow, says Jesse Hull, president of Sportsmen Products, in Boulder, Colorado. And if they were that wide, they'd overlap.

With two big round things on your feet you'd have to walk with your legs far apart, like a duck. You'd be a mockery, even more so than usual.

Why wasn't there a left-handed heavyweight boxing champion until 1994?

Left-handed baseball pitchers are a dime a dozen—okay, more like $3 million a year—and left-handed presidents are almost as common. Five out of forty-three presidents have been sinistral, including three of the last five. But left-handed boxers are rare.

There have been, coincidentally, forty-three heavyweight champs recognized by at least one boxing association in the last century, but there wasn't a southpaw among them until Michael Moorer defeated Evander Holyfield in 1994.

Come over closer and we'll whisper a big secret: Even Moorer isn't left-handed, really. He boxes left-handed, but otherwise he's a righty.

So's Marvelous Mavin Hagler, the great middleweight champ: He writes right, throws right, boxes left (jabbing with the right hand, keeping the left close to the body, coiled for the power punch).

True lefties have won titles in boxing at lower-weight classifications, but the boxing records show that only three lefties (including Moorer) have ever even had a shot at the heavyweight title.

There's a simple reason, says Bert Sugar, editor and publisher of *Boxing Illustrated*: "Managers would turn them around."

You know how years ago schoolteachers would force left-handed kids to write right-handed? The same has been even more true in the boxing world. Managers knew that lefty boxers actually had an advantage over righties, but this was mitigated by a disadvantage: The righties wouldn't fight them. A big part of boxing is simply getting someone to agree to fight you. No righty wants to fight a lefty: It scrambles the choreography of a bout.

"Your foot movements are different, your counterpunches are different, your leads are different, everything you do is different. And you have to constantly think about it, whereas you have been almost by rote programmed to fight right-handers," says Sugar.

Sugar points out that Holyfield had fought only one lefty before Moorer. Holyfield had another problem: "Moorer was the first man to win a title while the other man was having a heart attack," says Sugar.

Holyfield complained of pain in his shoulder during the second round. After the fight he was diagnosed as having a heart condition. Sugar says Holyfield himself now thinks he had a mild heart attack during the second round.

You see what you get for fighting a lefty.

Why are the biggest, baddest computers still unable to beat the top human grand masters in chess?

L et's not get smug. It's true that in 1989, world chess champion Garry Kasparov easily whipped a machine called Deep Thought. But the machines are getting bigger, smarter, hairier.

The fact that humans can still beat machines illustrates a fascinating difference between the way the human mind works and the way a computer works. A computer chess program uses a "brute force search" to look at millions of possible outcomes to any given move. Deep Thought II can look at 6 million chess positions every second. By 1992 it was among the top thirty chess players in America. By the time you read this, a computer may have succeeded in beating everyone.

How does a human stand a chance against these silicon monsters?

By discriminating, for starters. A human player focuses on a few possible lines of attack (or defense) and totally ignores most possible moves.

"We haven't been able to figure out how to get the computers to concentrate on just the good moves," says IBM computer scientist Murray Campbell. "The grand masters, since they're only looking at a few positions, can do a deep analysis of the consequences of those few positions."

Why can't the computer simply figure out every variation on a given game? Because chess is designed so that there are gazillions of possible permutations. There are far more possible games of chess than there are atoms in the universe. So although the computer is crunching away, it can't look at every eventuality.

Humans have another advantage: We know how to break rules. You might decide that losing a rook in a certain situation will make long-term strategic sense. A computer doesn't have the luxury of being illogical, quirky, artistic. Computers don't think, they just do what they're told to do. They can only play as well as they are taught to play by the computer programmer.

Dan Edelman, assistant director of the United States Chess Federation, says, "Chess is a game of outwitting one's opponent, rather than just deep calculation all the time."

And computers are, alas, witless.

Eventually, no doubt, a machine will rule the chess world. IBM computer scientist Feng-Hsiung Hsu has designed a computer called Deep Blue that might be able to analyze a billion positions per second.

It's a real brute. We think it may beat Kasparov. We think it may, in fact, take over the world. Unplug it now is our advice.

THE SEXES

Why are people so obsessed with thinking, talking, hearing about sex? And why do they care so much about the sex lives of famous people?

Some people would argue that our minds have been poisoned by the filth of the modern mass media. They'd say that sleaze perpetuates sleaze, an endless, escalating cycle. But scientists put forward a simpler explanation: Sex matters. Sex, in fact, is the most important thing we ever do, even more important than accumulating money and power.

Sex is so important that we need to be fascinated not only by our own sexuality but also by the sex lives of total strangers because of the odd chance that some piece of knowledge will affect our reproductive success.

"It's important who's doing what with whom. It matters whose children are whose. It matters which relationships might be ending. It matters which relationships might have powerful influence," says Randolph Nesse, a professor of psychiatry at the University of Michigan.

Helen Fisher, anthropologist at the American Museum of Natural History, says, "We're interested in sex for our own competitive reasons, and we're interested in comparing our family values with the family values of everyone else, so we can see how we're doing, so we can measure our moral blood level with everyone else's moral blood level."

Lionel Tiger, an anthropologist at Rutgers University, says

this is an ancient trait: "Who the dominant males are having sex with is a matter of considerable concern in a primate community. Males compete among each other in order to acquire access to females and to the genetic future."

Thus, in the primate community of modern America, we have practical, natural reasons for knowing about Woody Allen's relationship with Mia Farrow's daughter because we might someday want to have a child with Woody Allen, or with Mia Farrow's daughter, or with Mia Farrow, or with Mia Farrow's ex-husband, Frank Sinatra, or with Frank Sinatra's ex-lunch partner, Nancy Reagan.

The strange thing is, you are probably more intrigued by the whiff of scandal than by the precise details of the sexual liaison itself. John Money, a professor of medical psychology at Johns Hopkins Hospital, says people love the hint of sex, the rumor that soon we will learn something tawdry, but the sexual facts themselves quickly lose their power to titillate.

"You always gossip about something that you've got wind of but you're not quite sure about," says Money.

Thus the Gennifer Flowers/Bill Clinton miniscandal no longer is interesting because Flowers no longer is mysterious. What sank Gary Hart's presidential candidacy in 1987 was not his relationship with Donna Rice so much as the way the story broke: that initial hurricane of allegation, denial, confusion, doubt, debate, all that guesswork and suspicion. A great scandal requires mystery—otherwise all you have is yet another guy with a midlife crisis and tickets for a cruise to Bimini.

Why are there so many people now being treated for sex addiction?

It's hard to believe, but there are actually people out there who feel compelled to engage in sex three, four, five, or even six times a year. And sometimes they drag a *partner* into their sick little game.

The fact is, the Why staff is under the distinct impression that most people would not rank at the top of their list of complaints about daily life "Partner Wants Sex Too Often." Nevertheless, there seem to be a lot of people out there who suddenly have discovered that they are sex addicts and are trying to cure themselves of this . . . *illness*. A new organization called Sex Addicts Anonymous has five hundred chapters around the world. Members of such groups go through a twelve-step program, as in Alcoholics Anonymous, that does not "cure" the problem but puts the participant "in recovery."

We spoke to one member, "Douglas," at the SAA headquarters in Minneapolis, who said that before he got help he suffered from preoccupation with sexual thoughts, demanded sex frequently from his girlfriends, cheated on them, and even exposed himself in public. Now, while recovering, he said, "I've got strict parameters around being sexual with people I am dating. It is no longer okay for me to date a woman and have sex with her until I've been dating at least six months."

When he stopped "acting out" his sexual cravings, he said, he went through withdrawal. He couldn't sleep at night. He was irritable. It is clear to him that he "used sex as a drug."

What do sex experts (we will resist the temptation to call them "sexperts") think of this phenomenon?

They say it's bunk.

"We don't buy it," says Elizabeth Allgeier, editor of the *Journal of Sex Research*.

"There's an industry out there promoting sexual addiction," says Michael Perry, a sex therapist in Encino, California. "I think it's motivated by profit and also a moralistic stance."

But aren't some people sort of disgustingly oversexed?

"Someone who is oversexed, or someone who is a nymphomaniac, is just someone who is having more sex than you are," Perry says.

The sex experts say some people may be sexually compulsive—in the same way that some people feel compelled to wash their hands a hundred times a day—but that's not the same thing as a physical addiction. Compulsive behavior is a psychological problem, not a neurochemical problem, like heroin addiction.

We received a lot of mail on this topic after we originally wrote about it, and many readers passionately declared that the addiction is real. Some of this might be a semantic debate over what the word "addiction" means.

But the key thing to keep in mind is that sex is a biological activity that is constantly judged by others. Too much sex, or sex with the wrong person, creates a disturbance in the social fabric. Thus a "sex addict" may merely be someone who feels he or she has behaved wrongly, or has been told, by someone else, that his or her behavior is improper or even abominable. The sex experts we spoke to say that most "sex addicts" are normal people who feel guilty about what they're doing or haven't been willing to take responsibility for the negative consequences of their actions.

"They just don't want to deal with the discomfort of saying no," says Marty Klein, a Palo Alto, California, sex therapist.

There are advantages to being a sex addict. Nothing is your fault. You are a victim of a disease, possibly one created by an abusive parent. Many therapists do not require that the abuse be remembered because it can be inferred by the existence, years later, of the sex addiction.

Says Klein, "People are saying, 'I couldn't help it, my addiction did it. I really didn't want to sleep with that woman, honey.'"

They used to say, "The devil made me do it." Now we just call the devil an addiction.

THE MAILBAG

A San Diego reader who identifies himself as a recovering sex addict wrote to object to our explanation of sex addiction:

"Addictions are compulsive drives to engage in destructive behaviors that an addict can't seem to avoid, no matter how hard he or she tries . . . I used masturbation with pornography as a compulsive escape from reality—avoiding healthy sex and intimacy with my wife, and healthy friendships with women—until I found Sex Addicts Anonymous and began to develop a new healthy sex life in my marriage and new ways of relating to women."

Dear Anonymous: We think it's grand if people join groups that help them improve their lives. Self-help books, group therapy, psychoanalysis—whatever works for you is what you should do.

Our job here is to explain why the world is the way it is, and that means that sometimes we cannot subscribe to explanations that merely make people feel good. Psychoanalysis, for example, is not a science, even though it may help some patients improve their lives. Just because someone engages in behavior that is crude or indecent or even self-destructive doesn't mean that the behavior is pathological. It's a sign of the times that millions of healthy, sane Americans are walking around under the impression that they are dysfunctional and diseased. That's just crazy.

Why are women historically considered the willing agents of Satan?

Let's be on record that we, ourselves, do not consider women to be on the payroll of the Prince of Darkness. If anything, he works for *them*.

What is true is that, in addition to all the other grief that women have suffered through the ages, they have been accused far more than men of being engaged in Satanic behavior.

This goes back to the biblical story of the Garden of Eden. The Devil wants Adam and Eve to disobey God's order not to eat the fruit of the Tree of Knowledge (we heard recently that scholars think it was a tomato, though we'd like to see the footnotes before we sign off on that). So what does old Beelzebub do? Disguised as a snake, he tempts Eve. The woman is the conduit to the man. Eve succumbs, then seduces Adam into eating the fruit as well. Chaos erupts: They realize they're as naked as a couple of jaybirds, they get booted from the Garden, and eventually the federal debt reaches $4 trillion.

The mythical prejudice had horrifying results in real life: The vast majority of people executed in the Salem witchcraft trials three hundred years ago were women; the men were, in most cases, relatives or associates of women suspected of witchcraft. The same pattern held true in the even bloodier witch hunts of Europe.

To blame this on misogyny seems too simplistic. Carol Karlsen, a professor of history and women's studies at the University of Michigan and author of *The Devil in the Shape of a Woman*, says there also may have been an economic motive. Many of the women accused of being witches at Salem had no sons or brothers, meaning that they were in line to inherit family wealth, Karlsen says.

"There is a real fear of female power that's increasing in the sixteenth century," agrees Tom Robisheaux, a professor of history at Duke University. He says that priests feared female sexual power and the way women could use sexual power to control men. Protestant reformers promoted a new morality centered around the family, with the woman as a symbol of order and piety; anything that did not fit the mold (such as an independent, unmarried woman) was suggestive of diabolism.

One other theory: During most of human history there weren't many doctors, and so women were pressed into the role of healers. They often practiced medicine in ways that by their—and today's—standards *would* look like black magic. And a few witchcraft scholars argue that some of the victims of witch hunts were, in fact, practitioners of witchcraft.

You know that argument: They asked for it.

Why do some marriages last for years and years even though the husband and wife clearly despise one another and the kids are long gone?

It's sad when a couple gets divorced or separates. But it's even sadder, and a whole lot weirder, when they stay together even though every time you go over to their house you see hemi-disks of dinner plates jutting from the walls. Why do couples who seem to abominate one another hang together for so long?

There are four reasons, according to Robert Sternberg, professor of psychology at Yale University:

1. Attachment. This is an emotion distinct from love. "It's like being attached to a blanket; it gets old and grungy, it gets smelly, you really don't need it anymore, but you don't want to give it up."

2. Fear. Life could be worse. A known evil is sometimes preferable to an imaginary evil.

3. Secret rewards. Some people like fighting. Or they like being able to go to their friends and tell war stories. Or misery confirms their self-image: They figure they deserve this.

4. Love. If you really love someone, you can tolerate the fact that you also hate him.

We are surprised to learn that divorce is most likely to happen to people in their twenties. For women, 82 percent of divorces occur before the age of forty-five, says Helen Fisher, author of *Anatomy of Love: The Natural History of Monogamy, Adultery and Divorce*. She says, "Divorce around the world is for the young."

People get married because pair-bonding is an evolved trait of the species, a strategy for successfully raising children. The marital stakes are highest, therefore, when people are in their youth, having babies and raising them. Common sense would tell you that couples would be more likely to split after the kids leave the nest, but competing against that is the biological reality that they aren't likely, as older persons, to have more children with another mate.

Fisher also gives a neurochemical explanation for why couples stick it out:

"There are two stages of love, the first being attraction. During that stage, you get a brain bath of three chemicals that are natural amphetamines. You can stay up all night, and talk till dawn, and feel giddy and euphoric.

"In time, these wane, and the second stage of love kicks in, attachment, and that's associated with a different brain chemistry, the endorphins, which have natural narcotic-like qualities," she says.

So over time, you become narcotized in a relationship. The cocaine buzz of infatuation gives way to a dull, blissed-out heroin addiction. (We know, we know, we should get a job writing Hallmark cards.)

Why do we close our eyes when we kiss?

Well, obviously, people don't look so great up close. You discover millions of new hairs. The eyes turn into goopy pools of slime. And even the most modest blemish suddenly becomes Mount Pinatubo.

The basic problem is that we're too visual to begin with. As predatory, analytical creatures we are designed to rely on our vision more than any other sense. Diane Ackerman, in her book *A Natural History of the Senses*, notes that 70 percent of the body's sense receptors are clustered in the eyes.

"Lovers close their eyes when they kiss because, if they didn't, there would be too many visual distractions to notice and analyze—the sudden close-up of the loved one's eyelashes and hair, the wallpaper, the clock face, the dust motes suspended in a shaft of sunlight."

Also this enables you to pretend that "John" actually is "Bruce."

Why do humans have a period called adolescence, even though no other species seems to suffer through this?

Adolescence, defined in scientific terms, commences when an organism reaches puberty and concludes when an organism no longer thinks that keeping the price tag on one's clothing is a nifty "fashion statement."

We had assumed that this period was an invention of modern society, a kind of post–Industrial Revolution madness with an underlying economic motivation, such as restricting the supply of available labor. There is, indeed, some artificiality in the institution of adolescence; as a society, we don't expect young adults to have meaningful jobs or to do much of anything other than trudge off to an architecturally hideous high school and try to avoid serious substance abuse. That said, adolescence is by no means a modern quirk.

"This is practically universal among humans. It's not a product of the Industrial Revolution," says Alice Schlegel, coauthor of *Adolescence: An Anthropological Inquiry*. She says there were adolescents in ancient Rome, Babylonia, you name it. There is a usefulness to this period: Humans survive through a strategy

And I thought he was ugly when he was a **baby**

Adolescence in Mole Rats

of intelligence and complex social behaviors, and the extension of childhood allows a person more time to learn the tricks of living (although we haven't figured out where trigonometry fits into the picture). And it's not true that there aren't "teenagers" among other species. Research on rhesus monkeys has turned up some provocative findings: When a male monkey reaches puberty, usually at the beginning of his fourth year, he either leaves his troop voluntarily or is kicked out. Where does he go? He finds other male adolescents. You betcha! For up to two years, he and his gang run around like outlaws, get in fights, try to make time with females, discuss the tedious construction of brassieres, etc.

"These guys are not always viewed with a lot of enthusiasm by long-standing troops," says Stephen Suomi, an ethologist at the National Institute of Child Health and Human Development. Eventually the male monkey joins a troop and settles down. The females, meanwhile, stay for their whole lives with their mother's troop.

"One has to be cautious in making generalizations from one species to another," Suomi says, "but there seem to be some basic principles that you see in many of the higher primate species. Dramatic and extended changes in social roles following puberty and preceding full adulthood is a general rule." Maybe someday humans will evolve beyond adolescence, and this whole "teenager" thing will be phased out. Except the trend seems to be going in the opposite direction.

More Incomprehensible Physics Than You Can Shake a Stick At

Why do squirrels get zapped by power lines sometimes, but not other times?

At the risk of actually dispensing some responsible advice, we'd like first of all to encourage everyone to assume that power lines are unbelievably dangerous and that it's basically insane to allow them to run across our neighborhoods and directly to our houses. What follows is not a guide to How You Can Play with Power Lines and Live.

Power lines are insulated. The problem is, they're insulated by air. Air is a good insulator, just like rubber or porcelain. This means that power lines usually are naked and exposed as they run from pole to pole. Sometimes, in areas with lots of trees, a "tree wire" will have a thin plastic insulation, but that doesn't necessarily make the wire safe to touch. The lines to a house may have heavier plastic insulation, but you shouldn't mess with them either.

A squirrel can run across an exposed power line because it's not touching anything else. The electric current has no reason to divert itself through the squirrel's body. The squirrel isn't giving the current a shortcut anywhere. "Short circuits" happen because an electrical current finds a better, faster route than the one it's supposed to be traveling.

SPARKY SQUIRREL SAYS

Kids! Don't scamper on power lines or chew through insulated cords!

American Council for Not Scampering on Power Lines

But let's say a squirrel climbs up the utility pole and stands on top of the transformer. That's dangerous. The transformer is that can up there on the pole, just under the power lines. A 13,000-volt wire is going into the top of that can, then passing through lots of coils, such that the voltage is diminished to a couple of wires with a total of 220 to 240 volts. Those wires and a neutral ground wire lead to your house.

The squirrel can't get hurt if it just sits on the can. Nor is it necessarily dangerous for the squirrel to jump through the air and land on the high-voltage wire. The problem comes when the squirrel, while standing on the can, touches the wire. It thus bridges the gap and makes a short circuit. It's toast.

Why are big dams curved, with the convex side toward the water?

You think you know this. You are thinking: It's stronger that way. And that is true. But why is it stronger? Simple: Dams are made out of poured concrete. Concrete is a brittle substance. That has a technical meaning: It cracks. That's how it fails, by cracking. When something cracks you don't want to put it under tension, pulling it apart, but rather under compression, pushing it together.

The water compresses the dam. If the water were pushing against a concave surface (bowing away from the water) it would put the concrete under tension instead of compression.

If you could build a steel dam it wouldn't matter because steel isn't brittle, it's ductile; it can be put under tension or compression. But steel is expensive, it can't be poured like concrete, and it rusts.

Why is gravity invisible?

Our own theory is that gravity doesn't even exist. We are praying that someday a group of eminent physicists will hold a press conference to announce that all supposedly "gravitational" phenomena are merely the result of static electricity and the reason things fall to the ground is that the Earth has "somehow been rubbed."

Scientists like to say that gravity is a distortion and squeezing and stretching of the geometry of space-time. Ignore them. That's just cocktail-party talk. It's just as fair to say that gravity is a force of attraction that affects all matter.

Modern physics predicts that there should be gravity waves and gravity particles (gravitons), but so far we haven't actually found these things. We aren't even sure how quickly gravity propagates across space. We desperately want to capture gravity, measure it, read it, but at this point we can't do a whole lot more than pull out the bathroom scale. Gravity remains invisible.

Here's the problem: Gravity penetrates everything. It goes right through you. It plows through brick, steel, lead. It blows through the Earth. The gravitational waves of the Big Bang are still scurrying around the cosmos with almost no disruption. Since nothing stops gravity waves, there's no way to make a machine that detects one of them.

"Since they don't interact with anything, since nothing stops them, it's also hard to trap them and measure them," says Robbie Vogt, a professor of physics at Caltech.

The reason vision works is that light doesn't entirely penetrate objects; some light waves are reflected, back into your eyes, and so we see things. If light didn't reflect, we wouldn't even have eyes. (We'd look *really* weird.) Gravity doesn't reflect at all. This is actually a good thing, perhaps. If you work in a room with metal walls, while you won't pick up radio signals because electromagnetic radiation is deflected by the metal, at least the gravity waves won't be blocked; if they were, you'd float around the room.

Why gravity is like this is something we can't answer, other than to say that that's the kind of universe we live in. If it were otherwise—if the universe were not permeable to gravity—then it would be such a differently configured place that perhaps no intelligent life would arise to ask questions like this.

The big news is, we may soon capture some gravity and use it to look at the world in an entirely different way. Vogt is director of LIGO, for Laser Interferometer Gravitational Wave Observatory. The project is designed to measure the very slight contraction of space that represents a gravitational wave passing through the Earth.

Here's the idea: Suspend two quartz cylinders with mirrored surfaces 2.5 miles apart. Then watch 'em. Closely. What the scientists want to see is some indication that they are being affected by the powerful gravitational waves created by collapsing supernovas and colliding neutron stars and other exotic events far away. These waves will pass through them only for a moment. Vogt estimates that the 2.5-mile separation between the cylinders will be changed by about a hundred-millionth of the diameter of a single atom.

How could anyone measure such a tiny distance? It's hard. It hasn't been done yet. But they will use lasers, and mirrors. The mirrors bounce the laser beams back and forth thousands of times to magnify the measurement, and so forth.

In any case, if we learn to "see" the universe through the "gravitational wave band," there's no telling what we'll discover. When radio astronomy was invented after World War II, we discovered that the serene universe seen through telescopes was an illusion. Radio astronomy showed us a violent universe of quasars and pulsars and cataclysmic change.

Vogt says, "We're trying to read the symphony that is on the gravitational waves."

Which is what you should tell yourself the next time you get an unfortunate reading on the bathroom scale.

Why is there so much noise when you put your head underwater in the bathtub?

Y ou can try this experiment at home if you promise not to breathe down there.

Take the plunge and the first thing you'll notice is the sound of your washing machine throbbing down in the basement as it goes through the spin cycle, or maybe the hum of your refrigerator's compressor, or maybe just the amplified splashing of water in the tub. Why's it so noisy? Because the tub is like a giant hearing aid.

Water has more density than air and puts more pressure on your eardrum (or on the little pocket of air right next to your eardrum). The water also conveys the vibrations of various machines in your house directly into your skull. Your skull becomes a resonant chamber. Some of those sounds you hear have the weird inside-the-head quality that you also experience with your own voice as it vibrates up from your throat.

The more important thing to realize is that water transmits sound much better and faster than air. Sound moves seven to eight times faster underwater than in the atmosphere. And it travels much farther. If you go outside on the street and shout, you will be heard for only a couple of blocks. But sounds can travel for hundreds or thousands of miles underwater. In one astonishing experiment two years ago, scientists proved that a sound could travel more than ten thousand miles underwater, about halfway around the world.

The remarkable durability of sound underwater is due to several factors. For one thing, there's no wind. Wind, and the chaotic motion of air molecules in general, has a drastic effect on sound (try shouting into the wind sometime).

Also, as sound travels through the air, some of the energy is transformed into heat. The same thing happens underwater but to a far lesser degree because water is a thousand times denser and molecules don't have as much room to get all hot and bothered.

One other thing: When you shout, the sound moves outward in all directions. But in the ocean, sound can be reflected by the surface above and by the thermocline below (that being the depth where the water suddenly and dramatically gets colder). You can feel the thermocline in a lake if you dive toward the bottom. You also can, come to think of it, hear distant motorboats when you're underwater, even if you can't hear them in the air.

Whales understand all this. We're told they can communicate across three thousand miles of ocean. Their signals don't get drowned out, as it were.

"With the advent of mechanically powered ships, the ocean has become noisy, and the ability of whales to keep track of each other has greatly diminished," says Robert Pinkel, an oceanographer at the University of California at San Diego. "We must have awesomely affected their social life."

So you can see why they must hate us. They can't hear anything. Plus, we kill them.

Why is the interior of the Earth still hot after 4.6 billion years of letting off steam (and lava)? Why doesn't this thing ever cool down?

We're not hand-wringers, not at all, but lately we've been having trouble sleeping because we're worried that the Earth will get so cold inside that all the volcanoes will die out, and no new mountains will form, and the continents will erode away until finally they will be as flat as a table and right at sea level and one day there will be a bad high tide and we'll all drown.

Think about it: The planet was formed 4.6 billion years ago (though our watch runs about five minutes fast), and ever since then it has been giving off heat in the form of volcanoes and deep-sea vents and geysers and so forth. So shouldn't it be cold by now? Why is Earth still bubbling and churning and doing that magma thing?

There are three reasons:

1. There aren't as many volcanoes as you think. "Heat loss by vulcanism is not very important," says Peter Olson, professor of geophysics at Johns Hopkins University.

2. There are radioactive elements that, as they decay, increase the heat of the interior.

And most important:

3. Rock is a good insulator. If you could take the Earth's overall temperature, it would be about 3,200 degrees Fahrenheit, but the rock of the outer crust doesn't conduct much of that heat to the surface.

The fact is that the Earth has probably cooled only a few hundred degrees since it formed, says Olson. If the Earth ever did cool down, the mantle, the thick layer of the planet below the crust, would stop convecting and there'd be no more earthquakes or volcanoes or ocean-floor spreading, no new mountains, no continental drift, and yes, after a couple of hundred million years the land would be eroded away by wind and rain and ocean.

By the way, we always picture the mantle as gray, like your average rock, but in fact it's green. Seriously. "Sort of an olive," says Olson. Our planet, the Earth, is mostly olive-colored. ("How fabulous!" you are probably thinking. "It matches the drapes!")

Why can't you make an atomic bomb out of lead, or silver, or gold, or Mars bars for that matter? Why can you make a bomb out of uranium or plutonium but not out of neptunium, the element between them on the periodic table?

We posed our brain-dead questions to Henry Kendall, a professor of physics at MIT who, at the end of our conversation, politely noted that he had recently shared a Nobel Prize for discovering quarks. So he's what you'd call an expert.

The main thing you need to know is that lots of atoms can be split, but few are as inviting as uranium and plutonium. These two elements are special because they're really big. They have obese nuclei, just waiting for someone to take a potshot at them (with a neutron). Big atoms have lots of energy that can be released if the atom is split.

"The reason this doesn't work with silver or lead or zinc or copper or anything else is—among other things—there's not enough electricity in there to really take over if you try to split the nucleus," Kendall said.

Neptunium is big, too, but it's virtually nonexistent in nature because after a couple of days it tends to decay into a simpler kind of atom. Plutonium also isn't found in nature, but you can make it inside a nuclear reactor, using uranium, which can be yanked out of the ground by the ton.

There's another factor: Only certain types of uranium and plutonium are good for making bombs. You want one of the more rickety isotopes, a type of uranium or plutonium that has an atomic structure that's unstable and is easily split apart. "You need a certain incipient instability in the nucleus," Kendall said.

Finally, to achieve either nuclear power or an explosion, you need to have a chain reaction, which is tricky, in part because of the danger that you might suddenly be vaporized. A nuclear chain reaction is when a neutron strikes an atom and splits it in a way that creates more loose neutrons, which in turn split more atoms. They do this slowly in nuclear power plants; in a bomb, you design it to happen in a fraction of a second.

We find all this to be fairly reassuring: Those nuclear forces, so fundamental that they are found in every fragment of matter and so powerful that they can level an entire city, are not poised on a hair trigger, waiting to annihilate us. It's certainly true that there's enough energy bound up inside a Mars bar to turn your neighborhood into a smoking ash heap. But go ahead and bite into it anyway.

THE MAILBAG

Jim Musumeci of Washington, D.C., has a rather daunting physics question: "Relativity tells us that if I travel off in a spaceship at close to the speed of light, I may come back to find I have aged only a few minutes while you have aged years. But relativity also says there is no absolute frame of reference, so from my perspective you are moving away from me at close to the speed of light and should age only a few minutes while I age several years. Obviously both can't be true. How is the apparent discrepancy between these two physical laws explained?"

Dear Jim: Thank you for not asking us why time dilation occurs. It has something to do with the speed of light, that's all we know.

Here's your problem: The second principle you cite (that there is no absolute frame of reference) applies only to "inertial frames" moving at constant speed relative to one another. It doesn't apply when one element, in this case the spaceship, is accelerating. The spaceship is not in an inertial frame because it is accelerating away from Earth. The person on Earth remains in an inertial frame (for this discussion we can ignore the effects of the planet's orbit around the sun and the sun's movement around the galaxy). Even if the astronaut is able to leave Earth by latching onto a passing high-velocity rocket, thus avoiding any gradual acceleration, at some point out there in space he will have to stop the rocket and come back, a maneuver that requires deceleration and acceleration.

It is easy to detect whether you are the one who is moving or the one who is staying still. The astronaut is plastered by G-forces against his seat, while the person on Earth is swinging in the hammock in the backyard swilling rum drinks (plastered in a different way).

Rich Friedman of Arlington, Virginia, asks, "If an individual in a falling elevator jumps at the precise time the elevator is about to hit bottom, will the individual save himself from injury?"

Dear Rich: It was thinking about elevators that helped Einstein develop his theories of relativity, which is a nice way of saying that your question isn't quite as silly as it sounds.

Einstein imagined an elevator somewhere out in space, in zero gravity. It would be accelerating in the direction of the ceiling, moving up at thirty-two feet per second per second, that is, g, the rate of acceleration of an object falling toward the Earth due to gravity. He asked: If you were inside this elevator, and there were no windows, could you tell that it was accelerating in space? Or would you think you were standing in a normal elevator on Earth and that heaviness you felt was just the planet's gravity? If you had enough scientific instruments, could you detect the difference between gravity and acceleration?

He concluded that there isn't any difference. Gravity *is* acceleration. That's his equivalence principle.

As for jumping: It won't work. One of our favorite physics 'sperts, Robert Park of the University of Maryland (eventually we will have to start paying him), worked out the equations.

Startling conclusion: If the elevator is free-falling toward the bottom of the elevator shaft you can't jump at all. You have to have weight to jump, and in a falling elevator you're weightless. "You can't jump. You're floating," Park says.

Normally, when you bend your knees to get ready to jump, your body drops. But in free fall, if you bend your knees your feet will simply come up off the floor. In order to jump, you'd have to grab the walls, push yourself with your arms so that you were in a crouch, then spring upward.

But let's say the elevator falls so far that, due to air resistance, it reaches terminal velocity. You will stop floating and resume standing normally. You can jump then. But the amount of velocity you can generate by jumping is tiny compared with the velocity of the falling elevator. "You're still going to be mush and the top of the elevator's going to hit you. Terminal has another meaning here," Park says.

As an added problem, when you jump, you push down on the floor of the elevator and make it fall slightly faster (you increase its terminal velocity). So the top of the elevator is going to come at you a little harder. Moreover, you are putting energy into the whole system of the elevator. That energy has to be dissipated upon impact. Park says the overall "mess" of the crash will increase if you jump.

So think about the cleanup crews. Just stand there and take it.

John Peck of Kissimmee, Florida, writes, "The spot which I occupy is traveling at about 1,000 mph as Earth rotates around its axis, and the entire planet is moving at about 67,000 mph in its orbit around the sun. Since my speed in relation to the sun varies by about 2,000 mph from the midpoint of 'day' to the midpoint of 'night,' why don't I feel the change of velocity as I do on a carnival ride which features movement around two axes?"

Dear John: You are thinking too much. Gear down a notch.

When you go on a carnival ride you endure sudden and severe accelerations through space. The motions of Earth, both its spin and its movement through the orbital plane, are gentle by contrast.

You are right to wonder if there are slight accelerations and decelerations that affect you. The planet is always accelerating toward the sun, and you, personally, accelerate faster when you are closer to the sun than when you are farther away because gravity gets weaker with distance.

But these kinds of things are tiny, tiny factors compared with Earth's own gravitational field. And even Earth's gravity isn't so terribly strong. That's why you leave the ground when you jump. One would hope.

TIME, THE UNLIKELIEST DIMENSION

Why does it just so happen that you are alive now, near the end of the second millennium? Why weren't you born during prehistoric times or in the distant future?

We started wondering this back in '69. It was when *Apollo 11* landed on the moon. We wondered: How come we're alive during such an interesting moment? Is it just plain luck? Surely, we thought, there have been billions of people who lived in much more boring times, when the only interesting thing to happen was, say, the invention of the dinner plate or an unusually bad plague of boils.

The question is, should we feel special? Are we lucky to be alive during a time of rapid technological change and good dentistry?

The answer is: No. The reason you are alive today is that this is what would be expected, according to statistical probabilities.

First, you have to realize that there are more people alive today than at any other time in human history—about 5.4 billion people. There have been roughly 70 billion human beings born since the appearance of *Homo sapiens* about 200,000 years or so ago. This means that about 7.7 percent of all human beings who have ever lived are alive today.

You might argue that we're lucky to be in the 7.7 percent and not in the 92.3 percent who are dead and gone. But that's

the wrong logic—by that reasoning, we'd be lucky to be alive at *any* point during the long tenure of the human species. You should *expect* that we would be alive at a time of high population rather than low population—and we are. So there's nothing unusual about it.

There's also nothing remarkable about watching the first moon landing. High population, like moon landings, is a function of modern technology. Technology permits human beings to proliferate and do wacky things like build *Saturn V* rockets. So it's no coincidence that amazing technological things happen at a moment when there are lots of people watching.

Another example: You should expect to live in a country with a higher-than-the-median population, such as the United States or Canada. The median population of nations on Earth is something like 6 million. Half the countries have a higher population, half have a lower population. But about 97 percent of the people live in the countries with the higher population. So if you live in, say, Kansas City, Missouri, there's nothing remarkable about that (except perhaps the fact that it's in Missouri and not Kansas).

Now let's get into a weird area. What do statistical probabilities tell us about our future as a species? Basically they tell us we're doomed.

Richard Gott, a Princeton physicist, recently published a

fascinating paper in the journal *Nature* in which he argues that human beings are unlikely ever to colonize the galaxy and will probably undergo a massive decrease in population.

Gott bases his argument on the Copernican principle. Copernicus, you recall, is the guy who said the earth wasn't the center of the universe. The Copernican principle says we shouldn't presume we're special in any way. Just as there's nothing special about the location of the earth in the cosmos, there's nothing special about our location on the time line that marks the history of the human species.

If you could somehow step back and make a chronological list of all the human beings who have ever been born, and ever will be born, we should be able to find our names somewhere in the middle of that list, rather than at the very beginning or end. That's what the Copernican principle tells us. In fact, there's a 95 percent chance that we will find our name in the middle 95 percent of the list of human beings who will ever exist.

So why does that mean there will be a depopulation of human beings? Because if we simply continued to have a population increase, or even if the population leveled out at, say, 10 billion people, eventually our list would stretch into the many trillions of names—and those of us around the 70 billion mark would be among the very first on the chronological list. We'd be violating the Copernican principle! So the principle tells us to expect that the species will eventually go into a period of extreme depopulation.

"It would be very unlikely for you to turn out to be so lucky as to turn out to be in the first one-billionth of human beings," Gott says. Oh, sure, it's *possible*. The Copernican principle doesn't say you can't be really lucky. It just says you probably aren't going to be really lucky. To think you'd be in the first billionth of the human population over time, Gott says, "is like someone who has $2 in their pocket saying, 'I'm going to be a billionaire someday.'"

It's also unlikely that we'll colonize space, for two reasons:

1. Space travel is a new trick. For us to colonize space over many thousands of years would mean that we were lucky to be alive at the beginning of a long period of space travel. Sure, that's exactly what most of us believe (the "Star Trek" myth), but the Copernican principle warns against such presumptuousness. Gott says we're probably in the middle of a brief window of space travel opportunity.

2. Our ancestors weren't aliens from space. If intelligent species had a good chance to colonize their galaxy, then most people in the galaxy would be descendants of colonists. "The interesting thing is that you and I are not having this conversation on a colony of some galactic empire. We're living on the home planet," says Gott. And thus it's unlikely that we will *just happen* to be born on the home planet of what will become a vast galactic empire.

The painful truth, he says, is that we're probably (not definitely, but probably) in the middle of a relatively brief population spike for the human species. It's a statistically based argument, but creepily matches the dire warnings of environmentalists and biologists who are working with real evidence of ecological peril.

We ought to feel horrible about all this. But for some reason we don't. The Why staff believes in human ingenuity. We're not just a randomly proliferating species, we're the kings of adaptation, resilience, and manipulation of the environment. We're going to put our money on the long shot here. Sometimes you just have to blow on the dice and roll 'em.

Why do we have daylight saving time in the summer even though that's when there's no shortage of daylight?

Admit it: You always assumed daylight saving time (or Daylight Savings Time, as we'd call it if our stylebook weren't so darn fussy) was an elaborate way of warding off darkness. That daylight saving time somehow converted nighttime into daytime. But mostly you just don't think about it. You are a sheep, following orders, biannually turning your clocks forward or backward and struggling to calculate whether this means you can sleep late.

Well, dig this: We have daylight saving time in the summer because in the summer we have *too much* daylight.

The whole point is to shift light from morning to evening because it gets light so early in the summer months. We don't need it to be light at five in the morning unless we are farmers. Farmers don't like DST much. Daylight saving time originated in England in World War I as a way of saving electricity in the evening. For the same reason we adopted the time system in America in 1918. Daylight saving time has steadily expanded since. The Daylight Saving Time Coalition, which represents softball associations, the charcoal industry, people with night blindness, and so on, is trying to get Congress to start daylight saving time in March rather than the first Sunday in April.

What would happen if we didn't "save" all that daylight? Hell on Earth, basically: In Washington, D.C., just to take a city randomly out of the atlas, the sun would have risen at 4:43 A.M. on June 21, 1994, according to astronomer LeRoy Doggett of the U.S. Naval Observatory. That means that "civil twilight," when it would be light enough to do outdoor activities, would have begun at about 4:11 A.M., when the sun was six degrees below the horizon. The first light in the East would have appeared about half an hour before that.

Yes: Three-something in the morning. You can see the ghastly possibilities: You wake up in the morning without checking the clock, make coffee, shower, drive to work, and suddenly discover it is only 4:15. In order to prevent that, the government makes sure every year to alter time itself.

Why did geologists come up with names and dates for geologic time periods that no one could possibly ever remember?

Every so often we'll ask a scientist how old something is, and the scientist will say, "Well, it goes back at least to the Miocene, possibly to the Oligocene." And then we'll say something like, "Wasn't that the time of the Romans?"

Pleistocene, Pliocene, Paleocene, Permian, Paleozoic, Proterozoic, Phanerozoic, and Precambrian—you can't even get the Ps straight! Why is there a Tertiary period but no Secondary period? *Who concocted this mess?*

No one. That's the answer. It wasn't invented in one motion, the way, say, the metric system was, or the dimensions of a baseball diamond. It was pieced together, a fossil bed here, a stratum of rock there. Devonian was named by a scientist working on some rocks in Devon, England. The Mississippian and the Pennsylvanian periods got their names in the same way. Tertiary is left over from another scientist's attempt in the 1700s to come up with a simple geologic time scale system, but the primary and secondary periods were given other names by other scientists. The English never recognized the terms Mississippian and Pennsylvanian—they just call that period the Carboniferous.

All the words mean something to someone. Proterozoic, for example, means "before animals" (from the Greek). We are going to guess that Carboniferous was when they did a lot of barbecuing.

The point is, rocks and fossils aren't organized in the ground in a neat way, so it took a long time to see the entire geologic picture. They kept adding pieces; at one point, they had to insert the Oligocene between the Miocene and the Eocene. Though it's all just a little Obscene if you ask us.

Why is Thanksgiving always on a Thursday?

Christmas always is on the 25th of December, Valentine's Day always is on the 14th of February, and the Fourth of July always is on the 4th of July. So why can't Thanksgiving just pick a day and stop roving up and down the calendar?

We have no problem with Labor Day being on a Monday every year. As anyone with historical understanding of the labor movement knows, Labor Day is specifically in honor of the working person's inalienable right to stay home on a Monday in early September. Easter also roams, but at least Easter is determined by a complex astronomical calculation involving the moon and the spring equinox.

But why is Thanksgiving on a Thursday, one of the silliest days of the week? And finally, why is it in late November even though the fall harvest is weeks or even months earlier?

The answer revolves around fish (wouldn't you just know!). James Baker, a historian at Plimoth Plantation, a museum in Plymouth, Massachusetts, says there were "fish days" back in the early seventeenth century. A fish day was a day when you couldn't eat meat. Elizabeth I wanted to bolster the fishing industry in England and so decreed that people couldn't eat meat on Wednesdays, Fridays, and Saturdays.

The Pilgrims in Plymouth and Boston, though not bound by that old rule, nonetheless were influenced by it. They tended to fast a lot, particularly on Wednesdays, Fridays, and Saturdays. But they decided to make Thursday their market day, when they'd trade their goods in town and stock up.

Thursday, you might say, became the big meat day.

So when the civic authorities declared a day of thanksgiving, it was on Thursday. Except in Connecticut. In Connecticut

Elizabeth I plans the nation's menu.

they had Thanksgiving on Wednesdays. The Massachusetts way of doing things won out when Thanksgiving went from being a regional holiday to a national holiday in the late 1700s.

But it wasn't always in November. The national Thanksgiving declared by the Continental Congress in 1777 was held on December 18. Why so close to Christmas? Because back then they had the common sense to know that the date of Christmas didn't have any scriptural basis (there's nothing in the Bible that suggests December 25 was the day Christ was born). Christmas, our hugest holiday of modern times, didn't catch on until the 1840s or so.

The first real day of thanksgiving was in the summer of 1623, after a providential rain. What people think of as the first Thanksgiving, the famous feast with the Indians at Plymouth, actually was a three-day harvest festival in early October 1621. That's why we associate Thanksgiving with the harvest. But the harvest festival was a one-shot deal. Never repeated. You gotta get this stuff straight.

Lincoln in 1864 ordered Thanksgiving to be held on the fourth Thursday in November. But that wasn't made an official rule until Congress passed a law in 1942. Franklin Roosevelt previously had decreed that several Thanksgivings (or "Franksgivings" as people called them) be held the *third* Thursday because he wanted to lengthen the shopping season. (He'd do anything to get us out of the Depression.)

Here's one last thing to consider: Before the mid-1800s, Thanksgiving was not an annual event. A "Thanksgiving" was declared only when events merited. It was not a blandly automatic holiday. You had a Thanksgiving when you were really thankful about something. Now the dang thing is shoved down our throats. Literally.

THE MAILBAG

There still seems to be some fretting about the millennium, not just because of the usual reasons (the Apocalypse, the Final Judgment, the terrible hangover) but also because people aren't quite sure when to party. The night of December 31, 1999? Or the night of December 31, 2000?

There's no disputing when the new millennium begins: January 1, 2001. That's because there wasn't a 0 year. The year 2000 is the last year of the twentieth century, as surely as the number 10 is the last of the first 10 positive integers (natural numbers).

The problem is, people don't want to be losers and wait an extra year to celebrate if the rest of the world doesn't care about these numerical technicalities and decides to party the moment the big 2 pops up on the calendar.

For example, Gail Simmons of Washington, D.C., writes, "Some friends of mine and I the other night were talking about what we would like to do to inaugurate the new millennium. Someone asked about how the last millennium was celebrated. No one knew. I feel certain you would."

Dear Gail: You might want to track down a book called *Century's End: A Cultural History of the Fin de Siècle from the 990s Through the 1990s* by Hillel Schwartz. He says there's a widespread belief, repeated for centuries, that Christians in the year 999 were terrorized by the millennium, that they freaked out, abandoned their homes, assembled under open skies with their crucifixes at the ready. But it's not true, he says. Pure nonsense. He writes, "Thus far, each century's end has been a comedy: we have always made it through, and we have regularly been surprised at just how we did it."

We went to the Library of Congress and pulled the microfilm of newspapers from January 1, 1900, and January 1, 1901 (we can't help but feel sorry for the people who lived back then, forced to get their news from microfilm, which is so hard on the eyes!). What we found surprised us: The new century was celebrated the night of December 31, *1900*.

That night, for example, City Hall in New York City was bedecked with a huge sign saying "Welcome 20th Century." The lead story in the January 1, 1901, *New York Times* was headlined "Twentieth Century's Triumphant Entry" and began "The Century is dead; long live the Century!" (We searched for the Abe Rosenthal byline but couldn't find it.)

What did people do the night of December 31, 1899? Not much. The Germans, we learned, actually did celebrate the new century a year early, but the Germans were extreme troublemakers back then as we recall. The pope declared that the year 1900 was a Holy Year of thanksgiving for the blessings of the nineteenth century (this was back at the height of the belief in "progress," before despair, cynicism, and victimization became chic).

So it should be clear: They waited last time until *January 1, 1901*. If the twentieth century is going to last a century, we can't pretend a new century and a new millennium have begun until 12:01 A.M. on January 1, 2001.

Nonetheless, the Why staff's policy is to party early and often. So we may decide to jump the gun. The world is different now—it's less disciplined, and people are less likely to obey an official government policy or a papal decree.

Besides, these are just numbers. Numbers have whatever meanings we assign them. We assign 10 and 20 and 30 and 2,000 special meanings only because we happen to have 10 fingers and thus invented a base 10 number system.

Thus an anniversary or millennial celebration is basically an *aesthetic* matter, and perhaps we should celebrate the arrival of the year 2000, which has an aesthetic charm that the following year lacks.

Besides, the twentieth century has been dragging on a little too long anyway.

John V. R. Williams of Rockville, Maryland, asks, "Why do we perceive ourselves as perpetually at the crest of a universal time wave, apparently leaving all past and future time lifeless or even nonexistent (!), unless or until we grace it with our consciousness?"

Dear John: Your fears are justified. The past does not exist. The future does not exist. The "present" is a useful but arguably silly and self-defining concept. Indeed, time itself does not really exist the way we typically think it exists.

You know the old story about Samuel Johnson being asked how he could refute Bishop Berkeley's statement that the world was an illusion. "I refute it thus!" he said and kicked a large rock. He was right: The rock was real. But you can't kick time. It's just an intellectual construct that's handy for describing rocks, authors, and the action whereby an author kicks a rock.

We spoke first to Freeman Dyson, the visionary physicist, who said he didn't buy the idea of past, present, and future. "It's a statement about us and not a statement about the world," he said. Dyson said physics had nothing to say about these issues, that they were matters of philosophy.

Fortunately we reached David Park, a retired professor of physics at Williams College and author of the book *The Image of Eternity*. Park assured us that the things we remember happening in the past really did happen, or at least that it's "amazingly probable" that they happened, but nonetheless the past does not exist. Abe Lincoln is not the president of the United States, even though someone with a really great telescope on a planet 135 light-years away might be able to catch a glimpse of Abe pacing around the White House. The past leaves behind evidence (for example, reflected light), but that doesn't mean President Lincoln still exists.

"You get into an awful lot of trouble if you say that time exists. What exists are things," said Park. "We are surrounded by things, and they *do* things. What exists are events. Things happen. We're part of it. We happen. We do things. We experience things happening all around us. And I think we then construct the idea of time as a sort of verbal or philosophical framework for our thoughts."

It is easy to imagine a universe without time: It doesn't move. It is always the same. It's frozen. The coffee cup is poised halfway to your mouth as you stare at this sentence, eternally. The cat is stretched out motionlessly with mouth agape, a hairball ready to be hawked up on the carpet. To describe this universe you have no need to invent so daffy a notion as "time."

We don't live in that kind of universe, but rather in one that is dynamic. It keeps changing, in very tiny increments. It has inertial energy. The dynamic personality of this universe is a function of the Big Bang, or the Creation if you prefer. That "initial condition" remains beyond our explanatory powers at this moment. If you have any ideas, operators are standing by.

On the off chance that this hasn't been perplexing enough, we should point out that we don't actually live in the present. Light and sound and heat and all the other things that stimulate our senses move at finite speeds. It then takes time to process stuff mentally. Science journalist Timothy Ferris points out that our optic nerve does not bombard our brain with continuous images of the world but rather creates individual snapshots, fewer than twenty-four a second, which is why you don't notice the twenty-four individual images that create a "motion picture."

So even if the present is a real thing, you ain't there. You are in the past.

Which doesn't exist.

The Readers Respond

Robbin John Herman of Phenix City, Alabama, writes: "Time exists. In purely scientific terms, time is measurable and quantifiable. The time fuse burns for thirty seconds. The rocket flight lasts for a duration of ten minutes. Carbon dating measures the age of fossils. Atomic half-life is a measure of time. That scientists use time all the time should remove any doubt about its existence. Here is where one approaches the level of sophomoric philosophical debate, so common of a late night back at the dorm after the keg has been drained."

Dear Robbin: Seems like we mostly debated whether we could find more beer. In any case, we are compelled to note that you are not, in fact, describing what time is, but rather you are using time as a conceptual tool for describing other things. Atomic half-life is quite definitely not a measure of time; time, rather, is the conceptual instrument by which we measure the decay of a radioactive element in relation to other events.

Sorry to be so argumentative, Robbin, but, although we readily admit that the past really happened and the future will happen, we are not willing to admit that time *exists* (in the way that other things exist) until someone shows us at the very least a grainy Polaroid snapshot.

Next comes a sage letter from Gerard L. Field of Annapolis, Maryland: "When scientists, science writers, and philosophers say that 'time does not exist,' or 'the past does not exist,' they are playing a kind of word game that only confuses the readers. The past doesn't exist so far as if it existed then it would be now and not the past.

"However, the past does exist if we acknowledge that we use things and inventions and ideas from long ago. We use mathematics that is mostly 2,500 years old. And if we listen to a Beethoven symphony that means that his ideas are here and now, which is really the same as if he were here and now. Of course we cannot observe Beethoven eating a plate of spaghetti, but we have the good stuff."

Dear Gerard: Intellectually, we agree. Emotionally, we are holding out for Beethoven eating spaghetti.

David Sansom of Rio Rancho, New Mexico writes, "I remember reading somewhere that according to one of Albert Einstein's theories of relativity, all time—past, present, and future—is essentially happening simultaneously, and therefore, we should be able to remember the future as well as the past. How 'bout it?"

Dear David: Actually one of Einstein's best riffs was pointing out that no two events are ever truly simultaneous. He nuked simultaneity.

What he might have said, only in German, was something like this: Time and space are intertwined in a seamless fabric called space-time, in which objects can be described as having temporal and spatial coordinates and in which no position is superior to or more remarkable than any other.

No physicist has ever said we "should" remember the future as well as the past, but many physicists have wondered why we don't. There's nothing in the laws of physics that says that time must flow from past to future.

Physicist Sidney Coleman of Harvard told us that the psychological arrow of time, that sense we have of going from past to future, is dependent on the thermodynamic arrow of time, which is the law of entropy, the tendency for things to go from "order" to "disorder" (ice cubes melt, dropped dishes shatter, the Why bunker gets messier).

The thermodynamic arrow is, in turn, the natural result of the cosmological arrow: The universe began hot, smooth, infinitely dense, a condition of very low entropy, and so the only direction it could head was toward greater entropy. And that's what happened. We call it the Big Bang. The universe dramatically surged from order toward disorder—expanding, cooling, getting lumpier and messier. This process is what created space and time as we perceive it.

So basically the Big Bang gave time its past-to-future spin. Let's just hope that if the Big Crunch happens—the universe collapsing again into a hot dense wad—time won't run backward. Because there's no way we're going through tenth grade again.

A Thematically Diffuse Chapter

Why is dryer lint always gray, even though it comes from clothes of many different colors?

Lint is not always gray. Check your belly button. Belly-button lint hews to the hue of your shirt. (We believe the collection of belly-button lint is exacerbated by stomach hair but have not confirmed this in the lab.)

Dryer lint is usually gray because gray is what you get when you mix fibers that are red, yellow, blue, green, black, white, etc. If all your clothes were red, you'd have reddish lint, but since you probably have a multichromatic wardrobe, the lint filter tends to be gray. "It's just the combination of bunches of color you see," says Eva Konopacki, supervisor of testing for the International Fabric Care Institute.

You can check this by using a "lint roller" on various garments; your gray lint will reveal itself to be individual fibers of different colors. By the way, we were planning to give up lint for Lent because we thought it was such a funny concept, but our associates convinced us to give up jokes.

BONUS LAUNDRY ITEM!

A mysterious K.P. of Cocoa, Florida, asks, "Why is it that when you accidentally put something in the wash that fades red/pink dye on other garments, this same red/pink dye that came out of the original garment so easily will not, in a million washings, come out of the faded-upon garment?"

Dear K.P.: We immediately contacted The Soap and Detergent Association (they stipulate that it's "The," in uppercase; we're tempted to call it "the The Soap and Detergent Association"). The association put us in touch with the American Association of Textile Chemists and Colorists. They, in turn, pointed out that dye is designed not to wash out of fabric. That explains why your underwear still is pink. The reason that the dye left your original garment is that it had too much dye to begin with, and that excess dye was just sitting there on the surface, waiting to run amok in your washer. When you discover that all your drawers have turned pink, don't put them in the dryer and bake the dye; instead, soak them and wash them again.

Laundry tips. What have we come to?

Why is Muzak everywhere even though people claim they dislike "elevator music"?

Over the years Muzak has become for most people a generic word for the bland, reprocessed, instrumental music that you barely register as you are shopping at Wal-Mart for multipacks of Jockey briefs. The word Muzak is such a joke that the Muzak company considered changing names in 1987. But it didn't. Maybe because it has, as of last count, 200,000 customers and about 80 million listeners a day.

Isn't there a paradox here? It's easily solved. Muzak's customers are businesses, not music buffs. The music is not there to be listened to; it exists to alter your behavior.

In fact the whole idea of environmental music is that you don't really hear it. You are enveloped by it, the way The Blob enveloped its victims. Muzak is simply part of the late-twentieth-century environment, like chlorofluorocarbons.

Elevator music was invented many moons ago when elevators were new contraptions, not much more than cages. They rattled you. The music was designed to be soothing so you wouldn't focus so much on whether the elevator cable would snap.

The Muse of Muzak calls on Beethoven

The Muzak company, founded in 1934, now has twelve different channels, but the most popular is still the environmental music channel, "today's instrumental favorites, hits and standards tastefully arranged and recorded especially for Muzak and programmed in Muzak's proprietary Stimulus Progression format," according to a Muzak brochure.

Stimulus Progression allegedly increases worker efficiency. The hour is divided into fifteen-minute segments, increasingly up-tempo, so that over the course of the hour you are whipped into a high-energy, "Feelings"-hummin' monster of productivity. Muzak also tries to counteract the fatigue that workers feel in midmorning and midafternoon. When you're down, Muzak's up!

Does it really work? Muzak has reams of studies showing it does. And there's no reason why it shouldn't. Nor is Muzak the only way to stimulate workers. Bright lights help, and even some kind of white noise is better than silence. (The Why bunker uses a tape loop of a gurgling coffee percolator.)

Now here's the big news: Muzak is getting funkier. Steve Ward, Muzak's manager of broadcast programming, says the baby boomers want a different sort of aural wallpaper than did a previous generation.

"We've tried to make that channel more hip and more

nineties, and we've changed the types of songs that we're selecting," Ward says.

Voices are, of course, still deleted, since voices are too much in the foreground, too distracting. But now the occasional guitar lick can stay. The new rules, says Ward, may allow even "a mellow Led Zeppelin tune."

So get ready. Any day now you may hear the Muzak version of "Stairway to Heaven." Just think of it as "Elevator to Heaven."

Why do movie directors need a slate that goes "clack" before each scene is filmed?

We had always assumed that the "clack" was just an affectation, a neat way of telling everyone that the film is rolling. But why not simply use a foghorn? Or a whistle? Or a starter's pistol?

Because the clacking sound is crucial to the synchronization of the soundtrack and the film. That "clack" takes place in less than one twenty-fourth of a second, so on the soundtrack it will match up with a single frame of film (the first frame where you see the clacker arm meeting the rest of the slate).

Wooden slates have been largely replaced by plastic—or worse, by a digital gadget that goes "beep" as a red light flashes. This, and the temporary closure of the Beverly Hills Hotel, have basically destroyed Hollywood as we knew it.

Why don't you see phone booths anymore?

There was a time when making a phone call was a civilized ritual performed within a comfortable environment. You would enter a booth, close the door, and a light would come on. You dialed the operator, gave a name, and after much switching you reached a person who reacted to your call enthusiastically, as though, indeed, it were the most remarkable piece of communication received by humans since the Ten Commandments.

Now, you go to a bank of phones stuck on a wall, punch some buttons, get a "menu" of options, punch more buttons, get "voice mail," and talk to a machine while everyone around you listens in. Civilization begets barbarism.

Phone booths began to die in December 1963, when the Bell System began advertising a coin telephone "shelf" similar to what you see today. The next stylistic blow to the booth came with the decision to make them out of glass and metal instead of wood; wood didn't match the new glass-and-steel architecture of the modern city.

At one point in the early 1970s, there appeared a phone booth that required no hands. The caller spoke into a microphone; a speaker in the ceiling projected the voice of the person on the other end. The experiment failed because people insisted on shouting at the ceiling.

The official death of the phone booth can be dated to 1978, when the first *Superman* movie hit the theaters—there's that scene where Christopher Reeve can't change into his Superman suit because the pay phone lacks a booth.

Why did booths go out of fashion? Three reasons:

1. "People use them as toilets. Or little offices. And they became very difficult to maintain," says Paul Hirsch, a spokesman for Pacific Bell in San Francisco. (The toilet problem surely has always existed, but in the last two decades there has been an increase in the number of homeless people in big cities and a proliferation of "Restrooms for Patrons Only" signs.)

2. Space. Phone booths take up a lot of room. They don't meet modern standards for efficient use of space.

3. Access for the disabled. You can't negotiate a booth if you're in a wheelchair. This was the specific reason that Pacific Bell cited in 1977 when it replaced booths with phone stands.

The phone booth now is a museum piece, a blast from the past. Let's just hope they leave the table booths in restaurants. Because if you're ever going to cut a major deal over lunch, it simply has to be in a booth.

Why do "f" and "s" and "p" and "t" sound so similar over the phone?

Let's say you work for the Why staff and you want to call up an expert on Spam. You call the people at the Spam headquarters, but when you ask about the delicious canned loaf of pink meat product, some dumb bunny says, "Stan?"

Another difficult day on the Hairball Hotline.

And so you have to go through the whole alphabetic deconstruction. "No," you say, "Spam—"s" as in sphincter, "p" as in pfennig, "a" as in aesthetic, "m" as in mnemonic." It's really a hassle.

According to AT&T Bell Laboratories, the two letters hardest to distinguish over the phone are "f" and "s." This sounds odd since in regular face-to-face conversation there's no difficulty at all in telling the difference between words like "fizzle" and "sizzle" or "fly" and "sly."

What you don't realize when you are talking to someone face to face is that you are unconsciously lip-reading, hence the difficulty when you talk over the phone. When you make an "f" sound, air rushes through a small opening between your teeth and your lips. With an "s," air rushes through a small opening between the tip of your tongue and the back side of your front teeth. Since in both cases you have air rushing through a small passage, the sounds are similar, and especially so over the phone.

Moreover—and here's the crucial part of the answer—the "f" and "s" sounds are emitted at high frequencies, between 3000 and 6000 hertz. But the telephone system only handles frequencies between 200 and 4000 hertz. Thus most of the "information" in the "f" and "s" sounds, all the nuance above 4000 hertz, is lopped off by the telephone. The phone usually captures just enough of the difference to allow you to distinguish

an "s" from an "f," but people still make a mistake about 10 percent of time, says David Roe, head of the applied speech
research department at Bell Labs.

After the "f" and the "s," the two sounds hardest to distinguish are "m" and "n." For our money they don't even deserve
to be separate letters. (We're told that the "m" and "n" sounds
come out of the nose. But we did a test. We discovered that we
use the mouth for them. Maybe we're just doing it wrong.)

The third most ambiguous pair is "p" and "t," fourth is "b"
and "d," and fifth is "g" and "t."

Now, you might ask, why doesn't the phone company invent
a telephone with broader bandwidth so that it could pick up
the subtleties above 4000 hertz? Roe says that it's possible, but
not economical, because the whole system has been set up on
the old standard, which is perfectly adequate for delivering almost the entire range of human intelligibility.

So stop complaining. That's "s" as in syzygy, "t" as in
tsunami, "o" as in oeuvre, "p" as in psalm.

Why are there still pennies?

Whenever we drop a penny on the ground, there's an an-
guished moment of indecision. We wonder: Is it
worth picking up? By "worth" we don't mean its value
in commerce, but rather whether the failure to pick it up will
be costly in terms of other people's perceptions. A penny is
garbage, it's a slug at this point, but if you don't pick it up
you'll be seen as a snob, an elitist, a monocle wearer. Solution:
Pretend we didn't notice we dropped it.

There have been movements in recent years to ban the
penny. But the Rounding Act of 1989, which would have made
merchants round off prices to the nearest nickel, never got
anywhere (we want to say "never made it off the dime"). The
public still likes pennies. A survey in 1988 showed that 63 percent of Americans wanted to keep them. It didn't say why. We
do know that Americans are quite conservative when it comes
to their coins and currency. Another argument against banning
pennies is that it would cause inflation. You think merchants
will round their prices *down*?

On the other hand, making pennies is expensive. The mint
makes billions of them a year, at a cost of about six-tenths of a

cent per penny. The mint has to keep making them because people, annoyed with the darn things, take them out of circulation, dumping them in jars and bowls, hoping that someday Grandma will roll them up and take them to the bank.

One last thing: The zinc industry has hollered about every suggestion to do away with pennies because the little coppers are 97.5 percent zinc. The American Zinc Association, by the way, tells us that it's a myth that swallowing a penny will cause instant death. "Zinc is a very benign metal. You have to have a certain amount of zinc a day to be healthy," says AZA spokesman John Lutley, though he could not tell us precisely how many pennies a day we should be swallowing.

Why did people once upon a time believe in vampires?

We are pleased to report that the answer is not simply, "Because they were a bunch of superstitious numskulls." The strange, chilling truth is that vampire myths are based, in part, on real scientific phenomena. Specifically, they arise from a misunderstanding of what happens when you drive a stake through the chest of a corpse. (This item will be intellectually stimulating but also kind of yucky.)

In places such as Bulgaria and Romania, a vampire was not necessarily a sensual, pale, Bela Lugosi–like bloodsucker who roamed around at night hoping to do some "necking." A vampire was the spirit of a dead person and could do all kinds of nefarious things, like alter the weather or prevent a farmer's cows from giving milk. (People would say, "Is it raining again? Damn vampires!")

It was pestilence and plague that drove the vampire myth. According to Paul Barber, author of *Vampires, Burial and Death: Folklore and Reality*, survivors of plague would hunt for a scapegoat, and the most obvious candidate would be the first person who had died from the mysterious malady. This person was presumed a vampire, and there would be an excited rush to the grave to exhume the body and kill it again.

You would think that when the frightened villagers dug up the body they'd just find a rotting corpse and then would realize the absurdity of their fears. Not so, says Barber. What they'd find was a fairly well preserved body, bloated as though gorged with blood, with blood on its lips. A corpse in the ground does not decompose as quickly as one exposed to the elements; the swelling of the body is caused by gases released by microorganisms. The blood comes from the lungs, which are squeezed by the bloating of the body.

So people would say: "Hey! This guy must be a vampire! Where's that darn stake?" Or whatever. There are many written accounts of these incidents, and they are consistent in describing what happens next: The vampire killers would drive the stake through the heart and—lo!—the corpse would appear to spring to life and utter a cry. How very scary!

Are these tales merely fiction? No, says Barber; they are describing what really happens. The movement is a normal case of Newtonian physics as the stake hammers through the body; the cry comes from air being forced through the throat.

"The vampire lore was a folk hypothesis intended to account for the events of death and decomposition," Barber says. "I don't think it shows any kind of unintelligent perception of the world. Their observations are clinically accurate."

Why are Americans today so enraptured by vampires? "People admire their power," says Norine Dresser, author of *American Vampires: Fans, Victims and Practitioners*. She adds, "Sometimes people like to feel powerless. He [a vampire] takes them under his control. Sometimes it's great not to be the one in charge."

But to this day in Eastern Europe, there are people who prefer to bury their dead "staked," says Dresser. It's an ounce of prevention, apparently. (We intend to ask that we be staked *and* cremated, just in case.)

Why is there doubt about whether Shakespeare really wrote Shakespeare's plays?

Nothing is as strong in human beings as the craving to believe in something that is obviously wrong. Nonsensical beliefs are surely unique to our species: Dogs and rabbits and squirrels haven't evolved to the point where their brains could possibly come up with something as stupid as the movie *JFK*.

Nevertheless, many learned, decent people fiercely believe that William Shakespeare didn't write Shakespeare's plays and sonnets. This notion first appeared in the 1800s, when the

"Baconians" argued that Sir Francis Bacon really wrote *Hamlet* et al. Today the most vocal group is the "Oxfordians," who say that Edward de Vere, the Earl of Oxford, wrote the plays and allowed Shakespeare to put his name on them.

Why do they think this? Because, as with almost any other controversial historical event, the official record has huge gaps, which invite speculation and alternative theories.

The official history of Shakespeare is based on sparse information: some land and tax records and a few contemporaneous references in the writings of others. But he was no celebrity by modern standards because there was no celebrity machinery, no "Entertainment Tonight," not even *The New York Review of Books*. We know that there was a "man from Stratford" who was known variously as Shaksper, Shaxpere, Shagspere, Shakespere, Shackspeare, and Shakespeare and that he was an accomplished actor. That his name itself was confusing is one reason people are not so certain he wrote the great plays. His name wasn't even on some of his early plays originally.

But after a few years his name did start appearing on the plays. Moreover, in 1623, seven years after his death, his colleagues put together a "folio" of his collected works, which featured a glowing introduction by fellow playwright Ben Jonson. There's no sign in that introduction or in that folio of any confusion in 1623 over who wrote Shakespeare's plays. No one was going around saying, whoa, something's fishy here. No one said, "*That* bozo? You think *he* wrote them plays?"

The skeptics point to the gaps in the record: Hardly a word of praise or homage during his lifetime, and nothing at all upon his death in 1616. The skeptics say the man from Stratford was weirdly unheralded.

"A genius that is obvious to us could hardly have been wholly hidden from the cultivated persons who made the Elizabethan age synonymous with an outpouring of poetry, drama and music," writes Charlton Ogburn in the seminal Oxfordian text *The Mysterious William Shakespeare*, which is nearly nine hundred pages long. "It is scarcely conceivable that they could have failed to appreciate in Shakespeare the supreme voice of their generation—the soul of their age."

The Oxfordian theory is that Edward de Vere, as a nobleman, couldn't allow his name on something so vulgar as a stage play. So he recruited this hack Shakespeare as his cover. The bard was the beard, you might say.

Alas, poor Yorick, the anti-Stratfordian theories are stained by their own intrinsic elitism. At their core is the belief that some people are too low-class and uneducated to produce great work. These theories invariably note that Shakespeare didn't go to a university and thus didn't have the education necessary to have written such great plays.

Barbara Mowat, editor of *Shakespeare Quarterly*, says, "I think it shows with what reverence these people hold the plays, that they want to find someone more important or more educated or richer to have written them, but all the documentary evidence that has come down to us links the plays to William Shakespeare." David Bevington, a professor of English at the University of Chicago, says Shakespeare's notoriety—the cultish immensity of his stature—contributes to these fringe theories. "It's clearly a cult," he says of Shakespeare fans in general. "When you have cults people are going to get suspicious and resentful."

We should note that there is one major colossal hitch with the Oxfordian theory. This de Vere fellow died in 1604. This is an inconvenient fact, given that someone apparently continued to write plays for roughly another decade under the name "William Shakespeare."

Call us crazy, call us wild-eyed maniac dingdongs, but we

have a hunch that "William Shakespeare" and William Shakespeare were one and the very same person.

THE MAILBAG

After we said the works of William Shakespeare were written by William Shakespeare, the "Oxfordians" wanted to eat us for lunch and wave our leg bones in the air like medieval kings signaling the vassals for more drumsticks. Here's a sample response, from James M. of Milpitas, California:

"The works of Shakespeare give evidence that their author was well traveled, was especially familiar with Italy, was on familiar terms with the court and nobles of Queen Elizabeth I, was intimately familiar with falconry, had a surprisingly detailed knowledge of the medicine and law of his day, was completely educated in Latin and Greek, and had a vocabulary that was truly astonishing. . . . There is not one shred of evidence associating the man from Stratford with any of the above characteristics. There is, on the other hand, specific evidence that all of the above characteristics applied to Edward de Vere."

Dear James: A more striking characteristic of Edward de Vere, though, is that his name does not appear on the title pages of *Hamlet* and *Macbeth*. Nor did he claim to have written those works. Nor did anyone until the twentieth century even suggest that he wrote them.

James writes, "There is no record that [Shakespeare] ever claimed authorship of the Shakespeare works." Jim, that would seem to us far more true of de Vere than Shakespeare. Shakespeare's name is on the plays and sonnets. That's a pretty ostentatious form of claiming authorship.

Yes, we admit you can nevertheless construct a theory that says de Vere, for social and political reasons, wrote the plays and persuaded Shakespeare to put his name on them. And it's true that Shakespeare is kind of shadowy. But that very shadowiness might be the key to the puzzle: There's no evidence he knew about falconry or Italy or whatnot precisely because there's not much information about him, period.

We will try to keep abreast of breaking developments in the Stratford versus Oxford debate. But frankly we'd rather worry about more pressing mysteries, like why banks put their ball-point pens on a theft-proof leash even though they don't work half the time.

Why did Kafka want all his writings burned after his death?

We expect literary geniuses to be eccentric. We expect them to be tormented, emotionally fragile, tubercular when at all possible. Literary geniuses are not supposed to be well-adjusted suburbanites who mow their own yards and tinker in the basement on their Black & Decker Workmate.

So one of the things that have cemented Franz Kafka's literary reputation is his request that his writings be burned after his death. It's such a . . . such a . . . *Kafkaesque* thing to do. Talk about a coincidence!

But he probably didn't mean it. It is significant that he gave the instructions to Max Brod, his friend and greatest fan.

one

two

"He was well aware that Brod would be the one man who would never burn his manuscripts," says Ernst Pawel, author of the Kafka biography *The Nightmare of Reason* (still another potential Why book title that's already been taken).

So why'd Kafka even make the request? One is tempted to argue that Kafka was merely posturing, that he was intentionally trying to be perceived as bizarre and self-loathing and avant-garde. Pawel argues that Kafka was just being ambivalent about himself, as always. This was a man who could never finish a novel and was constantly changing his mind about getting married.

"He wanted them destroyed, but he didn't want them destroyed," says Pawel. "He never could make up his mind, and he suffered from that. He always saw not two sides of every question but five sides."

Frederick R. Karl, author of the biography *Franz Kafka: Representative Man*, says Kafka's desire for literary self-destruction reflects both positive and negative impulses—self-hatred and

Three

self-mockery on the one hand, a sense of pride on the other. "Kafka set this impossible high standard for himself, one that he couldn't possibly maintain," Karl told us. Kafka did burn some manuscripts during his lifetime, but this probably was more a form of editing than self-negation. "If he had really wanted everything destroyed he could have done it himself," says Karl.

Was he as weird as people think? Probably not.

"He was neurotic but not all that strange," said Pawel. "He was a very regular guy with a great sense of humor."

He looks like an assassin in most photographs, but was in fact a rather handsome chap, tall for that period, and he held down a good job as an insurance executive. Right, an insurance executive. He was the man in the gray flannel suit. Someday we'll find out he could drive a golf ball farther than John Daly.

The downer was that he never made any money with his writing. Not until after his death did Kafka emerge as one of the literary giants of the century. Once, he found out that a bookstore had sold eleven copies of one of his books. He was puzzled. He had bought ten, he said, but who in the world bought the eleventh?

Why is the Oval Office oval?

Rex Scouten, curator of the White House, says the original house had three oval rooms and most of the presidents during the 1800s used the oval room on the second floor as their office. When Theodore Roosevelt built the West Wing in 1902 he set himself up in a normal, rectangular office, nothing too fancy.

But that got to be a problem since so much of what the president does is ceremonial, and Roosevelt kept having to troop back over to the main building to shake hands with ambassadors and war heroes and so forth. So when Wiliam Howard Taft enlarged the West Wing a few years later he made the president's office oval, so it would seem more White House-ish.

(Funny how no one cares that William Howard Taft used three names, but if the president's wife wants to be Hillary Rodham Clinton it's an act of unspeakable arrogance.)

Why don't rivers and lakes get absorbed into the ground?

They do, sometimes. There are "ephemeral" streams all over the western United States, streams that literally get soaked up by the ground. In Saudi Arabia, dry riverbeds are called wadi, and they contain water only when there is a torrential rain.

In other places, there's way too much water rushing through a river channel, or pouring into a lake from tributaries, to be absorbed. The extent to which a river or lake infiltrates the ground depends on the type of mud or rock at the bottom. Sandstone and limestone are more porous than granite. "You can think of the ground as a sponge, but there are different kinds of sponges," says Debra Knopman, a hydrologist with the U.S. Geological Survey. "Some sponges work better than others."

But there's another basic answer to our question: In many places, the water doesn't seep from the stream to the ground, it seeps from the ground to the stream. The surface of the stream often marks the top of the water table. That's why even in the middle of droughts, some streams keep on chugging—they are supplied not by rain but by groundwater. You might say they invent themselves out of thin ground.

Why do we all agree where "left" and "right" are? Why isn't our "left" hand on our right side instead of being on our left side?

Imagine what life was like in prehistoric times, when people lived in caves or mud huts and had not yet agreed upon a universal designation for left and right. One of them would be lining up a putt and his caddy would have to say something like, "I think this one breaks six inches from the side of the green with the big sand trap to the side where we drank the blood of the gazelle."

There's a reason left is left and right is right. What's the most important instrument in your life, other than the remote control? Your two hands. And, if you're like 90 percent of the population, your right hand is your strongest. The left is weaker and less adept. Thus the words for the weaker hand and the stronger hand have always reflected, quite bluntly, this bias.

"Left" comes from the Old English word "lyft," meaning weak and useless. So it is that the stronger hand is called

= Binky =
drawn right-handed

= Binky =
drawn left-handed

"right," an unabashedly positive word, with various roots connoting strength and straightforwardness. If you are nimble-fingered you have great dexterity, from the Latin "dexter," meaning right. If you are a klutz, perhaps you have "two left feet," as the cliché goes, which would make you freakishly, doubly "sinistral," from the Latin word for left and not coincidentally the root of sinister.

"This looks like it's something that's deeply ingrained in the psyche," says David Jost, the senior lexicographer for *The American Heritage Dictionary*, who was surprised to see that the nasty terminology goes way back.

So far as we know there's never been anyone who actually had two left feet or a left foot transposed to where the right should be and vice versa. Surely that would be a story in its own right. Right?

Why is the Golden Gate Bridge red?

As a smart person you need only scratch your noodle for a few seconds before realizing that "Golden" adjectivally modifies "Gate" and not "Bridge," and, thrilled by your deduction, you can then decide that it refers to all the gold in them there hills in California, which, of course, is wrong.

The name Golden Gate was coined in 1846 by Captain John C. Frémont, a couple of years before gold was found and the rush began. The entrance to the bay reminded Frémont of the Golden Horn of the Bosporus, that narrow passage at the eastern edge of the Mediterranean Sea, dubbed "Chrysoplae" (golden mouth) by the Greeks because it led to Byzantium and the riches of the Orient beyond.

"It's golden only by analogy," says Charles Fracchia, president of the San Francisco Historical Society. The thinking was, "This is a great port, this would lead to mercantile activities, to prosperity. It had nothing to do with the metal gold."

It's a good thing the bridge isn't gold. The bridge is so dramatic, so heroic, it needs a color that contrasts with the surroundings. Gold would be washed out in certain light and would get lost amid the surrounding hills during the drier months. The navy thought it would look nice with alternating yellow and black stripes, which sounds like it would exacerbate seasickness. The bridge designers considered gray, but that was becoming a cliché by the 1930s ("I'm tired of those battleship gray bridges. They are boring," chief engineer Joseph Strauss supposedly said). Eventually they stuck with the standard red paint that already was on the steel that came from the plant in Pottstown, Pennsylvania.

And the bridge isn't red, officially. It's "international orange." It sure looks more like brick red to us ignorant Why staffers. Allen Temko of the *San Francisco Chronicle* has written, "Variously described as a kind of vermilion, it is largely a mixture of orange and lamp black, which produces the burned reddish-orange that responds so eloquently to changing light, in sunshine or mist, from soft dawn to violet twilight."

Which is the nice way of saying that it looks good in that damn fog.

Why are Impressionist paintings so much more popular than any other style?

Y ou got an art question, you talk to us. We do highbrow, we do lowbrow. In fact we are the only people we know who have *Les Demoiselles d'Avignon* in a velvet version. When that dang Picasso gets dusty we just take it outside and (KA-WHOMP) shake it like a rug.

Recently we were tooling around the National Gallery in Washington when we noticed that huge crowds were packing into the Impressionism galleries. Van Gogh in particular was putting people in a dither. Monet, Gauguin, Renoir, Pissarro, Cézanne, Toulouse-Lautrec, and that whole gang seemed to have people hypnotized.

Maybe the crowds were driven by the auction-house hype of recent years, when the Impressionists were selling for obscene sums, tens of millions for a single painting. People may have it in their heads that these paintings are worth more than others, that there's some kind of official index (money) by which they are judged superior.

But the real answer is probably in the paintings themselves: They depict a dreamy world of exaggerated gorgeousness—the world as we would wish it to look.

"They were beautiful. The palette was more highly keyed, that is, the color was brighter, than the paintings of a previous generation," says Charles Moffett, director of The Phillips Collection in Washington.

The first Impressionists, such as Claude Monet, were making a break with academic painting, with the strictures and formulas of the art schools. They began to experiment with abstraction and distortion, without abandoning recognizable subject matter; you might say it's a form of modernism that's easy on the eye and brain. (An 1872 painting by Monet, *Impression, sunrise*, gave name to the movement; van Gogh, Gauguin, and Toulouse-Lautrec are more properly considered post-impressionist.)

"People enjoy the flirtation between illusionism and abstraction, which is what Impressionism is about. There's a tension between the style and the subject," says Moffett.

And speaking of subject matter: It's hard not to like a painting that shows people lolling around a park or drinking coffee in a Parisian café.

"Their subjects were from everyday modern life: people relaxing in the country, eating, boating, picnicking, or people in the city, going to the opera, the theater, walking on the boulevard, sitting in cafés," said Elizabeth Streicher, head of the Department of Modern Painting at the National Gallery. "It's the romance of Paris too."

And finally, Impressionist paintings appeal to the painterly aspirations in all of us. They don't look that hard to do, unlike those baroque and rococo masterpieces. We fantasize not only of being in that field of sunflowers, but being there with a palette and brush. We could be the next van Gogh! But with ears intact, of course.

Why is Jesus traditionally depicted as a skinny guy with long hair?

The Gospels don't describe what Jesus looked like, and Jewish law prohibited the making of graven images, so there are no contemporaneous paintings, no statues, no Polaroids. Lacking textual or graven evidence—someday we will find out what "graven" means—religious iconographers have had no choice but to make stuff up.

Western civilization is filled with images of a thin, white-skinned, long-haired Jesus because, according to Hershel Shanks, editor of *Biblical Archaeology Review*, "he was painted by slender white men with long hair."

If you survey different cultures, though, Jesus comes off as the man of a thousand faces. He's white, black, lanky, burly, effeminate, brutish. He's what every culture wants him to be, a mutable Jesus.

The long hair may be the one feature that is historically accurate. Romans cut their hair short. The Jews may have let their hair grow as a way of distinguishing themselves, as an act of defiance, biblical scholars say. They were letting their freak flags fly.

Was Jesus skinny? He did fast for forty days in the desert, according to the Gospels, and he may have come from an ascetic tradition that emphasized self-denial. It's a fair guess that he wasn't obese. Whether he was "white" or "black" or something in between is an issue contaminated by our own rather bizarre conceptions of what such terms mean. "He probably was a person of color, just because of the ethnic and racial mixes in the ancient Near East," says Marcus Borg, a biblical scholar at Oregon State University. Of course, "person of color" is a modern term; Jesus and his followers showed no interest in racial labels.

Some scholars have gone so far as to claim that Jesus was married. Or a widower. Or gay, a hypothesis first floated in the 1960s by an Anglican priest. All these theories are based on the absence of any mention of a wife for Jesus, which was unusual for a Jewish man of that era, when there wasn't even a word in Hebrew or Aramaic for "bachelor."

Jesus was perhaps a bit diminutive by our standards. "He was about five feet tall," postulates Borg. "That was the average height of a man in the Near East in the first century."

In all this, scholarship is intertwined with speculation and supposition. Guesswork should never be treated as the gospel truth.

Why is the elevator always there? Why do you never get the shaft?

It would stand to reason that every so often, maybe once every three or four months, just because of random mechanical failure, you'd fall down an elevator shaft and die. But for some reason the elevator always seems to be there, which is good, because as a person of dignity you don't want people knowing that your last words on Earth were something like "There's this great little deli over by the woh-woh-*woooohhhhhhhhhh*."

Obviously there's a simple economic reason why elevators are reliable: If they weren't, no elevator company could stay in business. There might be a freak accident here and there, the odd shafting of some poor soul, but basically these things are extremely reliable. Our question is, what's the mechanical safeguard?

Here's the key thing you need to know: The doors to the elevator shaft can be opened only by the doors on the elevator car. There's no independent mechanism to open the shaft doors. The doors are kept shut by a powerful spring. If you pry them open with a crowbar, they will spring closed again. Because there's no way to open them mechanically without the presence of the elevator car, you don't have to worry that one day you'll hit the elevator call button and have it mistakenly open the doors onto an empty shaft.

The motor that opens and shuts both sets of doors is on top of the elevator car. When the car gets to within about an eighth of an inch of the correct floor, the shaft ("hoistway") doors are unlocked electronically and simultaneously snagged by the opening car doors.

"It is the safest means of transportation in the world," says Jim Christensen, spokesman for Otis Elevator Company. "Statistically it is safer than walking."

That's right. Because of the manhole danger.

Why do some words have two radically different meanings? Why does "box" mean both a pugilistic act and a rectangular container?

If you have small children you probably feel guilty sometimes about bringing them into a world that has so many wars, ancient hatreds, incurable diseases, and English-language homonyms.

Let's say you're reading *One Fish, Two Fish* by Dr. Seuss, and you come across the part where the kids play Ring the Gack. How do you explain that "ring," as in a circular object that can be thrown on the Gack's antlers, is not the same thing as the noise that the telephone makes?

And when the little boy in the book boxes with the Gox, how do you explain that "box" in this case is not related to the toy "box"?

(Answer: Plop child in front of "Sesame Street" and let Big Bird sort it out.)

The container "box" comes from the Greek "puxis," which also refers to a type of tree. In Latin the word became "buxis," and by the time it reached Middle English it was simply "box," the same spelling and pronunciation as the word meaning "to slap." This convergence was probably due to nothing other than a mangling of the foreign word, from "buxis" to "box." This has always happened, which is why "Detroit" is pronounced the way it is rather than in the Frenchy way that makes it sound as though you're trying to spit out your dinner.

Once the convergence takes place, it's hard to pry the two

words apart because spelling is far more rigid than meaning and there's no way to pronounce one "box" differently from another "box."

"If our spelling system were less fixed than it is, we wouldn't have so many of these homonyms," says David Jost, senior lexicographer at *The American Heritage Dictionary*.

We forgot to ask him to look up "Gack" and "Gox."

THE MAILBAG

We adore letters, even the one that said, "You are worse than Dormer, or whatever the man's name was that chopped up those boys and ate them."

The Why column is an "interactive" medium, which means that readers write questions to us and we, in turn, interactively, let them pile up on the desk for *years*. Chronic self-delusion has convinced us that we will write back to each person, individually, at some point in the future. Unless the letters turn to mulch first.

A typical letter comes with a list of twenty-five questions, a self-addressed stamped envelope (for our convenience, apparently), and the admonition "Please write back to me directly with the answers as I do not subscribe to the newspaper." We are always amazed that they do not offer to let us come over and shampoo their pets.

Sometimes we get just a scrap of paper with a single question on it. Postcards are big. Once we got an envelope utterly empty but for a small yellow Post-It note stuck on the inside flap, saying "A piece of crap!" We presumed that was more of an answer than a question.

Another common missive is the equation-filled tome. This is the letter that comes from someone who has become the world's foremost amateur expert on, say, Fermat's Last Theorem. Such a letter will often show conclusive, exhaustive, irrefutable proof that the Why staff has produced an incomplete answer to something. And that the letter writer does not have a life.

Dear Mr. Achenbach,
There's this guy I think
likes me but my friends
all say no way! Help!
P.S. You are the
Teen Advisor, right?

Wiseacre comments aside, our readers are astonishingly smart, curious, and perceptive. The readers have kept the Why staff on its tippy-toes. They've asked many of the questions included in this book and probably most of the questions that are any good. (The Why staff itself comes up with the questions that no one has ever pondered in the history of sentience. For example, the other day we were wondering if there had ever been a person who had only a sense of smell, with no other senses. We were certain that if such a person had ever existed he or she would have invented a personal odor–based language. We're still checking.)

Sometimes we have felt as though the Why column is too limited, too *focused*, and so we've thought about changing the name to something like Fire Away! and dealing with more personal concerns, stuff like this:

Q: I have a mysterious pain in my right side, below the ribs. What should I do? *Jacki in Tucson*

A: Have that kidney removed immediately.

But until we make that format change we will stick with the dismal grind of explaining how the universe works.

Here's a classic MIRVed letter, from a certain Timmy

Metal plate in skull

Stamp breath

Disgruntled Postal Worker

Fake Rolex

Recognizing Beasley for Beginners

Fount of Frederick, Maryland, who managed to cram an awesome list of questions on a thin strip of paper: "In 'Blondie,' why do the mailman and Herb Woodley look like twins? What's the difference between ketchup and catsup? What does YKK stand for on a zipper? Other than Pearl Harbor, why didn't Japan or Germany directly attack American cities in World War II?"

Dear Timmy: We heard a nasty rumor that Herb Woodley *is* the mailman. It's not true. The mailman's name is Mr. Beasley. (In fact his name is Beasley Beasley, he once admitted. His father was lazy.) Beasley and Woodley do look astonishingly alike. Dean Young, who took over the strip when his father, Chic Young, died in 1973, readily admits that the two characters are deep into "Separated at Birth?" territory. Same mustache. Same sideburns. Same build. But Young notes that Herb has a slightly more pronounced jawline and a cleft chin. Keep in mind that many cartoonists have characters that look alike—all the men in "Doonesbury" have pencil-like noses, for example.

Ketchup and catsup are the same thing. Another variant is catchup. In the United States "catsup" was preferred until this century. A few years ago Del Monte became the last national brand to switch to "ketchup." These are just alternative spellings and pronunciations of the same word, a noun that in precise speech should usually carry an adjective—tomato ketchup, mushroom ketchup, etc. The Chinese first concocted something called *ke-tsiap* in the eleventh century. It was a mixture of pickled fish, shellfish, and spices. How it would taste on a corn dog is frightening to contemplate.

The YKK stands for Yoshida Kogyo Kabushikigaisha. The company is named after the Japanese founders. The Why staff has discreetly checked its own zippers—people don't always believe you when you say you're engaged in a scientific investigation—and has discovered that they say Talon.

Further checking reveals that Talon is a brand name that replaced Hookless Fastener in the 1930s when the Hookless Company realized that a term like "hookless fastener" sounded hopelessly old-fashioned, particularly since B. F. Goodrich introduced the catchier (no pun intended) name "Zipper" in the 1920s. "Zipper" was so catchy, in fact, it quickly became the generic name for a slide fastener. "Slide fastener" is still what the folks at YKK call their product, by the way.

Now let's make a delicate transition to this Pearl Harbor business. Pearl Harbor was a stretch for the Japanese. Planes in that era couldn't easily fly long distances, and you certainly wouldn't send a fleet of ships on a suicide mission across the vast ocean. The Japanese did bomb Dutch Harbor, in the Aleutian Islands, and later they sent incendiary balloons across the ocean, which started some forest fires out West. German submarines sank a lot of boats off the East Coast.

But basically the U.S. mainland wasn't attacked because you couldn't get here from there.

Now let's just rifle through the mailbag looking for treasures. One thing that's really frustrating is that after all these years no one has written us with the question "How many angels can dance on the head of a pin?" We happen to know that the answer is "It depends on the dance."

Here's a classic so-dumb-it's-brilliant question from Patrick

McGuire of Washington, D.C.: "What does the inside of your nose smell like?"

Dear Pat: We spoke to Charles Wysocki, a neuroscientist at the Monell Chemical Senses Center in Philadelphia, and he said that you can't smell your nose because, to the extent that your nose has a smell (and it may have a smell if you have an infection), you've become adapted to it. But that's obvious. What's interesting is that no one is certain exactly how a nose can become adapted to a smell, such as the stench of a paper mill or a paint factory.

We always had heard that it takes seven minutes to get accustomed to a smell, but that's not true. Adaptation can take mere seconds for some odors or take months or even longer for a noxious stench, such as a landfill. Put your nose to a freshly sliced pear: You register a lovely scent. But after about fifteen seconds (the time varies from person to person) you probably can't smell much of anything.

It's not clear if this adaptation is happening in the nose or the brain. It may simply be that your olfactory receptors send signals to the brain only when they first make contact with the odoriferous compound. Or it may be that your brain itself is filtering out the information and you simply are not conscious of the smell, in the same way that you can read an entire newspaper column and come to the end and have no idea what it was that you just read. (To recap, we said, "It smells like chicken.")

Janet Cherry of Baltimore asks, "Would you be weightless at the center of the Earth?"

Dear Janet: Sure would. With the planet's mass equally distributed around you, gravity would be canceled out.

David Thomas of Denver writes, "Everyone knows what happens when you put a bottle filled with water in the freezer—the water expands, turning to ice, and breaks the bottle. What would happen if you filled a very strong safe with water and dropped the temp below freezing? What if the safe was too strong for the freezing water to bulge out the walls of the safe? Would it be able to freeze at all?"

Dear David: The water would not freeze, at least not right away. You'd just have very cold liquid water. The reason is elementary: As pressure rises, the freezing temperature drops. Inside the chilling safe, some ice crystals do form, increasing the pressure and keeping the remaining water in a liquid state. That remaining water will freeze if you can get the safe colder, down to about –20 degrees Celsius or so, according to physicist Robin Blumberg Selinger of the University of Maryland. And then the solid ice, being under great pressure, will be denser than the stuff you have in your freezer and won't expand as much. (Ice is not all the same.)

You can see this phenomenon illustrated by putting a beer in the freezer. The beer is under pressure. Pull it out when it is still liquid, pop the top off, and—if it's cold enough—it will freeze up in a few seconds.

Karl Peters of Highland, Maryland, writes: "Is it entirely fortuitous that the apparent size of the sun and the moon are nearly identical from the Earth, which beautifully enables us to observe the sun's corona during a solar eclipse? Or did God plan it this way?"

Dear Karl: Not even the Why staff would presume to read God's thoughts. But as far as any scientist can see it's just a big-time coincidence. On no other planet do you have so close a match between the "angular size" of a satellite and the sun. The two appear to be the same size because the sun is roughly four hundred times farther away from the Earth than the moon and is also (concidentally) four hundred times larger in diameter than the moon.

The moon is, from our perspective, just a wee bit larger, which is why it blocks out the sun during most eclipses. But to give you an idea of how close they are in apparent size, there are occasional eclipses in which the moon's disk is smaller than the sun's, leaving a thin ring of the sun's surface visible, rather than just the corona. These "annular eclipses" (from the Latin *anulus*, meaning ring—though the Why staff must confess that we always thought it meant "butthole") are the result of the moon's elliptical orbit, which makes the distance between the moon and Earth vary by about 14 percent.

Speaking of perspective: Charles Jones of Norfolk, Virginia, writes, "Why do objects appear smaller the farther we move from them?"

Dear Charles: Some nerds will tell you that the apparent size of objects is a function of straight-line geometry, and they'll draw diagrams of triangles and cones. They'll point out that if you double your distance from the wall clock, its diameter will span half as many degrees of your field of vision as it did originally. But ignore all that. These are the nineties, an age of heroic action and positive thinking. The new rule is, when objects recede they don't get smaller—*you get bigger*.

Heather West, age six, of Glendale, Arizona, asks, "How did the beach get so much sand?"

Dear Heather: Sand is rock that's been beaten up for years, until all that's left are little pieces. It's minerals in miniature. It comes from mountains, down rivers, into the ocean, then gets thrown up onshore, over and over for millions of years.

The term "sand" refers to the size of this stuff, not the precise composition. If it's between two microns and sixty-four microns in diameter, it's sand. If it's smaller than that, it's silt.

Sand is coarse to the touch, and silt is gritty. If the particles are really small, that's called clay, which feels smooth.

Most beaches have lots of quartz in the sand. That type of rock won't break up into pieces smaller than about sixty-four microns. It has a "terminal size." "Quartz is the most stable material," says Stephen "Dr. Beach" Leatherman, a geographer and sand expert at the University of Maryland.

You might also find garnet, feldspar, and magnetite in the sand. Pink beaches are made of crushed coral. The black beaches of Hawaii have sand from volcanic rock. Sand Beach in Acadia National Park is made up almost entirely of ground sea urchin spines. (We're glad the sea urchins have finally been put to practical use.)

Michelle Pase of Phoenix asks, "What happens to your umbilical cord inside you once you are cut from your mom? I mean, does it just disintegrate, or does it stay hooked to anything?"

Dear Michelle: The weird thing about the umbilical cord and the placenta is that they don't look remotely human. Of course, babies at birth don't really look all that human either. Many a parent has looked at the doctor in the delivery room and said, "No, no, we wanted a *human* child. Put it back."

The cord is a bit of a management problem, but there are natural forces at work that help the situation. As you know, the cord is cut at birth and clamped. If the cord isn't clamped, the baby can lose a lot of blood and even die. But that's not too likely because there's an adrenalinelike hormone in the baby's body during delivery that causes the blood vessels inside the umbilical cord to collapse. Neat trick!

These blood vessels inside the cord stump close up so tightly that they are sealed off from the rest of the baby's circulatory system. Eventually they disappear completely. So what you have is an external stump that dries up and falls off in a few weeks and an internal stump that collapses and vanishes.

The bottom line is that the baby is undergoing a radical change in circulation, the old system instantly collapsing under the hormone stress even as the new system, employing lungs, kicks in. What will they think of next?

Mitch "Chubbs" Greger of Bowie, Maryland, writes, "Why don't they take a really, really fat guy, like the late Walter Hudson, or

even Bill Clinton, pad him up, and make him a goalie in the NHL? Isn't it possible, with padding and stick, that someone is fat enough to block every square inch of the goal?"

Dear Mitch: That's a really impractical idea. For one thing, as you even point out, Walter Hudson's dead. And Bill Clinton, though capable of quickly skating left and right, never would agree to wear a goalie's mask because people would think he was not only a tax-and-spend Democrat but also Jason from *Friday the Thirteenth*.

Here's your real problem: You are forgetting that people are three-dimensional. When someone adds "inches" to his waist it is a reference to circumference, not diameter. For example, when Walter Hudson reached his top weight of 1,200 pounds, he had a girth of 113 inches, according to a newspaper clip we found. But girth is not the same thing as width; he was probably only about three feet wide (we're assuming a round physique and dividing 113 inches by pi). A hockey goal is six feet wide and four feet high. This means that Hudson couldn't have sat in front of the goal and blocked every shot. Even if he had lain on his side, the "top shelf" of the goal still would be exposed and the skilled players of the NHL would have had no trouble flicking the puck into that space.

(Naturally this is a discussion of physics, not the professional possibilities of the morbidly obese; we assume the late

Mr. Hudson would have had no desire to be pelted by hockey pucks at 110 miles an hour.)

Arthur Pincus, spokesman for the National Hockey League, notes that goalies are not just obstacles to the puck. They usually have quicker reflexes than anyone else on the ice and are the best skaters. Some of the best goalies in the country weigh under two hundred pounds. They're in constant motion as they play defense.

One other thing: All hockey players have to wear skates. We assume that employing a sled would be in violation of the rule book.

Bob Boorman of Phoenix asks: "Does empty space exist, and where did it come from? Does the Big Bang theory answer this question?"

Dear Bob: The real mystery is, why is there never enough closet space? You know?

As we speak, there's a U.S. space probe hurling toward the interstellar void, far beyond Pluto, and even out there it runs into stuff. *Pioneer 10* is about fifty-eight astronomical units (AUs) from the sun (Earth is one AU and Pluto, with its crazily elliptical orbit, ranges from thirty to fifty) the last time we checked, and it's still feeling the meek gusts of the sun's solar wind, which essentially is a bunch of ionized hydrogen atoms. There's about one atom per seven thousand cubic inches of space out there.

More dense yet are the cosmic rays, which are atomic nuclei that are flying at us from all over the galaxy. You find one of those every three hundred cubic inches or so. If Daniel Boone went out there he'd probably complain that you can't find elbow room anywhere.

(By the way, there's a great word for the point where the sun's solar wind finally stops: the heliopause. You should try to use this in a sentence, such as "He's got the worst toupee this side of the heliopause.")

If you ever left the Milky Way galaxy you'd find yourself in the intergalactic void, and that's much emptier. But even if it was devoid of all matter, it wouldn't really be "empty space" because it's permeated with radiation and gravity. If radiation didn't span the void we wouldn't be able to see stars and galaxies, since light is a form of radiation (electromagnetism). Gravity, too, shapes galaxies and galactic clusters and galactic superclusters. So "empty space" is a chockablock with energy.

The Big Bang does explain the origin of space. The creation of space, and time, is what the Big Bang *is*, and it's really an ongoing creation. The Big Bang theory says the universe was once hot and dense and then began to expand and cool. "The reason there's space at all is because the universe is expanding," says Kenneth Sembach, an MIT astrophysicist.

As the universe expanded, matter clumped together and left behind "empty space" where it had been. So the void beyond Pluto has not always been so void. It's just void where matter is prohibited.

George Wilk of Chagrin Falls, Ohio, asks, "What is the origin of the game tic-tac-toe?"

Dear George: Glad you asked, because tic-tac-toe has always driven us crazy. It's such a dumb game. Every game ends in a draw, unless you or your opponent has tofu for brains. "Go fish" is a game of genius compared to tic-tac-toe.

But now that we've insulted it, we have to reveal that, according to Claudia Zaslavsky's book *Tic Tac Toe*, it really is a very sophisticated game. Originally from ancient Egypt, it has spread around the world. It's called noughts-and-crosses in England, Ecke Mecke Stecke in Austria, and Tripp Trapp Trull in Sweden.

It's a kid's game, obviously. The reason it has been so widespread probably is because it's a great way for kids to learn how to play games in general. There are tricks involved, decisions to be made, pitfalls to be avoided. The first player has a huge advantage. If the second player doesn't put a mark in the right place, the first player can set a trap that ensures victory. Kids have to learn to play defense, to see those traps coming. In so doing, strategic thinking is born.

Those kids go on in life to invent more glorious games. Where do you think we got Mutual Assured Destruction?

Mitzi Swift, a high school chemistry teacher in Coronado, California, asks, "Why is urine yellow?" She explains why she's so curious: "I've checked what resources I have available to see what solutes are in urine and have determined that the substances are colorless."

Dear Mitzi: For years we've struggled to explain why something is one color rather than another; ultimately it's a physics question involving the absorption or lack of absorption of certain wavelengths of light (and these things always end up seeming kind of arbitrary). Dealing with the chemistry of the matter is easier. Helen Free, president-elect of the American Chemical Society, told us that the yellow comes from "urochromes," which are just some of the many molecular compounds that get filtered out of the blood.

She said that it all starts out red. The bright red hemoglobin is broken down into orangy bilirubin, which is eventually broken down into the yellowish urochromes. "It goes from red to orange to brown to yellow," she said.

(You mean . . . purple's not normal?)

Randall Zagata of East Pointe, Michigan, writes, "I've heard that in a few years, seven of our planets are going to line up. And if this happens it will cause disasters worldwide. What will happen to the world with the gravity pull and all?"

Dear Randall: Planetary alignments are usually a sham. The planets don't really line up!

For example, the Grand Alignment of 1982, which was supposed to result in cataclysm as a result of something called the Jupiter Effect, was in fact not particularly grand. What happened was merely that most of the planets were arrayed across about ninety degrees of arc in the sky. So they weren't aligned at all, they were just near each other in the sky from our vantage point.

It's true that there will be an "alignment" again in the year 2000. (We will let everyone know when they can stop calling it "the year 2000" and simply call it "2000.") On May 5, 2000, the sun, Mercury, Venus, Mars, Jupiter, and Saturn will be arrayed over about thirty degrees of arc. The Earth will be on the opposite side of the sun from those planets. That means you probably won't be able to see any of them because they'll be washed out in the sun's light.

As for gravity-induced disasters: Don't worry, you won't be ripped sideways out of the stuffed chair in your living room. LeRoy Doggett, a U.S. Naval Observatory astronomer, investigated the alleged Jupiter Effect back in 1982 to see if these alignments actually exert much gravitational force. He found that if we could perfectly line up all the planets to generate the maximum tidal force on Earth, it would be about 0.0001 of the ordinary tidal forces that we have every day due to the sun and moon.

Doggett says the alignment in May 2000 hasn't been named yet. Obviously we should christen it the Millennial Alignment.

Though "Alignment of Doom" is also pretty catchy.

A reader in Rockville, Maryland, asks, "Why hasn't natural selection eliminated homosexuality?"

Dear Reader: We don't want to offend all the missionary-position enthusiasts out there, but people find pleasure in all sorts of things that don't directly spawn offspring. We're sexually diverse. Even the terms we use, like "heterosexual" and "homosexual," imply a standardization that doesn't really exist—the point being that there are a lot of "unproductive" sexual activities that natural selection hasn't eliminated.

But it's still a good question, and there are several possible explanations.

For starters, we'd point out that homosexuality isn't a classic genetic trait, like blue or brown eyes. Yes, there is evidence linking homosexuality to genetic factors, but it's not that simple, because there are also hormonal and environmental factors. Human sexuality is largely shaped in the womb by hormones, and hormones aren't precision instruments. There's some slack built into the system.

Another thing to think about: Homosexuals do sometimes have children. Moreover, they play a role in their families. Rutgers University anthropologist Lionel Tiger told us, "Many homosexual people are very much involved in their relatives anyway and there's a phenomenon in biology called helpers-at-the-nest."

Two nephews are worth one son. That's the equation, says Tiger. He had some other theories that were really interesting and potentially highly offensive and so we'll just let them sit in our computer for a few months or centuries until we find the right time to spit them out.

Celia Alvyn of Miami writes, "Why don't we fall out of bed more often?"

Dear Celia: A corollary to your question is, why do kids fall out of bed, but not adults?

We spoke to Mary Carskadon, editor of the *Encyclopedia of Sleep and Dreaming*, and she said that you don't fall out of bed because you aren't totally asleep when you toss and turn. Your brain detects the edge of the bed.

"When we do roll over, we are somewhat aroused," she says. "Our brain, in order to initiate that movement, has come closer to an awake state, where there is some sensory processing."

So the brain processes the edge of the bed and says don't roll over any further. What's interesting is that when you wake up later and find yourself in some strange position, you have no memory of how you got there. That's due to another phenomenon: You lose memory of events right before you fall asleep (or fall back asleep when slightly aroused in the night). It's as though the act of falling asleep purges the last few sensations and thoughts.

Kids do often fall out of bed, probably because they are much deeper sleepers. You may have noticed that sleeping infants can be lugged around like a sack of potatoes, dragged across broken glass, exposed to fire, and still won't wake up. They also sleepwalk more than adults.

"Sleep is so intense in young children that it almost defies our normal description of what sleep is, which is a quickly reversible behavioral disengagement from the environment," Carskadon says.

We can think of one other reason adults don't fall out of bed: The forces affecting two people in the sack are often centripetal, not centrifugal.

Bernhard Schopper of Alexandria, Virginia, asks, "Why are condemned prisoners executed with 2,000 volts over several minutes, instead of 20,000 volts over several seconds?"

Dear Bernie: One reason is, we no longer believe in burning as a way of execution. The stake, the rack, the iron maiden, and the gibbet all are out of fashion, and likewise we do not choose to execute people with so much voltage that the contact points will catch on fire.

Ron Wright, the Broward County, Florida, medical examiner, calculated that the average human being, with a resistance of 500 ohms, would pull 40 amps at 20,000 volts, which translates to 800,000 watts. You don't have to know what the numbers mean to realize that it's a tad excessive.

"You'd actually cook the person," says Wright.

The State of Florida uses about 4,800 volts for a minute. The current is cut off and then resumed a minute later. This happens three times as precautionary measures. The first jolt renders the prisoner instantly unconscious and raises the temperature in the brain to the point where the brain is destroyed.

The problem is, the heart often still beats after the high voltage is removed. The Commonwealth of Virginia deals with this by using a two-phase process: high voltage first and then low voltage, which puts the heart into irreversible quivering, called ventricular fibrillation.

We think Wright put it well: "The whole thing is, in an odd sort of way, both high-tech and barbaric."

Taki Telonidis of Washington, D.C., asks, "Why is it called the funny bone and why does it seem to be neither a bone nor funny?"

Dear Taki: You have a lot of nerve. Har! The funny bone is the ulnar nerve, of course, and when you whang it you feel numbness and tingling in your pinkie, half your ring finger, and your palm. Why they put the darn thing in an unprotected spot is something you'll have to take up with management (next time: testicle trivia). Suffice it to say that it comes from your spinal cord, over the shoulder, down the arm, and through the slot at your elbow, leaving it exposed to certain kinds of jabs, especially those associated with doors, which have penetrating edges. The source books say that "funny bone" is a pun on the "humerus" bone that goes from the elbow to the shoulder, but we've never seen proof.

Terrel Stewart of Columbus, Georgia, asks if miracles really happen. "Does the mere fact that there are natural events have to automatically mean that there are never any supernatural events?"

Dear Terry: Whenever we manage to turn in a column on time our editors react as though it were a supernatural occurrence. Our dictionary says that something is supernatural if it "depart(s) from what is usual or normal so as to appear to transcend the laws of nature." By that loose definition, something can be termed "supernatural" if it's presently inexplicable.

But what you want to know is if the supernatural "really happens," and all we can tell you is that if we were to observe a supernatural event, and verify that observation experimentally in a theoretical framework superior to all other known theoretical frameworks, and write up our results in a prestigious journal such that you would be convinced this really happened, then it wouldn't be all that supernatural, would it?

Barb Meluch of Maple Heights, Ohio asks, "What do they do with the blood after they embalm a person? Can it be used again?"

Dear Barb: Other than as a cocktail mixer in the House on the Haunted Hill there's no good use for cadaver blood. The cells in the blood rapidly die after the host departs this earth. We called a funeral home in the District of Columbia and were told that they dump the stuff down the drain, which frankly shocked us. Blood is, obviously, a vector for disease. But we've been assured by a mortuary science professor that the chemicals in the sewage treatment process render blood harmless.

In any case, don't go hanging around the sewers of D.C. (unless you're trying to find your congressman).

Timothy DeMerle, age ten, of Buffalo asks, "Why don't police officers wear running shoes? I think it would be easier to run after criminals and capture them."

Dear Tiny Tim: Sneakers are against the dress code. For instance, the "Footwear" section of the Detroit Police Officers Association guidelines requires "solid black, plain toe, lace type shoes; black military type lace boots; or over the ankle, black, plain toe Wellington boots." It adds, "In all instances, the shoe or boot must be capable of taking a high degree of polish."

But let's go beyond that. Why so dressy a shoe? Why not something more practical? This really gets into the whole history and theory of uniforms. The redcoats in the British Army in the Revolutionary War were probably asking these same questions, wandering around the American wilderness in their starched collars and powdered wigs. There are several major reasons why uniforms were adopted:

1. Uniformity helps discipline. A war is no place for rampant individualism; every soldier (or police office fighting a different kind of war) is supposed to be part of a larger, cohesive unit.

2. It's cheaper to supply clothes for an army if everyone wears the same thing.

3. A uniform announces your identity. Otherwise, when the battlefield gets smoky you might accidentally bifurcate your bunkmate.

4. Intimidation. "You're cowing the enemy with your power, which stems in part from your clothing," says Les Jensen, museum curator for the Center of Military History in Washington.

There's no need to chase after a criminal if you can merely intimidate him into surrendering. Those spit-shine shoes announce to the world that The Law has arrived. They add luster to the profession.

Jim MacNabb of Columbus, Ohio, wants to know why NASA doesn't seem interested in making spaceships and space stations that spin, to create artificial gravity for the astronauts, just like in the movie *2001: A Space Odyssey*.

Dear Jim: The movie accurately shows how centrifugal force can create "artificial gravity," but the space shuttle is way too small for that trick. It'd have to spin like a top. How would it rescue ailing military spy satellites?

We could rotate a really big space station, but what Stanley Kubrick and friends didn't realize was that one of the main reasons NASA says a space station is worth the tens of billions of dollars it would cost is that it would create a zero-gravity work space where fancy high-tech materials could be manufactured. (We always imagine fibers of some kind.) NASA would never spin the thing just so that astronauts would be able to walk around. Heck, they can do that here! We could send them on a field trip to the mountains and save a bunch of money!

We'll entertain any question here in the Why bunker, including this one from Everett Johnson of Washington D.C.: "Why are home toilet seats generally a closed circle, while 'institutional' toilet seats are generally an oval open at the front?"

Dear Everett: We spoke to Nancy Deptolla, of the toilet-making Kohler Company, and she explained that public seats are governed by health codes and have that opening "for sanitary reasons." We can safely report that those reasons are unspeakable. The bottom line (ha!) is that public seats are designed to be not-all-there because even though you probably can't catch anything from a toilet seat, you definitely can't catch anything from a gap in a seat.

John Caffo of Albuquerque says he likes "Golden Oldies" from the fifties and early sixties and asks, "Why aren't there any songwriters and singers out there today who are coming up with new, original music of the same style?"

Dear John: Because most musicians have pride. They'll "cover" an old tune, sure, but anyone with enough artistic skill to write terrific tunes isn't going to have so little artistic pride that he or she is willing to duplicate shamelessly that old sound.

We hate to break it to you, John, but new styles of music sell much better than the old doo-wop and rockabilly and whatnot. People have children. Those children transmogrify into teenagers and young adults. They buy music with a passion. Thus it is that the big acts in the world in the early 1990s were Pearl Jam, Dr. Dre, Nirvana, and a bunch of others that we'd name except we're pretty uncool too these days (it *is* "Dr. Dre," isn't it?).

We called Anthony DeCurtis, a rock critic for *Rolling Stone*, and he pointed out that some artists do emulate old styles, whether intentionally or not. There's a band called the Posies that sing pretty songs with harmonies, just like the Hollies (yuck!). The Stray Cats did retro rockabilly. Boyz II Men sing group harmony tunes. "R.E.M. for many years was criticized for sounding like the Byrds. And every other band you hear sounds like the Velvet Underground," says DeCurtis.

One last thing: The Rolling Stones toured in 1994. So did the Eagles. As DeCurtis puts it, "One of the reasons people aren't making this kind of music anymore is that the people who made it in the first place are still making it." That's the X-factor in all this: Keith Richards, against all odds, still isn't dead.

Gregory Porter of Glen Burnie, Maryland, writes: "Please help settle a dispute between my wife and me. When it's cold outside, I 'warm up' the car and I turn on the heater full blast. My wife waits until the car has warmed up, then turns on the heater at medium. I think my way heats the inside of the car faster than her way. Do you know if this theory has ever been imagined or tested? I think my wife doesn't like to have the heater on full blast because it blows on her somewhat exposed, nylon-clad ankles."

Dear Greg: Let's make a deal. You get to be the winner of the dispute, in terms of the engineering question. But then you have to promise not to blast cold air on the ankles of your wife. This issue requires both an understanding of machines and an understanding of human beings.

The car heats faster if you blast the heater from the very start. We are assured of this by John Kill, chief engineer for climate control subsystems at Ford Motor Company. In American cars, the heat comes from the engine coolant. That's right: As the coolant warms up, it warms the heater core. The heater core is like a radiator, with little metal fins. Air blows across the heater core, then onto your legs. The coolant starts warming immediately. By running the heater full blast you maximize the heat transfer, even when things are still pretty darn cold. This will warm a car about 20 to 25 percent faster than if you wait until the engine is warm and then turn on the heater, Kill says.

But obviously in the meantime you have to endure the wind chill on your legs. Why endure several minutes of discomfort, and get in squabbles with your spouse, simply because you want the interior of the car to be toasty in six minutes instead of eight?

You could always ask your wife to ride in the backseat, however. You could pretend to be her chauffeur.

As fans of undersea cables—we just think they're cool—we were delighted when Elaine Morrell of Puyallup, Washington, wrote, "What is the current function of the Atlantic cable? I'm particularly interested in knowing if the gutta-percha covering is still holding up."

Dear Elaine: The gutta-percha is probably doing just fine, says Jim Barrett, vice president of engineering and marine operations for AT&T Submarine Systems.

But it doesn't actually matter. The gutta-percha, a resinous, rubberlike substance, was used on telegraph cables laid in the 1800s. They're still down there, buried in mud and silt, but are unused. Now we use telephone cables, which have been laid since the 1950s, about ten of which cross the Atlantic.

The real question is, how do they repair these blasted things? The Atlantic has an average depth of about 2.2 miles. What if something happens down there? Is the whole cable ruined? Not at all. First, they have to find the location of the failure. Because of the distance across the ocean, devices called "repeaters" are used to boost the signal, and these repeaters send out alarms if there's a break in the line. This guides the repair ship to the general spot where the problem is.

Then they drag the ocean floor, slowly and carefully, with a grappling device that's capable of hooking the cable. They can also use a remote-control vehicle. Once hooked, the cable is snipped in two, again by remote control. It has to be cut because there's not enough slack to haul it to the surface (it would be too heavy to pull up intact). The cut ends of the cable are then separately raised and spliced together after the failed portion has been removed.

Now then, you might think that satellites would have replaced these undersea cables, but it's not so. Communications satellites are 22,300 miles in space, in geosynchronous orbit—definitely our personal favorite brand of orbit—and that's so far away that it creates a slight pause in a phone conversation or data transmission while the microwaves are doing their space travel. The speed of light is fast, but not that fast. Thus, many elite, fussy organizations actually request dedicated cable lines for their overseas communications.

We intend to be that way from now on. We'll tell the operator, "Excuse me, but can you please make sure this one goes under the ocean?" It's a sign of sophistication, like having the salad dressing on the side.

Noel Agler of Cape Coral, Florida, asks, "If you were to present me with one pound of plutonium, in what form would it be? How would it be contained? Feel to touch? Smell? Color?"

Dear Noel: Excellent idea for first prize in our next reader participation contest! We turned to the U.S. Department of Energy, which makes nuclear weapons for the Pentagon. Spokesman Sam Grizzle says he's seen a ball of plutonium and that it was silver and shiny. Plutonium would probably be warm to the touch.

"When it's fitted into a weapon it's in the form of something called a pit, and I can't get into the exact size and shape of it, but we use something like a bowling ball to describe it to somebody," says Grizzle.

Plutonium can also exist in powder form, but you don't want to get near that stuff because you might inhale some, which would be deleterious to your health (we are guessing you would develop exploding tumors).

Michael J. Auer of Crofton, Maryland, asks, "Who determines what time sunrise and sunset are?"

Dear Michael: The government, who else? The U.S. Naval Observatory has gone to elaborate measures to calculate the sunrise and sunset in thousands of cities. Not every newspaper or TV station or weather bureau uses these figures, but many do.

The Naval Observatory first uses Census Bureau data to find the geographical center of a city's population—which isn't the same thing as the geographical center of a city as described by official boundaries. In Washington, D.C., for example, the Naval Observatory locates this point at longitude 77 degrees, 1 minute, and latitude 38 degrees, 53 minutes. (Our map shows that as being near the Federal Center SW Metro stop, a few steps from the north curb of E Street SW, halfway between Third and Fourth streets. But we have to note that this is hardly a major population nexus. Maybe it's just near the center of the bureaucracy.)

In Detroit it's longitude 83 degrees, 5 minutes, latitude 42 degrees, 23 minutes. San Francisco is longitude 122 degrees, 26 minutes, latitude 37 degrees, 46 minutes. The observatory, noting that the sun is a disk and not a point, defines sunrise as the moment when the leading edge (or "limb," as they preposterously call it) of the disk breaks the horizon. Sunset is when the trailing edge vanishes. The time is rounded to the nearest minute. The sun would set a couple of minutes earlier and rise a couple of minutes later if the Earth had no atmosphere. The air bends the sun's light, the same way a straight stick inserted into a swimming pool seems to bend at the point of contact with the surface.

We should add that, in our opinion, the moment of sunrise and sunset is something that should be determined by each individual. Our view is that sunrise occurs at the first suggestion of luminousness in the East, far before the sun actually appears, in that moment of promise, hope, challenge, resurrection.

Fran Voelker of Golden, Colorado, writes, "What is the scientific thought on the meaning of (a) Creation (b) Cosmos (c) Universe. I simply do not believe my dictionary!"

In civilian life it's probably safe to use "universe" and "cosmos" as synonyms, but "the cosmos," to our ear, refers not merely to a thing (the universe) but to a system of things (galaxies and stars and planets) that comprise the universe. Thus a "cosmologist" studies the way the universe is put together.

"Creation" is a term of both natural and supernatural significance. Religious scholars have long debated whether the Creation was a singular event or an ongoing process that continues today. Scientists are a bit confused too: Their Big Bang theory seems to resemble the religious notion of Creation, but when you look more closely you see that the preexpansion universe is so dense that space and time are dimensionless and effectively nonexistent. If there is no time, it's hard to figure out when the universe "began."

Saint Augustine once wrote that God created the world with time but not in time. Fortunately this chapter has run out of space. (Just in time.)

A Final Note About Truth

Recently someone asked us, "Do you think there is such a thing as Truth?"

We said we'd check.

And so we did. We can now confidently answer, yes, there is Truth—more or less.

Richard Rorty, the eminent philosopher from the University of Virginia and author of *Objectivity, Relativism and Truth* (precisely the title we would have chosen for this book had it not already been taken), tells us that no philosopher doubts that truth exists. Rather, the big split is between the common-sense types who say that truth exists absolutely—that there's one and only one way that the world is—and the "pragmatists" like himself who say that there are ways of looking at the world that are *useful* but that don't necessarily reflect an absolute truth.

"True beliefs are the ones that get us what we want," he explains. "Belief in particle physics gets us the ability to build bombs. But there's no point in asking, 'Does it correspond to reality?' "

We'll paraphrase: Truth exists within self-consistent systems. Thus it is "true" that Fred Flintstone and Barney Rubble have no necks, even though, in the nonanimated system we call the real world, these people do not exist and if they did they'd be required to have necks.

INDEX

About the Author

Joel Achenbach was born in 1960 in Gainesville, Florida. He attended Princeton University, worked at *The Miami Herald*, and since 1990 has been a reporter for the Style section of *The Washington Post*. His column "Why Things Are" is nationally syndicated by The Washington Post Writers Group. He is a regular contributor to National Public Radio's *Morning Edition*.